ACT
VERBATIM
for Depression & Anxiety

◆ Annotated Transcripts
for Learning Acceptance &
Commitment Therapy

MICHAEL P. TWOHIG, PH.D.
STEVEN C. HAYES, PH.D.

Context Press
New Harbinger Publications, Inc.

Publisher's Note

This publication is designed to provide accurate and authoritative information in regard to the subject matter covered. It is sold with the understanding that the publisher is not engaged in rendering psychological, financial, legal, or other professional services. If expert assistance or counseling is needed, the services of a competent professional should be sought.

Copyright © 2008 by Steven Hayes and Michael Twohig
New Harbinger Publications, Inc.
5674 Shattuck Avenue
Oakland, CA 94609
www.newharbinger.com

All rights reserved. Printed in the United States of America.
Distributed in Canada by Raincoast Books.

Acquired by Catharine Sutker; Cover design by Amy Shoup;
Edited by Elisabeth Beller; Text design by Tracy Carlson

Library of Congress Cataloging-in-Publication Data

Twohig, Michael P.
   ACT verbatim for depression and anxiety : annotated transcripts for learning acceptance and commitment therapy / Michael P. Twohig and Steven C. Hayes.
      p. ; cm.
   Includes bibliographical references.
   ISBN-13: 978-1-57224-523-5 (pbk. : alk. paper)
   ISBN-10: 1-57224-523-9 (pbk. : alk. paper)   1. Acceptance and commitment therapy--Case studies.   I. Hayes, Steven C.   II. Title.
   [DNLM: 1. Cognitive Therapy--methods--Case Reports.   2. Emotions--Case Reports.   3. Self Concept--Case Reports.   WM 425.5.C6 T974a 2008]
RC489.A32T96 2008
616.89'1425--dc22

                           2008003620

10 09 08
10 9 8 7 6 5 4 3 2 1
First printing

To my wife, Katie, for supporting me from the beginning.
—MPT

To my wife, Jacque, for loving me.
—SCH

CHAPTER 1

Contents

Dear Reader:

Welcome to New Harbinger Publications. New Harbinger is dedicated to publishing books based on acceptance and commitment therapy (ACT) and its application to specific areas. New Harbinger has a long-standing reputation as a publisher of quality, well-researched books for general and professional audiences.

ACT Verbatim is the first book of its kind to provide readers with an intimate window on the inner workings of ACT as it is applied, in real time, with a client presenting with anxiety, depression, and anger-related concerns. This is not a how-to manual on ACT, nor is it a book about ACT techniques. Rather, it is a book for those on the path toward developing greater competence in the flexible application of acceptance and commitment therapy. In short, ACT Verbatim is ACT demystified. Here's why we think this is so.

The authors, both seasoned ACT therapists and trainers, reveal the fluid application of ACT with a complex case over ten therapeutic sessions. The book is framed early on within the ACT process model of psychological health, suffering, and change. The model is then woven into the fabric of therapy, where the reader is given a unique opportunity to get into the head and heart of therapist and client alike as they move together on a journey out of suffering and into something more vital and new. This insider perspective is unique and helps to make ACT much less mysterious.

Clinically rich therapist and client transcripts provide a structure for much of the book. The authors guide the reader into the pulse of each session and gently point to the presence and absence of important ACT processes as they emerge. This, along with periodic discussion and commentary, also serve an important learning function by teaching the reader how to develop greater sensitivity to the ACT therapeutic stance and ACT-relevant targets of change. Each chapter ends with the authors reflecting on the previous session, with attention to ACT competencies, skills, processes, and therapeutic progress. The book demands that you work with it as you read, and if you do that, ACT Verbatim will help enrich your competency, clinical sensitivity, and flexibility as an ACT therapist. You may even benefit personally too.

There are many ways to learn about ACT and how to apply it in clinical practice. You can attend a workshop or two. You might read several excellent ACT books, join a reading or online discussion group, or perhaps follow the growing research literature. You may even take a class on the topic, observe training tapes/DVDs, or practice applying ACT under the guidance of an experienced ACT supervisor.

Yet, even with all of that, you may still feel unsure about what to look for at the process level and how to link those processes with therapeutic actions that are ACT consistent, flexible, genuine, and helpful. The authors of ACT Verbatim will help you fill in those gaps and round out your professional development as a more effective and skillful ACT therapist. This exceptionally well crafted book is not the way to do ACT, but will show you one of many ways to do ACT.

As part of New Harbinger's commitment to publishing sound, scientific, clinically based research, Steve, Georg, and I oversee all prospective ACT books for the Acceptance and Commitment Therapy Series. As ACT Series editors, we review all

ACT books published by New Harbinger, comment on proposals and offer guidance as needed, and use a gentle hand in making suggestions regarding content, depth, and scope of each book. We strive to ensure that any unsubstantiated claim or claims that are clearly ACT inconsistent are flagged for the authors so they can revise these sections to ensure that the work meets our criteria (see below) and that all of the material presented is true to ACT's roots (not passing off other models and methods as ACT).

Books in the *Acceptance and Commitment Therapy Series*:

- ✓ Have an adequate database, appropriate to the strength of the claims being made.

- ✓ Are theoretically coherent—they will fit with the ACT model and underlying behavioral principles as they have evolved at the time of writing.

- ✓ Orient the reader toward unresolved empirical issues

- ✓ Do not overlap needlessly with existing volumes

- ✓ Avoid jargon and unnecessary entanglement with proprietary methods, leaving ACT work open and available

- ✓ Keep the focus always on what is good for the reader

- ✓ Support the further development of the field

- ✓ Provide information in a way that is of practical use to readers

These guidelines reflect the values of the broader ACT community. You'll see all of them packed into this book. They are meant to ensure that professionals and the general public get information that can truly be helpful, and that can further our ability to alleviate human suffering by inviting creative practitioners into the process of developing, applying, and refining this approach to meet the needs of the human condition. Consider this book such an invitation.

Sincerely,

John Forsyth, Ph.D., Steven C. Hayes, Ph.D., and Georg H. Eifert, Ph.D.

Preface

The empirical evidence for the underlying processes of acceptance and commitment therapy (ACT) and supportive clinical outcomes is rapidly growing. As a result, so is professional interest in ACT. First-year graduate students as well as experienced clinicians are taking notice and desire to know more about it.

Ten years ago, it was very difficult to find any training in ACT, and most published pieces were theoretical and did not deal with procedures. People had to take fairly drastic measures, such as flying to Reno to be trained by the developer, to learn about ACT. This is now far less of a problem. There are experienced clinicians, professors, and trainers who are teaching people in ACT (see *www.contextualpsychology.org*). There are excellent books available that are extremely practical, not just theoretical. And several DVDs are being issued, either alone (e.g., Hayes, 2007) or in conjunction with books (Luoma, Hayes, & Walser, 2007), that show ACT sessions. There is still much more interest than existing trainers can address, however, and additional training resources are needed. People need multiple examples and multiple opportunities to learn to become proficient in the application of ACT.

This book is intended to help therapists and students learn the target processes in ACT. It will not be sufficient as the only means through which to learn them; you will need to read the basic texts on the treatment and use this book as a supplement. It is our feeling that reading these transcripts and comments will help solidify some of the knowledge acquired from other sources. It is sort of like watching a sporting event, where knowledge of the sport increases your appreciation of it. It allows you to see the small moves that are very important to making the final score, such as, "Why did the therapist target that process instead of the more obvious one?" or "Why didn't the therapist respond to that?"

This book begins with a description of the ACT model of psychological disorders and the ACT processes that counter these processes. It provides examples of when target processes are present and when they are not. To help the reader become more familiar with these processes in flight, the rest of the book contains ten sessions of edited transcripts of the work of a relatively proficient ACT therapist (who asked to remain anonymous) with a client who struggles with anger, depression, and anxiety. The transcripts were edited for confidentiality and training purposes. We note in the transcripts when ACT processes are present and absent; we discuss what we think is occurring in session; and we comment on the therapist's choices, both positive and negative. We hope that our comments help the reader become better able to differentiate between these processes as they are occurring. This is not meant as a shining example of ACT—it is just one style from one therapist who has both strengths and weaknesses.

Acknowledgments

Whether this is our first book (MPT) or thirtieth (SCH), it is still the product of many circumstances, events, and people. We want to thank our wives and children for their support of these projects. Writing this book literally took hundreds of hours, and those were hours that were not spent with those we love. So thank you Katie and Jacque for supporting us in this project. We both have little boys of the same age and we both experienced the struggle of taking time away from them to work on this project. We only hope that this book does some good in the world and that people become more effective therapists, better prepared to alleviate human suffering, as a result of reading it.

Additionally, we want to thank our colleagues and students (or classmates in MPT's case) for their role in the development of this book. We both participated in many Monday clinical supervisions and Friday laboratory meetings, all of which helped develop the ideas, concepts, and therapeutic moves that are presented in this book. Specifically we would like to thank the members of the ACT/RFT lab in Reno who were there during the development of this book, including Kara Bunting, Alethea Varra, Heather Pierson, Akihiko Masuda, Jason Lillis, Chad Shenk, Tuna Townsend, Jason Luoma, Lindsey Fletcher, Jennifer Plumb, Roger Vilardaga, Tom Waltz, and Claudia Cardinal. Additionally, we would like to thank Elisabeth Beller for her thorough edit of this book; her suggestions and comments greatly improved it and helped us clarify concepts that were difficult to understand.

Finally, we want to thank the client whose transcripts were used in this book. While you are one of many clients treated with ACT, your impact on us has been large. Witnessing your struggle and courage has taught us a great deal. Similarly, we want to thank all of our past clients for teaching us about the process of therapy and we thank the therapist who allowed this work to be held up to scrutiny by us.

To you, the therapist, we want to say that we hope that this book makes a difference. If you are an experienced ACT clinician, we hope that you pick up something useful from this text. If you are new to ACT, make room for what your mind tells you while reading this book and be open to what it might offer you. You deserve applause for diving into something new.

—Michael P. Twohig, Logan, Utah
    Steven C. Hayes, Reno, Nevada

CHAPTER 1

What Is ACT?

The aim of this book is to help therapists become more competent in acceptance and commitment therapy (Hayes, Strosahl, & Wilson, 1999). ACT (pronounced "act" not as "ay-cee-tee") is not so much a set of techniques as it is a model of psychological health, pathology, and change. There are important benefits for practitioners that come from having a clear and well-supported model, but the complexity of learning a new model creates a challenge for training. The largest issue is that this model differs in some notable ways from much of applied psychology. Thus, it may require a fair amount of work to gain competency in this approach. This book is organized to help overcome that challenge.

Most empirically supported psychotherapies are taught in a protocol-based fashion. You learn the first step, then the second, and so on. If you follow a certain set of procedures, in a set order, with a specific disorder, there is an expected outcome.

Such an approach has helped establish empirically supported treatments, but anyone who uses manualized therapies knows that the sessions often do not go as written. Important events occur between sessions, clients fail to respond to aspects of the intervention, or issues arise in the therapeutic relationship. Furthermore, clients usually come into treatment with multiple problems in multiple areas. Therapists have to be creative because manuals just cannot cover every event that might occur in treatment for every combination of clinical needs.

Flexibility is thus a necessary component of good clinical work, but it can undermine the basis of empirically validated treatments if innovation and flexibility are based on clinical whim instead of a sound theoretical or conceptual basis. We suspect this is why adherence to empirically supported manuals often does not predict outcome. The vision of empirically supported treatments cannot fully be realized unless clinical creativity is channeled.

That is why ACT is a model, linked to a basic research program about processes of pathology and change. If the model is correct, any method that advances the processes that ACT targets can be viewed as an ACT method. Practitioners are free to create, modify, and innovate once they understand the processes they are targeting. And indeed that is happening. Thousands of practitioners around the world are busy developing new exercises, metaphors, and techniques that facilitate ACT processes.

There are many great exercises and metaphors that are used by most ACT therapists, and more are developed each day, often tailored to specific problems (e.g., Dahl, Wilson, & Luciano, 2005; Eifert & Forsyth, 2005; Hayes & Strosahl, 2004; Walser & Westrup, 2007; Zettle, 2007). Any ACT clinician will need to read and understand books such as these. But using particular statements or exercises is not necessary to "do ACT." Even ACT exercises and metaphors are only consistent with ACT if they target the processes that are central to the therapy. Competent ACT therapists can go multiple sessions without saying anything that is printed in a book or a chapter and be completely ACT consistent.

This is a wonderfully liberating aspect of ACT work, but it creates significant challenges for training and for learning, especially for new ACT therapists. To be fully useful, ACT processes cannot be understood merely in an intellectual way. The opportunities and challenges occur too quickly in applied work.

The present volume is one of several that attempt to find new ways to teach ACT that will help practitioners acquire fluency in the application of the model. In this book we will describe the ACT model and the processes that are targeted within it but then will spend the rest of the book walking through segments from clinical transcripts of a proficient ACT clinician working with a specific client. There was no practical way to use the entire transcript, so we have selected parts that help reveal the process. As you will see, this is shown, warts and all—complete with errors, misreads, and dead ends. The transcript has been modified for confidentiality and training purposes. In a few areas, confidentiality or training concerns have required that we use pieces of transcript from other clients, or even just make up material, but this is still very largely an authentic example of real ACT work, and the substantial majority of the transcript is word for word what was said with this specific case. By showing these processes in flight, it is our hope that clinicians seriously interested in an ACT model can begin to see the opportunity for innovation within a consistent and empirically proven model of psychopathology and clinical change.

THE SIX CORE ACT PROCESSES

There are six interrelated functional processes that are targeted therapeutically in ACT: acceptance, defusion, self as context, contact with the present moment, values, and committed action (see figure 1.1). All are "processes" in the sense that they are functionally defined, ongoing psychological acts, not constant or static things. The first four—acceptance, defusion, self as context, and contact with the present moment—

constitute the mindfulness and acceptance processes within the model. A second grouping of four—self as context, contact with the present moment, values, and committed action—constitute the commitment and behavior-change processes. The middle two are in both sets because in either case we are speaking of a conscious person living in the present. The intended outcome of targeting these processes is *psychological flexibility*, which is the ability as a conscious person to experience events fully and without needless defense, and to persist or change in behavior in a given situation in the service of chosen values. Because the model can be arranged into a hexagon and has, as its core, psychological flexibility, the ACT community (somewhat tongue in cheek) calls the overall model shown in figure 1.1 the ACT *hexaflex*.

Each of these processes has a flip side, and taken together these constitute an ACT model of psychopathology: avoidance, fusion, conceptualized self, not present, unclear values, and inaction. Experiential avoidance and cognitive fusion are the flip sides of acceptance and defusion. Attachment to the conceptualized self is the opposite of contacting a transcendent sense of self. Dominance of the conceptualized past and feared future and weak self-knowledge are the inverse of contacting the present moment. Lack of values clarity, or choosing "values" in the service of *pliance* (following a socially derived rule) or avoidance, are the pathological counterparts to ACT values work. And inaction, impulsivity, and avoidant persistence are the unhealthy counterparts to committed action. Overall, the pathological core of problems from an ACT point of view is *psychological inflexibility*. This is shown in figure 1.2.

Because this is a book on intervention, not psychopathology, we will primarily speak of the six processes and their core targets using the therapeutic language of acceptance, defusion, and so on, but the pathological terms will also be used. Our purpose is to help ACT clinicians discriminate between each of these processes. To assist in this process of discrimination, in this section we will illustrate each of these processes in a number of ways: each will be defined; an example of an exercise or metaphor that teaches the process will be provided; examples of client behavior that would generally indicate that this process needs to be targeted will be provided; and a number of examples of behaviors that would indicate that each of these processes is being sufficiently targeted will be offered. Note, however, that the six processes are interrelated and none can be fully defined without reference to the others.

Acceptance

Acceptance involves actively embracing private events (thoughts, feelings, bodily sensations), while they are presently occurring, as ongoing private experiences. Acceptance is an action; it is not a feeling or way of thinking about private events. People can behave acceptingly or they can work to reduce or change a private event. Acceptance is different than tolerance or resignation, both of which give a sense that something is being done to someone—that the person does not have a choice in the situation. A person can make the choice to accept thoughts or feelings by not working to reduce or

Figure 1.1 The ACT hexaflex model of intervention

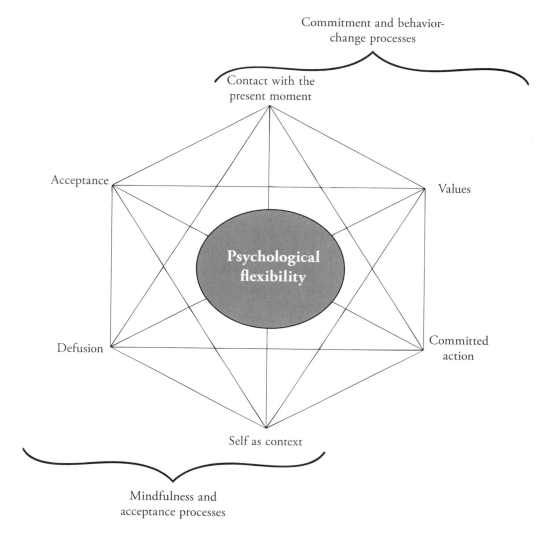

change them and by thinking and feeling them as they are, not as what they appear to be.

Acceptance is a skill and can be learned. Thus, a lot of time is spent in and out of session helping clients become more skilled and proficient at accepting private events that usually interfere with pursuing their values. Acceptance is practiced in session when difficult private events occur and can be taught directly through exercises and metaphors; it can also be practiced outside of session in a more graded, hierarchical fashion. This can look topographically similar to exposure therapy, except that the function is not to reduce the events but to increase openness to them and flexibility in respond-

Figure 1.2 The ACT model of psychopathology

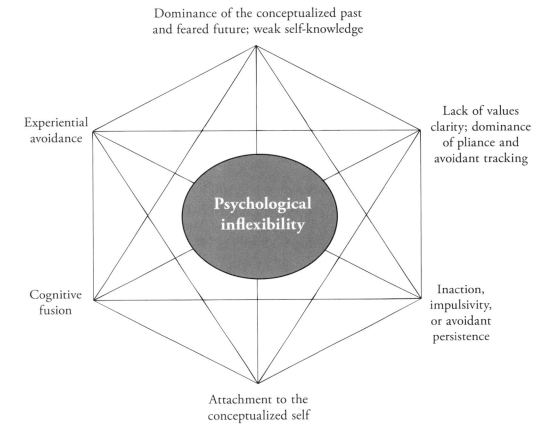

Dominance of the conceptualized past
and feared future; weak self-knowledge

Experiential
avoidance

Lack of values
clarity; dominance
of pliance and
avoidant tracking

**Psychological
inflexibility**

Cognitive
fusion

Inaction,
impulsivity,
or avoidant
persistence

Attachment to the
conceptualized self

ing to them. The goal is to contact thoughts, feelings, and bodily sensations without defense, inviting them in as if they were a friend or a relative you haven't wanted to spend much time with previously. Because it is a skill, clients generally get better at this as therapy progresses.

An example of an acceptance exercise could involve imagining a distressing experience, such as an argument with a friend, and working to sit with whatever feelings occur. An example of an acceptance metaphor is the two-games metaphor.

Therapist (T):   What if it works like this? There are two games in life. The first game is over here on this hand [therapist can put out one hand] and the focus is on decreasing whatever thought or feeling that you have been struggling with. If you win this game, these thoughts and feelings will be gone. Have you been winning this game?

Client (C): No way! I have been playing that game for most of my life, and the feelings are there just as much as ever.

T: It is sort of like you are playing against a professional team; there is just no way you can win.

C: Yes, that is what it feels like.

T: What would you get if you won that game?

C: I feel like once I get this part of my life under control, I can do the things I have been missing, like dating, changing my job, and being more active.

T: Here is my offer. There is another game over here that most people do not pay attention to [puts out other hand]. It is similar to the first game in some ways, but also different in other very important ways. To begin with, this game is fair. The more you put into it, the more you generally get out of it. Most importantly, instead of playing for control of your thoughts, you play for those things that you really want in life. Instead of getting your emotions under control before you move forward, what if we just started moving forward? What you would have to do is take your team from the first game and move them over to this new one. It might be a bit difficult because the players will want to look over there and see the score, maybe play a little more. When that happens you will need to notice it and bring your team back to the other game.

C: What, and just feel anxious?

T: I believe you already feel anxious. But this way you can feel your anxiety when you feel anxiety and continue to do the things that are important to you instead of sitting and waiting for your anxiety to change.

There are many indicators that *acceptance* needs to be targeted therapeutically. Here are a few indicators that the client may exhibit:

✓ Makes statements about needing to change, regulate, or control thoughts, feelings, or bodily sensations

✓ Avoids talking about things

✓ Changes the topic

✓ Purposely talks about easy topics (e.g., weekend activities rather than the treatment target)

✓ Makes jokes or is funny to break the mood

✓ Avoids eye contact

- ✓ Doesn't complete homework

- ✓ Isn't engaging in exposure activities

- ✓ Worries excessively

Here are some examples of a client behaving in a more accepting way:

- ✓ Is more willing to talk about difficult topics in session

- ✓ Brings up or asks to talk about emotionally difficult topics

- ✓ Engages in homework or other exposure exercises

- ✓ Talks about doing things just to do them or doing things for the experience

- ✓ Engages in behaviors that are new or have not been done for a long time

- ✓ Says, "I would usually not talk about this" or the like

Defusion

Thoughts do not present themselves as thoughts. Because of the relational and bidirectional nature of human language (as revealed in the basic work that underlies ACT—relational frame theory or RFT: Hayes, Barnes-Holmes, & Roche, 2001), thoughts appear to be what they are related to, not what they are. Generally, people are far more aware of the world structured by thoughts about events than they are of the events themselves.

Our culture adds to the inherent problem in language by teaching us that our negative thoughts are themselves dangerous or harmful. For example, it is normal to hear people say, "Don't worry about it" after a difficult event. What they are doing is attempting to protect us from our own thoughts.

There is nothing actually dangerous about any private event. Indeed, thoughts are both useful tools and indications of the relevance of history to the present moment. But it is difficult to relate to thoughts in this way if they are constantly taken literally. Few would run from the thought that "I am wearing khaki pants," but many surely would run from the thought "I might fail." Both are just thoughts, and seen that way, a wide variety of things might be called for in responding to them. Defusion exercises work to help the client experience thoughts as nothing more than might be experienced listening to an announcer at a sporting event; thoughts are not to be ignored, but they are not necessarily to be followed either.

Cognitive defusion involves altering the context in which thoughts are experienced, in order to undermine their automatic impact and importance, by seeing them as an ongoing relational process. More simply, cognitive defusion can be thought of as breaking down the literal meaning of one's thinking so that thoughts are experienced as just that—thoughts and nothing more.

Like all other ACT processes, defusion is not a particular technique. Many different procedures are used as cognitive defusion practices, some being more structured than others. There are unlimited numbers of cognitive defusion techniques in principle, and scores have been used in ACT protocols. Here is one example.

> T: Would you mind giving me an example of a thought that has really been getting in the way for you?
>
> C: The main one lately has been that I am a terrible father. I mean I forgot my daughter's birthday last week, and I have not really been there for her when she needed me.
>
> T: Do you mind if we do a silly little exercise with the thought that you are a terrible father?
>
> C: No. Go ahead.
>
> T: If that thought were a dog, what kind of a dog would that be?
>
> C: A big mean one, like a pit bull.
>
> T: What color would it be?
>
> C: Black and brown. [The therapist can go through a whole variety of qualities of the dog, including size, energy level, personality, obedience level, speed, and sound and volume of bark. Once the client has a good sense of this thought as a dog, the therapist can say something like the following.]
>
> T: Is this a dog that you need to get rid of? If this dog were yours, would you be able to take care of it? Is there anything useful or life enhancing you can do with this dog?

This exercise has a couple of functions. It helps the client see this thought (that he has been struggling with) in a different context, one which pulls for mere observation—as would actual dogs—instead of the cognitive overextension that people easily do with most events. By treating this thought as an object, it allows the client to see it as generally not threatening, but even if the object were threatening, the threat does not necessarily imply anything negative about the person perceiving it. This exercise helps produce a distinction between the person and the thought. The person is not the object; he is thinking about the object. It also increases the number of ways a client can respond to the thought. Held lightly, this thought might encourage better parenting. Held literally it will likely do the opposite because "What can be expected of bad people but bad things?"

Cognitive defusion is one of the key processes targeted in ACT, and there are many chances to use defusion. Here are some examples of client behavior that signals that this process may need to be targeted:

✓ Won't talk about something

✓ Says a thought is "scary" or "too difficult"

✓ Closes eyes or won't look at you when a difficult topic comes up

✓ Rigidly follows verbal rules that don't work

✓ Exhibits lack of spontaneity in behavior

✓ Says that she wants a feeling, thought, or emotion to go away

✓ Says he feels emotionally tight

✓ Loves and trusts her mind

✓ Is not enjoyable to be around

✓ Experiences problematic thoughts and feelings, elicited by many events

✓ States that he must understand something

And here are some indications that the client is becoming less verbally entangled and more cognitively defused:

✓ Laughs at things in session

✓ Begins to enter into a "right and wrong" story about others and hesitates and abandons the story midstream

✓ Talks about her mind as a separate thing (e.g., "There my mind goes again")

✓ Seems confused and is fine with it

✓ Comments flexibly on the functions of thoughts

Self as Context

There are three types of self as defined within ACT: the conceptualized self, the self as a process of ongoing self-awareness, and the observing self, or self as context. The *conceptualized self* is the self that is made up of your self-evaluations and categorizations. It would be as if someone asked you, "What are you like?" People define themselves as kind, helpful, mean, an outcast, studious, and many other things.

People often develop a protective attachment to a conceptualized self. For example, if a person has a belief that he is a good worker, he can work very hard to keep that true, even to the detriment of family or other things of value. Similarly, if someone believes that she is a failure and that her mother is to blame, she can also work very hard to keep that accurate by not changing what she does or changing how she relates to her childhood. The pull to be "right" means that the impetus to change is held back by the person's own concept of self. This is the most dangerous form of self, and in ACT, particular attention is placed on detecting and weakening the attachment to the conceptualized self.

Ongoing self-awareness involves a continuous awareness of present experiences where those experiences are noticed in a descriptive, nonjudgmental way. It involves noticing each experience as it is, as, for example, "I am thinking this; I am feeling that; I am seeing this." This is generally considered a healthy form of self-awareness. There are two main advantages to experiencing consciousness in the present: (1) we are more aware and sensitive to the present contingencies and our history with regard to them, and (2) consciousness itself is less threatening in this context than when experienced as a portrayal of ourselves.

The *observing self* is often the type that we are least familiar with, even though it has been there continuously since infantile amnesia fell away. Indeed, from an RFT point of view, development of such a sense of self is part of *why* infantile amnesia ended. This sense of self is the result of seeing that observations are being made from a consistent locus: I/here/now. In lay terms, it is the "you" that is "behind your eyes," the "you" aware of the experiences, not the experiences themselves.

In ACT we work to foster a sense of the observing self. This part of ACT helps create a psychological stance in which thoughts and experiences can occur without threatening one's self. It is not a threat because "I/here/now" is not defined by content. This cognitively established sense of self is the context in which private experiences occur. Because the limits of that context cannot themselves be observed by the person, the observing self carries with it a sense of transcendence and boundlessness. In a word, it engenders a sense of spirituality (Hayes, 1984).

There are a number of exercises that foster this process; here is one—an abbreviated example of the observer exercise—which is a common ACT practice:

1.   Help the client come into contact with the present moment by closing her eyes and getting in touch with her senses. Next, ask the client to try and observe the self that is experiencing these events at the moment.

2.   Then have the client picture a day, one week ago. It is easier to find an event that was somewhat memorable to the client, such as an argument or an enjoyable event. Help the client report on the experiences during that event and come into contact with the self that experienced that event. Ask if that is the same self that is here presently.

3.   Continue with this exercise by going back every ten years or so. Help the client remember events that happened when she was in her twenties, in

her teens, and in her childhood, if possible. Help the client really experience what was happening at these times. Once the client is in touch with these moments, have her notice the self that was there to experience these moments. Help the client compare that self to the one that experiences the present and see that it is the same self.

4. Help put this experience in a therapeutic context by pointing out that the same self has been present at all points in the client's life and has not been removed by events that have occurred. The observing self has always been there and always will be.

A sense of an observing self is part of many other ACT processes, so some of the list below could fit under a different process, given the correct context. Here are examples of times when self as context may need to be targeted:

✓ Is afraid of his experiences

✓ Does not want to change for fear of not remaining consistent

✓ Experiences events from her past as very dangerous to her self

✓ Is held back from moving forward by past experiences and attachment to the story about how they have affected him

✓ Thinks past experiences need to be changed before other changes can occur

✓ Must "know why" she is like she is

✓ Has a sense of not knowing who he is

✓ Has a poor sense of boundaries, especially a chameleon-like tendency to try to become what others think she is

✓ Is personally threatened by anxiety

✓ Has difficulty concentrating or sleeping

Here are some of the indications that a more transcendent sense of self is being established as a process:

✓ Feels as though he is comfortable with who he is

✓ Is comfortable in her own skin

✓ Shows a profound sense of empathy for others

✓ Shows unusual sensitivity to the psychological perspective of the clinician

✓ Perceives a deep sense of conscious connection between the clinician and client

✓ Has a healthy and nondefensive sense of interpersonal boundaries

✓ Can sense private events as ongoing processes that do not define him

✓ Talks about private events as "coming along with her" and not "dictating to her"

Contact with the Present Moment

Most of the time we are in the past or the future in our heads; we are usually thinking about things that have happened to us or about what we should do later. We spend much less time experiencing what is occurring right now. Being in contact with the present moment occurs when we experience thoughts, feelings, and bodily sensations as processes occurring now as opposed to events that refer to the past or are in the future. *Contact with the present moment* is generally defined as consciously experiencing internal and external events as they are occurring, without attachment to evaluation or judgment. Therapeutically, contact with the present moment helps clients experience the external and internal world as it really is, instead of the world as it is portrayed by one's symbolic behavior.

Work on contact with the present moment contains similarities to many mindfulness-based practices and therapies. It encompasses at least two skills: to openly and fully experience what is occurring in the present moment, and to label and describe these events without judgment. This is taught in many ways, the most common being more formal meditation and mindfulness practices. Not all such practices are completely consistent—mindfulness practices sometimes have a "control of emotions" component to them. In ACT, the focus of contact with the present moment is not to control any part of our private experience, but to more fully experience all parts of our experience.

Here is an example of one type of this exercise.

T: The focus of this exercise is not to help you feel calm or relaxed—if that happens, that is fine, but it is not our goal. The purpose of this exercise is to help you see the difference between looking at your thoughts and looking from them. There is a difference between a thought as a thought and a thought experienced as "you."

1. Sit comfortably in a position that you can maintain for about ten minutes.

2. You may close your eyes or stare at a blank area on the wall.

3. Start by paying attention to your breathing. Pay attention to a breath as it comes in and goes back out the other way. Pay attention to the temperature of the air as it comes in and see if it is different when it comes back out. Notice your belly expand and contract as you breathe. Really pay attention to these feelings.

Now, note that all the feelings that are associated with breathing have been there all day, but this is likely the first time that you have noticed them.

4. Notice the sounds in the room. There are the obvious ones like the air vents and the people in the halls, but there are smaller ones also. These sounds have been there the whole time that we have been in here, but this is likely the first time that you have noticed them.

5. Now move your attention to your body. Feel what it feels like to sit in your chair. Feel where the chair is smooth, rough, bumpy, and so on. Feel where there is tension in your body. Feel what it feels like to press against that chair. Again, you have been experiencing those feelings this whole time, but this is likely the first time that you are conscious of them. The reason that most people are not aware of their present experience is because they are in their minds all day.

6. I'm going to invite you to experience your mind in a different way. You are going to just watch your mind as a person would observe waves crash on a beach. Do nothing but observe your thoughts. If you have the thought that you are not sure what I am getting at, just observe that thought. If you are not sure if you are doing it correctly, observe that thought. If you find yourself wanting to hold on to one thought, don't do it. See if you can just observe them.

7. At some point you will no longer be watching your thoughts; you will have bought into one of them. You will not see the thought; you will be in the thought—looking from it. When that happens, please let that thought go and come back to the present. This is the point of the exercise, to see the difference between looking from your thoughts and looking at them. You spend most of your day looking from your thoughts. It is almost as though you have a colored glass ball over your head that you see the world through. Your mind clouds your experience in the same way that wearing the glass ball clouds your vision. You do not need to get rid of the ball, but you can become more aware that it is there so that you can experience the world as it is and not as your mind wants you to experience it.

Here are some indications from client behavior that contact with the present moment needs to be addressed:

✓ Seems to be in his head

- ✓ Does not pay attention

- ✓ Seems rushed and scattered

- ✓ Forgets things or daydreams in session

- ✓ Does not feel present in pleasurable activities

- ✓ Experiences the present moment clouded by thoughts and worries

- ✓ Is unaware of her own thoughts and feelings or can't describe them when asked

Here are some examples of client behavior that indicate that contact with the present moment is going well:

- ✓ Feels more present in the room

- ✓ Enjoys things again

- ✓ Can describe what he is feeling and thinking

- ✓ Exhibits behavior flexibly and effectively related to what the current environment affords

- ✓ Notes small events that transpire, or features of the room, with appreciation

Values

Values are the areas of life that we choose to pursue on a moment-by-moment basis, but we can never achieve or possess a value as an object. Said in another way, values are areas of importance that we recognize and embrace as guides of our patterns of action. They are not concrete goals, which are events with discrete beginnings and endings; they are not feelings or thoughts, which are mere side effects; and they are not just "what we want," regardless of why we want things, because they must be chosen, personal, and "nonavoidant" while many "wants" are none of these.

Suppose you value having loving relationships. Values in this case are like an adverb: to relate *lovingly*. We can never achieve this as a thing or possess it as an object. As a value, you don't just "get" love and then stop and have it the way you might "get" married or "get" to sleep with someone. Choosing the importance of relating lovingly is part of that very value, so the moment you own it, you have it. But because it is a quality of ongoing patterns of action, it never stops so long as the value is retained. No matter how much you lovingly relate to others, there is still more of that to do.

Values can function as a compass to help clients know which direction to move in; they provide a guide for behavior that goes beyond habits or momentary emotions and thoughts. There are many areas of life that one can use as a guide while pursuing values.

Examples include family, friends, social involvement, health, spirituality, citizenship, and work. Everybody values different areas in life, and an ACT therapist works to support the client's values without judgment. This almost always leads to the question of what to do if the client's values are highly inconsistent with the therapist's values. This situation is far more often imagined than actualized once clients dig down to deeply chosen values. If it does occur and cannot be resolved, then a therapeutic contract is not possible, and appropriate steps (such as referral) need to be taken.

Values are useful in that they can alter functional relations—most especially they provide an appetitive alternative to the usual patterns of avoidance. If someone who meets criteria for agoraphobia comes to realize that avoiding public places has been hurting her family, whom she values greatly, then the difficult process of exposure has a real importance beyond merely getting anxiety to go away. Values also provide direction for therapy. An ACT therapist will seldom work to decrease a disorder alone; the decrease in a disorder is always in the service of a value, or the decrease in the disorder can be secondary to pursuing a value.

There are many formal examples of values exercises, such as asking someone what he would want written on his tombstone or what she would like said as a eulogy at her funeral. Values work, like many of the other key processes in ACT, gets addressed in most sessions. Here is an example of some values-based dialogue with a client with OCD who has cleaning compulsions.

T: I am not asking you to be uncomfortable for no reason. I wonder if it might be worth it to be uncomfortable. Might there be something important in doing this?

C: Well, I could get control of my life again.

T: Why get control of your life? What are you missing because of your cleaning that you want to get back?

C: I want time back. I want time to watch TV, hang out with friends, do what normal people do, not spend my days cleaning.

T: It is hard to miss out on those things.

C: Very hard.

T: What is in the way of having those things right now?

C: I can't. The urge to clean drives me crazy when I do not clean. If I just ignore the urge, it is there all day.

T: And when you listen to it, you miss out on these things that are important to you. What do you really want?

C: My life back.

T: What if the urge is part of living your life? Are you willing to have that?

Here are some client behaviors that indicate that values need to be targeted:

✓ Exhibits a lack of direction

✓ Finds therapy lacks a sense of importance, relevance, or vitality

✓ Is unsure of why he should participate in therapy

✓ Exhibits behavior that is often in the service of controlling emotions or other avoidant processes

✓ Values things because others expect it

✓ Values things in order not to feel guilt or shame

Here are indications that valuing is occurring:

✓ Engages in activities because of their intrinsic value and the vitality they bring

✓ Is clear on what she wants

✓ Links previous pain to present purposes

✓ Exhibits behavior in the service of values

✓ Is more open or willing, seeing vulnerability as part of something deeply desired rather than as a burden to be removed

Committed Action

Committed action is at the heart of traditional behavior therapy, and it is at the heart of ACT. There's a statement in an ACT session that captures this: "Now that we are no longer manipulating your mind, let's get down to doing what is important to you."

In many situations the client possesses the repertoire to overcome the disorder—smokers know how to not smoke, people diagnosed with trichotillomania know how to not pull their hair, people diagnosed with depression know how to start living—but their minds get in the way. Many traditional behavioral interventions would be effective if the client could only follow the therapist's advice. A person would have a very good chance of decreasing an anxiety disorder if he would participate in exposure both during and out of session. *Committed action* involves defining goals along a certain path and then acting on these goals while practicing the other ACT strategies so as to build larger and larger patterns of healthy action.

The particular ways that committed action is practiced differ between disorders and individuals. Commitments are often made publicly with the therapist or with other individuals. The size and degree of the commitments generally increase throughout therapy, and a greater sensitivity to patterns of action expands as slips and failures are reacted to in ways that reaffirm desired processes of change.

The most obvious and commonly used form of a behavioral commitment exercise is graduated exposure, which is applicable to just about any psychological disorder. The client and the therapist should determine what the highest possible goal will be. For smoking cessation, this could be no longer smoking; for anxiety disorders, it could be encountering anxiety-provoking stimuli without avoidance; for a person who is feeling depressed, it could be being active and following her values throughout the day. Often this highest goal is used to create a rough hierarchy so that the person's ultimate goal can be pursued in small steps. The client can then work through the steps. As the client directly experiences how ACT processes participate in taking these steps forward, it is quite common to see the client willingly take greater or additional steps than were agreed on with the therapist. This occurs when the larger function of the exercises becomes clearer. There is a kind of transformation quality to the ACT message, and once clients truly experience it, they see that there is no reason to live inside mental cages of their own making. These steps are about things that are important to the client—not about getting rid of a disorder—and engaging in these activities often reinforces and perpetuates these new patterns.

Here are examples of client behaviors that indicate when committed action needs to be targeted:

- ✓ Is inactive

- ✓ Does not do homework or commitment exercises

- ✓ Is not feeling as though life has vitality

- ✓ Presents with no vitality or sense of immediacy

- ✓ Is not doing things that are important to him, has no plans to do things differently, or feels committed actions are heavy and burdensome

Here are examples of the client engaging in committed action:

- ✓ Spontaneously engages in new behaviors

- ✓ Completes homework and commitments

- ✓ Experiences life changes—especially in areas that were stagnant

- ✓ Experiences generalization to new domains

- ✓ Exhibits a sense of flexibility, responsibility, and empowerment

CLUSTERS OF ACT PROCESSES

As is shown in figure 1.1, the six key ACT processes can be gathered into two basic clusters, rotating around a central theme.

Mindfulness and Acceptance Processes

The mindfulness and acceptance processes fall more on the "cognitive" side of therapy. They are used as ways to work with the client's thoughts, emotions, and bodily sensations. These processes focus on altering the function of the client's problematic private events rather than their form, frequency, or situational sensitivity. They help get private events off the table as variables of importance and help shift the focus back to overt and meaningful behavior change.

Commitment and Behavior-Change Processes

Commitment and behavior-change processes are more consistent with traditional behavior therapy or behavior modification. These processes focus on helping the person change actions that do not work well in the long run. They differ from classic behavior therapy in that the changes are always in the service of something larger—something that the person finds meaningful. They are similar in that they focus on overt repertoire building and goal achievement.

Psychological Flexibility

The overall function of these six processes is to foster psychological flexibility. Psychological flexibility is observed when clients engage in new behaviors, or persist in behavior in the service of chosen values, and do so with a sense of openness, presence, and awareness. Part of psychological flexibility is the ability to experience private events from a different functional context. A thought experienced as just a thought is not dangerous, just as the feeling you get on a roller coaster is not usually experienced as inherently dangerous. It is fun.

The other part of psychological flexibility is the ability to continue moving forward in a valued direction while accepting the private events that are occurring. Most people are psychologically inflexible in that they do not pursue their values and instead work to control their thoughts and feelings. They act as though they must get their thoughts and feelings under control before they can move forward. Being psychologically flexible means that you can move forward at any time with whatever is occurring privately.

SUMMARY AND STRUCTURE OF THE BOOK

ACT is a set of core processes that are targeted in therapy, not a set of techniques. The ability to sense the need to address these processes, and being able to do so effectively, will result in the largest clinical gains when doing ACT. The ability to do so cannot be fully taught through a set of rules. Therefore, in this volume we will attempt to teach the discriminating techniques needed to notice the presence and absence of these processes.

We hope to help shape your ability to recognize ACT processes in flight and to recognize functionally useful responses to these processes. This will take time and practice, but we hope the book will help speed up that process.

This book consists of clinical transcripts of therapy sessions with a middle-aged male client who struggles with anger, depression, and anxiety and is being seen by an experienced ACT therapist. We will walk through each of several sessions, commenting on different processes as they occur and are addressed. We will note when we believe that a process has been effectively addressed and when one could have been addressed more effectively. We will mention alternative ways these processes could have been targeted. We will also write about what we believe is occurring in the therapy session and where we think things are going.

At the end of each chapter we will examine how much each process was advanced. This should give the reader a feel for the progression of therapy throughout the sessions. Many of these processes are addressed in multiple sessions, but the sessions follow a pretty typical order. There are a number of styles of doing ACT, however, and it is very important not to think that this sequence is the correct, only, or even typical sequence. What is most important is learning to see ACT processes in the client and having alternatives available for addressing the target processes that allow the sessions to move in the needed direction.

These choices then set up further work, and seeing that happen is a final purpose of the book as it is organized. For example, suppose a client diagnosed with obsessive-compulsive disorder says, "I would really like to just leave my house in the morning, but the obsessions are just too strong and will bother me all day if I don't do my routine." A response that focuses on defusion could be "It sounds like you are really buying into those thoughts … How close to you are they?" while a response that focuses on values could be "Where in your life is it costing you to stay home and do your routine?"

Similarly, responses could occur from every other point of the ACT model. The choices then set up further work—as we will see in the transcripts. We now turn to these sessions.

CHAPTER 2

Committing to Therapy and Beginning to Let Go of the Struggle

ACT is a nontraditional psychological intervention in many ways; it is primarily an acceptance-based intervention. Most clients come into therapy hoping that the therapist will help them decrease whatever emotion they are experiencing (e.g., anxiety, anger, depression). That is not the focus of ACT. ACT is about living a vital life, and sometimes that means living that life with difficult emotions, thoughts, memories, bodily sensations, or behavioral urges. In the long run, most clients want a vital, meaningful life, but they believe that negative private experiences must be taken care of before this can occur. They are so focused on getting control of their private experiences, and so fooled by the fact that attempts to do so sometimes seem to work over the short term, that they don't recognize that this effort is a detour that never gets back to the main highway.

ACT uncovers an experiential truth: the more we fight with our insides, the less control we have over life itself, and ironically, our inner world then becomes more negative, not less.

ACT helps clarify this paradoxical process, but the therapist needs some time and psychological space to do this. Therefore, initially in ACT, the therapist warns clients that what is about to occur will be different than what they expect and that it will take a bit of time to see if this approach is useful. To shift the focus from controlling emotions to living a vital life, the therapist helps clients come more into contact with the effects of their control efforts so that these can be examined without a predetermined conclusion that control is helpful or harmful in actual experience. That is the work we will be examining in this chapter.

TRANSCRIPT STRUCTURE

Most of the rest of the book is built around transcript sections. These sections do jump forward a bit at times—there are gaps. But we've picked sections that will give you a sense of the quality of the session—even after we have had to edit it for confidentiality and training purposes.

You will occasionally see words for each of the six primary ACT flexibility processes and the six ACT pathology or inflexibility processes that were described in chapter 1. When you see one of the six ACT flexibility processes (acceptance, defusion, present, self as context, values, and committed action) in brackets, it indicates that the processes are present. When you see one of the six ACT pathology or inflexibility processes (avoidance, fusion, not present, conceptualized self, unclear values, inaction), that means that we believed that the opposite was present in session. So, for example, if the person has taken an accepting stance, "[acceptance]" would appear in the transcript; if the client was very cognitively fused at a certain point, it would be indicated by "[fusion]." We also included the two indicators that many ACT processes are present (or many are not) by using "[flexible]" or "[inflexible]" in the transcripts. Hopefully, these indicators will help the reader better discern when these processes are absent or present, but we are not presenting this notation as a formal transcript scoring system. Such systems do exist for ACT (Khorakiwala, 1991), but often almost every statement can be scored, frequently with multiple categories, and that would be distracting to our present purposes. We are willing to stand behind terms actually presented, but the lack of terms is not informative. For example, a statement that reflects values may nevertheless not have the label "[values]" because we are only using enough terms to explain the flow of the session. Sometimes, if it seems necessary, a categorization will be followed by an explanation. If so, it to will also be inside the brackets.

DESCRIPTION OF THE CLIENT

The focus of this book is not on ACT case conceptualization, and we will spend little time on it here except as it appears in the moment-to-moment interaction in therapy (for more extended treatments of that topic see Luoma et al., 2007; Moran & Bach, 2007; Hayes & Strosahl, 2004).

However, a brief description of the client is needed. He is a middle-aged divorced male with three children, ages nine to sixteen, who live with him part-time. He has been struggling with depression, anxiety, and anger for many years. He owns a restaurant with an attached general store and works relatively long hours in the business.

Socially he seems tightly wound and somewhat stiff. His words can be clipped, and he casts occasional barbs at the therapist even in the earliest sessions. He has a few friends but he is lonely. Intelligent and well-dressed, he projects an aura of competence. In the assessment session he wanted to talk about external sources of his problems: his ex-wife, his employees, his former girlfriend, and past therapists, among others.

BEGINNING THE WORK: SESSION ONE

T: Okay. So, we've actually only met that one time. Have you been thinking about coming in here and seeing a shrink yet again? I mean, what's going on in your head about getting back into therapy?

C: Well, a couple of thoughts crossed my mind. One was that you weren't really able to describe in detail the type of therapy you will be using. I understand its purpose is to get out of the war instead of winning it—but I don't really know how you propose to do that. I thought that was very interesting because I've always believed that if you can't tell other people what it is that you do, or why you do it, then you don't really understand it yourself. I agree to go ahead, and I guess I understand it, but it makes me a bit worried, which I don't really like [fusion, avoidance].

T: Okay, yeah, that's some complex stuff. Can I make a distinction between two different kinds of talk that may help? One kind of talk is about describing something. The other kind of talk is to make a difference. And sometimes the one isn't the best avenue to the other. It's like the difference between a reporter and a coach. A coach can say any dang thing and be literally false. You know, like, "Float down the field," but you don't actually float. As long as the words do what they're supposed to do, well, then that's cool. That's what it's about. On the other hand, the reporter has to describe things accurately or he's not going to have a job very long. So in here, I want us to talk to make a difference. Do you play any kind of sports or music?

C: I ski.

T: Okay, have you ever been in a situation where an instructor talks too much?

C: Yeah.

T: And the next thing you know, you're thinking too much?

C: For sure.

T: The next thing you know, it's like, "Where do my feet go?"

C: Mm-hmm.

T: And you feel awkward and stupid. If I lay out some sort of big logical scheme right now, it could just be a big obstacle. One of the things I want in here is the freedom to be inconsistent, in a way, and to talk in whatever ways will help you accomplish what it is that *you* really want to accomplish by coming in here. Even if they're contradictory, paradoxical, confusing, as long as they get the job done. Then with another hat on, we could maybe talk logically about what we are doing—when it's safe to do so. But the progress comes first—then the understanding. Otherwise we will get all entangled in theory and take our eye off what we are really trying to do.

C: You are expressing yourself well, and you are talking about things with which I am not yet familiar. I'm willing to go on faith for a while here, even if it's a bit uncomfortable [acceptance].

It is pretty clear that the client is fused with his thoughts. He is treating this therapy situation like he treats most other situations in his life. He wants to logically figure it out. He wants to use his head; and after figuring it out logically he can decide if this will work for him or not. The therapist needs to sidestep this process because it is part of the same system that got the client stuck in the first place. In this case, informed consent has already been given—there is no benefit to trying to describe exactly and fully what will be done, and why, in a topographical sense. Instead of playing this game with him, the therapist asks the client to put the need for details to the side and to move forward without fully knowing. This is very different than how the client usually handles these types of situations.

There is also a "prove it to me" and judgmental quality to the client's comments about the therapist (for example, "You don't really understand it yourself" and "You are expressing yourself well"). The therapist models acceptance and defusion by not changing these judgments and the discomfort they may bring to the clinician. The judgments are simply sidestepped but without judging the client in return.

You can see even in these earliest interactions the attempt to create a different social and verbal context in therapy than occurs outside of therapy: one that actively instigates and models ACT processes. This is necessary because there are many practices in ACT that differ from the way things work outside of therapy. For example, an ACT therapist will try to elicit emotions without trying to save the person from them and will speak metaphorically and paradoxically. The therapist needs permission from the client to do this, or the client may not participate fully or could terminate therapy prematurely. In the previous assessment session, the therapist asked the client both to be open to new things and to purposefully evaluate this therapy in larger chunks as it moves along. This is a section from that session.

Therapeutic Contract

T: The other thing I'd like to do is carve out a time to do this work, small
       or large, without necessarily stopping to evaluate it at every step. You
       can set it to fit your comfort level. Then at that time, we'll sort of stop
       and look and see how things are going, and you can tell me (I won't tell
       you) whether we are moving ahead. Therapy can be kind of like cleaning
       out a glass that has sludge in the bottom—it's probably going to make
       everything look dirty for a period of time. You could very carefully pour
       out the water and pour some more in and it would look cleaner, but
       there's still the sludge in the bottom. It's like that. Sometimes people feel
       confused, like things are going backward. On the one hand, I want to
       make sure that you have control, in the sense that this is your therapy
       and you're not just buying something blind from some wiseass shrink. On
       the other hand, we want to make sure that we have the time to sort of
       get through some peaks and valleys.

Agreeing on the course of treatment and giving fair warning about some of the
difficulties likely to be encountered is important for informed consent in a treatment
like ACT because you cannot fully explain "what will happen" in a treatment that
changes how you view the world and your own psychology.

Looking to Experience

The following dialogue follows later in the first session. It is designed to help the
client begin to face the current situation and begin to let go of the struggle. In this
phase, the therapist is going to examine how successful each technique has been in
controlling the client's emotions and thoughts. The therapist is going to bring the client's past attempts into the present so that the client can really see how successful they
were. The point is not to judge but to validate the client's experience, whatever that
may be. Typically, a client feels that it's his own fault—that things have not worked—
without considering the alternative—that things have not worked because that is how
these things function. Functionally, validating a client's experience decreases the client's
cognitive attachment to what has not been working and opens up the door for a fundamentally different alternative approach.

T: It sounds like, in terms of general things that you've struggled with,
       depression has been a constant going back to adolescence, right? And
       anxiety, especially social anxiety and occasional feelings of panic. And
       then there's this anger issue. And I gather that is the additional kind of
       struggle that brings you in.

C: Yeah. I feel like I have proved to myself that I cannot control the depression even though I keep trying. Anxiety comes and goes, but I mostly just avoid it. I feel like the anger is something that I can control or should be able to control, and I don't understand it as well, and it bothers me and interferes with my life [avoidance, conceptualized self].

T: Give me examples of some ways that anger interferes with your life; what's the cost?

C: Cost … It derails me from whatever I want to be doing, whether it's working or what I am enjoying at any particular time.

T: Can you give me a couple of examples?

C: For example, being at work and having an employee do something or I see the result of something that showed that this person was careless or irresponsible or thoughtless or whatever, and instead of just going, "Zowie, this person was careless or thoughtless or irresponsible," I'm going, "Goddamn it! Why was this person doing this?" It happens over and over. You know, it's inconceivable to me for them to be so irresponsible—and it pisses me off and I resent that I have to live with it—that I can't get away from it, that I have to do something about it, that I have to take time away from things that I feel are more important, or are more enjoyable, to take care of this person's problem [fusion]. When I'm able to get away from work and I have time to reflect and think, this problem comes back around again and again, and I think, "What am I going to do about this?" Again, you know the resentment of why it's taking up my time, here I am on my leisure time, and it's still taking up my time [not present; he is giving us an example of how hard it is to stay present outside of session instead of drifting off into his mind].

T: How about switching to the other issues? I'm going to ask you the same thing. How about the depression and anxiety side: what is the cost?

C: The cost is similar. I spend too much energy trying to solve it, deal with it, cure it, trying to turn it into something manageable by squashing it, curing it, you know, whatever. It messes up my days off or causes me to not go to work. When I have a day off, I just lie in bed; I can't get up [avoidance, fusion, unclear values]. When anxiety hits, I just withdraw.

T: Yeah. And this kind of fix, cure, struggle, focus-on-a-plan, figure-it-out stuff that goes on in the anger area—"Why did he do this?" or "What am I going to do about this?"—is what's going on in depression or anxiety, essentially a form of that same kind of struggle?

C: Yeah. The methods are the same.

The therapist is beginning to lay the groundwork to tie these different behaviors into one functional class for the client—experiential avoidance. These last exchanges are designed to begin to foster acceptance over control, in part by highlighting the costs of trying to control depression and anger, and also by treating the client's experience in such a matter-of-fact way. This communicates that the outcomes being experienced are normal. Control should become less desired as a result of this work—not because the therapist says so but because the client's experience says so. The original commitment to control was as a means to a better end, but, in fact, the client's experience reveals that this is an end that does not come.

Eroding the Control Agenda

T: Yeah. And if you were to look over the last month, if anger can go from 0 (which is blissful absence of an anger moment) to 10 (in which you're ready to rip the heads off whoever walks by, or at least whoever pushes your buttons)—where would you say you are?

C: Mostly 1s and 2s with some very disturbing, you know, 7s, 8s, and 9s right in there. Depression is pretty much down most of the time—1s and 2s and 3s. Anxiety has peaks.

T: So, in that 7–8–9 range, if we were to create another scale, which is how much you struggle with that, how much you squash the anger, try to cure it or figure it out and so on, where would you put that scale?

Just in asking the question, the therapist is beginning to link the struggle with these emotions to suffering but without yet challenging the idea that the intensity of content is synonymous with suffering.

C: Well, as I sort of implied, I feel like I have the depression under control most of the time. When that's a factor, I fall back on medication, sleeping, exercise. Sometimes it's a struggle to do the exercise—I just don't feel like doing it [avoidance]. Sleeping is not usually a problem, unless I had too much of something, which also isn't usually the case, so that, on a scale, I probably am a 4, 5 maybe, with depression. It's maybe taking up half of my effort [avoidance].

T: Okay.

C: But when the anger comes, there's a lot more effort going into it because of its destructiveness. There is the potential to harm my business, hurt somebody else, get a big legal slap, hurt a customer in some way. You know, they've come in for some food and relaxation, and I not only don't help them relax but I'm upsetting them because they see how angry I am and I'm attacking my staff. There's something wrong with me when I get like that [fusion, avoidance, conceptualized self].

This last statement is a good example, one that shows self as *content* rather than a more healthy self as *ongoing process* or self as *context*. The general theme is that if he feels certain emotions, then he will do certain things, and it means something about who he is. In reality, the struggle against the emotion and its linkage to a conceptualized self is helping to lead to ineffective behavior. The emotion is not a mechanical cause—it is dependent on the client's relation to the emotion. But the client is missing this entirely.

> T: If you were to put a number on it, where would you say you tend to go, strugglewise, when anger is rocking?

> C: I try to match it, point to point [avoidance].

> T: Okay. What have you tried on the anger stuff? I mean, when you're in the middle of the struggle with it, what are you trying, or what are you thinking about? One of the things you've said so far is you try to talk yourself out of it.

Fusion and Emotion

The therapist is laying groundwork to help the client see his reaction to emotion as a key issue and to consider its utility. It is pretty clear that the client focuses his time and energy on decreasing the feelings of depression and anger. If you were to ask him if he needs to get rid of these things to live a successful life, he would say yes. Instead of directly attacking this, the therapist is slowly undermining this whole agenda. The therapist does not go right ahead and say, "Look, don't you see that control makes it worse?" Instead the therapist is slowly highlighting this relationship. This process is like the way that the waves wash the sand out from under your feet on a beach; eventually you'd fall over. The therapist is slowly washing away the supports underneath the client's whole agenda of controlling his emotions.

> C: First of all, I back off, you know, step aside from this emotion. Give myself a few minutes to think about what is really going on here. Usually it's a reaction to something that's been perceived that will make someone angry, a threat, an insult, a flaunting of rules. It takes the coolheaded party to back off and say, "Zowie, you thought I blasted you right there, and I can see that I—whatever I did—hit you the wrong way. I'm sorry, maybe we need to, or we don't need to go into what actually happened but, what's behind this, and usually it's the same old thing: I want too much or you don't want me to do this or whatever." I try to figure out what's going on, in other words [avoidance, fusion, conceptualized self].

T: Okay.

C: It's real hard for me to look at someone and realize that they seem to be happy just poking along, you know, just being there. They think that showing up for work on time, well-groomed, is enough. Maybe by the book that's enough. I mean, these folks are following the contract, but following the contract or not, I mean, "God dang, don't you want anything out of your life? If you're coming to work at a job, that doesn't mean anything to you? Don't you want to advance from here?" I've done this. I've worked my way up the ladder and now I even own the place. Now I can do things that are more valuable, worthwhile to others, and worthwhile to me. They don't, they don't care. I don't want to work with these people. They're not educated. They don't care about using their minds. They're blind. They're not ambitious. They're not fun because they don't see fun like I see it. God, I don't want to be with these people there. It's not that they have bad intentions or bad attitudes, they just don't have any. ... I don't know, so it pisses me off that I spend time with these people. I want to spend time with people who care about what they are doing [avoidance, fusion, not present, conceptualized self]. Of course I can't say that directly. I always have to patch it up. I need to or I wouldn't have anyone to staff the place. So when I go off, I have to stuff it and backpedal ... just to smooth things over [inflexible].

This is a good example of a cluster of ACT processes. We started out looking at anger and how he deals with it, and the next thing you know, we are talking about how people should be, how he is, how it's "pissing him off," how he tries to control it, and so on. He is doing his spiral from "anger as an emotion" to "angry judgments." He is doing it right in front of the clinician as he gets so emotional over a memory based on his categorization of himself and others. In essence, he is objectifying and dehumanizing both others and himself.

T: It seems very sticky. I can feel the pull of it even in these few moments of talking about it. And it sounds like some of what you then do is to try and just manage this situation and your reactions to it. I gather some of those things work to a degree.

C: Yes.

T: They manage the situation, short-term. What it doesn't do is remove the issue, yes? I mean, here you are, seeing me.

The therapist is trying to undermine a control strategy by pointing to its long-term lack of utility, thereby hoping to eventually increase acceptance of these types of thoughts and emotions.

C: Right.

T: That feeling is going to come back again and again, and when it comes back, it's going to be awfully intense for you. Has that been your experience?

C: Right. And the basic issue is that we have different values, different hopes and expectations, and I can't seem to put aside the fact that they're doing the best that they can or want to [avoidance, fusion, conceptualized self, unclear values; it is worth noting that the language of values is being used here, but it is different than the kinds of values we will pursue in ACT because there is very dominantly this "I'm right; you're wrong" quality, and probably if it were a choice, the client would not choose to be about that in his life].

T: Has this same issue shown up in other places, like close relationships and things of that kind?

C: It came up in that other situation I was telling you about, about the blonde in the convertible, just sort of waltzing through life.

T: Yeah.

C: She cut me off! Like don't you see that you just put two lives in danger? And people who litter—it's like, "Don't you care?" We all have to take some responsibility; we all have to care [not present, fusion, conceptualized self; the reason self is scored here is that inside the judgment of others there is an implicit entanglement with a conceptualized self, as if to say, "And *I'm* not like that!"].

Note that there is a lot of emotion showing up as this entangled, fused, judgmental language emerges. That can be very useful in ACT because it allows the material to be taught experientially. During this session the client can feel that this struggle has been around for a long time, and the therapist is gently orienting him toward this. It is a good idea for the therapist to use this emotion in the session directly, but this is early in therapy and more groundwork needs to be laid. Instead, the therapist leaves the emotion there, acknowledged but not unpacked, which is itself a kind of acceptance move. It is as if to say, "High emotion is welcome here—we don't need to do anything specific about it necessarily, just notice it."

T: Okay. In personal relationships? We just went by this very quickly in the last session, but you are going through a breakup with your current girlfriend, yes?

C: Yes.

T: And does anger show up there too?

C: Yeah. It was kind of a similar thing. It could be related actually. I felt that my partner wasn't doing her part holding up her end of the stick. I felt like I was making things happen, whether it was good stuff or bad stuff. My interest was petering out because it didn't seem like she was growing or contributing [conceptualized self; again, these judgments of others suggest attachment to a conceptualized self].

T: Okay. It does seem similar. Are there other things you do when you're angry or depressed? What kind of things have you done to deal with that when it shows up?

C: Well, one time I tried to kill myself because it was just unbearable.

T: Okay.

C: I would do it again if it became unbearable [avoidance].

T: It's always a way out.

C: For sure.

T: As far as we know, people don't hurt when they're dead [pause].

This is a very, very gutsy ACT response, and lots of books will tell you it is wrong, that suicidality should have been immediately explored, and so on. We think the move is powerful and well-timed. It gets at the function of his statement, and in an irreverent way. The client would commit suicide to end this suffering that he has been experiencing; it is an avoidance move. The therapist treats this as yet another way that the client has approached controlling his anger and depression. Suicide would probably end them, it is true, but it would have this small side effect called death. This irreverent response normalizes the struggle and also shows that this is a place where the therapist will not back off or run away screaming "The sky is falling," even when very difficult material comes onto the table. Instead, we will go into the pain and look at it honestly. It models and instigates acceptance and defusion as well because a functional approach to the meaning of the statement is inherently defusing.

Of course, this is a judgment call. The clinician is taking a risk here. If the client were immanently suicidal, other questions might need to be asked; and there are lots of experts who might be ready to question the approach taken. But a closer look at the actual data on suicidality suggests that many of our common practices to manage suicidality are inert or even harmful, and that the approach taken here may be helpful if well-timed (see Chiles & Strosahl, 2004).

T: What else do you do when you're angry or depressed?

C: Sleep. As I said, the depression kind of leads more toward the irritation part, and other times it's like, "I just can't; I just can't do anything." As time passes by, it's like, "Zowie, I have enough energy now; I can get up and fight" [avoidance, conceptualized self].

T: Tell me a little bit about your own relationship with emotions more generally—your emotional life. The sense I get is that if things are going on emotionally that are unpleasant, a primary move for you would be to go into your head: figuring it out, thinking about it, talking yourself out of it.

C: If it's negative, unpleasant, for sure [avoidance].

T: Right. If you look at negative emotionality in general, how much capacity do you have to stay with it or to do other things with it, other than the ones that you mentioned? I want you to tell me about your sort of emotional life and how you are as an emotional person—kind of what your model is, I guess; what you're supposed to do with it. What's it even for?

The Role of Emotion

Notice that the focus of therapy thus far has been on how well he can control his depression and anger. Now the therapist is opening the door to a larger universe of issues and asking for the client's views of what private experience is good for—emotions, bodily sensations, and other private events.

C: They help me figure out how I feel about what it is that I'm doing. If I'm not happy about going to work, and it's unhappy enough where I'm getting physical sensations—you know, I feel sick to my stomach—then it tells me that that wasn't a good thing; maybe work isn't where I ought to be right now. Maybe I should look into changing something. But if I can't, that's where I get into my head like, "I've got to put these feelings someplace else because they're interfering with my work, which is important right now" [avoidance, conceptualized self]. I have to do it, to stay alive, you know, to keep the roof over my head and my kids' heads—at least when they are with me.

T: Okay, so the first move is "I'm too busy to have time to do that, and then I've got to do something else with that, just not have it interfere too much."

C: Right. But sometimes good feelings are to be enjoyed, I mean, to let them wash over you and let them release tension for you. I was in a real interesting situation not too long ago at a dinner party at a friend's house. There were about equal numbers of males and females, and we decided we wanted to get a little crazy, you know. And we were playing with a balloon that was there from one of the host's kids—pretending that it could not touch the table or ground without moving your chair. There was only one woman who kind of played with us and said things like, "One, two, three, go!" and we'd whack the balloon. I was just laughing and the tears were coming down and we all, I think we all knew that, God, it had been a long week, and here we are at this party, we're just going to cut loose, nobody was really getting smashed, getting drunk or anything, we were just being really silly. Like little boys. And the women were looking at us like we were goofy. We had a good time. It made me wonder if they go out and have their own good time, but it wouldn't be like that I don't think [conceptualized self; note how the person is defining himself in a way that differentiates his experience from others, particularly women]. You know, being physical at the table and just letting your laughter come out. I mean I hadn't anticipated that happening, but I think that's one of the reasons I go to parties anyway; I like to be with people who are safe, that I can just say whatever I want to with, and be appreciated for you know, being me [avoidance, conceptualized self; both of these scores come because this comment implies that it is not acceptable to be yourself with your own reactions in other contexts, especially if others do not approve]. [Client begins to tear up.]

T: Okay. There's something in the room having to do with …

C: My conditioning.

T: Yeah. What stands between you and really living.

C: It's very powerful.

Notice how the client, when asked about the role of emotions and other experiences, moves back and forth from the importance of emotion to avoidance of emotion to values and then to the pain *that* brings: the pain of wanting to be free yet not really living life freely. It is early, and this lead will not fully be pursued now, but it will not be forgotten. This client objectifies others, especially women, and yet longs for a place to be appreciated for being himself. There is a value in there we will return to later. But we can already see how avoidance is costing the client dearly.

The Roots of Avoidance

The following section occurs a short time later. The therapist begins to explore the historical nature of avoidance.

T: Tell me about that. My sense is that this is an issue for you that sort of lurks a level down or something. It's old. Am I wrong about that?

C: I can see that, right there [pause]. I remember many occasions growing up where my father, not my mother, would say, basically, stuff it, whatever I was feeling. "Stop crying; save your tears for something important," and you know I could be completely wrong and he might have said something else, but that's what I heard. It's like, well, wait a minute, if this is important to me, now, then you've just invalidated everything I've ever felt up until I'm an adult, and you're telling me that nothing I feel is worthwhile. I didn't have those words when it was happening. I was just angry. It was like, you're telling me that what I'm feeling is not important, or not valid or not right, or incorrect. And I internalized that [avoidance, conceptualized self].

T: Right. Ouch.

C: So, I remember being pissed at him at the time but also realizing that my crying made him uncomfortable. He wanted me to come and sit down to dinner; he wanted everything to be okay, and I wanted to accommodate him and that situation [avoidance]. Many other experiences like that made me realize that I couldn't go to him when I needed to spill my guts, and there were many times that I knew that what I needed to spill my guts about was stupid. You know, it's like I'm being jealous or petty or greedy or something, and yet, I just wanted him to say something. I know he loves me very much, and we have a great time together, but I have learned to not talk about emotional stuff at all. It hurt to not be able to be myself with my parents [acceptance; it would be a better indicator of clinical progress if he saw that he was not willing to be himself around others, rather than not "able," but this is a step].

T: Right.

C: And my mom is too much like me, you know, she's in her head.

T: Right. So Dad is saying that, or giving the message that …

C: "This is scary, this makes me uncomfortable." So I back off [avoidance].

That little exchange helps put on the table that we are products of our histories and that these patterns of experiential avoidance are often not born with us—they are passed down. It helps make clearer that thoughts and feelings are not *us*; they occur *within* us. And the client is beginning see that he came by a pattern of avoidance honestly. There is a sense of sadness but also of kindness and self-validation that is emerging. It is tough to be human.

T: If a miracle were to happen as a result of what we do in here, how would things be different?

C: The thoughts that are running through my head are "Do I want to have a means or a tool to be able to instantly make my negative thoughts go away?" I'm not sure I do. Maybe to turn my negative thoughts around and get something out of them
[acceptance, defusion].

T: Part of you wants to say, "Go away," but part of you is a little suspicious of that and wonders what they have to teach you. Do I understand you?

C: Yeah.

T: You mentioned negative thoughts; is this an issue for you as well? I mean we've been talking about it in terms of the emotion side, but thoughts are slightly different.

C: For sure.

T: The same ball of wax but a different side of it?

C: Yes, and I think that thoughts are very powerful and I've tried to go from not saying things, you know, like "Fuck you," you know, and I don't. I avoid negativity [fusion].

T: Yeah.

C: I wasn't raised that way, or whatever, but I think that spitting out those negative words makes that negativity more palpable, and so I try not to think negative thoughts [avoidance, fusion]. Like "God, I hate you" or whatever. I say to myself, "I don't like this; okay, I'm going to do it and get it over with." Anything from going to the dentist, to, like I'm on the computer and I swear to God, my fingers are betraying me, you know, I'm trying to get something and I can't get the damn typing right.

T: Huh.

C: So, no negativity, just, just let it go, okay. Boy, this is really pissing me off, all right, things aren't going well, you know, let it go, let it go, just try to let it go [avoidance; in this case the words "Let it go" mean "Make it stop." It is not acceptance].

T: Okay. How does that work?

C: It helps.

T: Okay. Do you have an example?

C: For example, I also do things like, "Boy, you are so stupid; how could you have done that?" and then I turn it into, "Okay, yeah, I made a mistake, you know, but I'm still okay." So I try to turn it into positive tapes instead of negative tapes about me [avoidance, fusion, conceptualized self].

T: Okay.

C: Because when I get depressed it's like, I hate me [pause]. I hate everyone [conceptualized self, fusion].

T: Right. Nice. Very nice.... But then even that, the whole thing of talking your way out of self-criticism. In the long run, take a look. Even that doesn't work, yes?

C: [Pause] It doesn't. It all just seems to take me down further and further.

Control to Acceptance

This last move could have been a little difficult for newer ACT therapists to follow, and it easily could have been rejected by the client. But it worked.

There is a flow here. The therapist is subtly bumping the client forward. The sand (the control agenda) continues to be washed out from under the client's feet. The therapist expands the focus to thoughts and takes advantage of a seed of doubt in the client about the utility of suppression.

Notice that the therapist often does not at first directly challenge what the client is saying even when it is clearly a negative process from an ACT point of view. When the client says he avoids negativity, the therapist just says, "Yeah." Fusion is reinforced by being right—and thus trying to convince the client would only have fed the process. Instead, the therapist—a few turns later—asks "How does that work?" This is an inherently defusing question because it is not about literal truth but utility, which requires looking at thought in a different and less literal way. When the client says that it *does* work, even *that* is not challenged. Although ACT theory suggests that workability in this area is unlikely, the client's experience is always the ultimate arbiter, so it is important to be open to ACT guesses being incorrect. The therapist decides to explore this area a bit more but without conveying skepticism. The therapist just asks for an example.

Here, the clinician makes a bold move. The clinician senses doubt (probably due to pauses and tone of voice) of the long-term utility of self-affirmations and asks a rather forceful question: "Even that doesn't work, yes?" The client's last statement indicates that he is loosening his grip on the control agenda. He is starting to sense that all this work and effort at control is paying off very poorly.

This initial phase of the treatment can be a very important one because it sets up a lot of what happens in the coming sessions. There are things that could have been added that might have strengthened this phase. For example, it can be useful to go more deeply into the long- and short-term effects of these strategies. These control strategies can often work immediately in that they can control the feeling temporarily, but they can make the whole problem stronger in the long run. For example, we find it useful to ask how things are changing over the years. For example you might say, "Do you feel that this struggle is getting easier and smaller or more difficult and larger over the years?" Our guess is that the client would say that things were getting more difficult instead of less—or at least staying the same.

The client notices the crack in the system that the therapist has just opened up. This is reflected a few turns later when the clinician asks a question.

T: I'm back to the miracle question. At best, if a miracle were to happen, what would happen as a result of what we do here?

C: I would be happy and less angry and depressed than I am [avoidance].

T: Okay. The bottom line is that you'll know that you're doing well when there's less anger, less depression, and more happiness.

C: Yes. And I'm afraid that you're going to tell me that's not the way it works [present; this score is a judgment call, but it seems that the client is catching his reaction in flight].

The client seems to know by experience that that's not the way it works because just a few turns earlier he opened the door to that realization. But the client's verbal organ (his "mind") will never really get that. It is worth noting that his last statement is a kind of warning to the therapist. The therapist does not try to defend the idea against the client's beliefs. Instead the therapist takes it into the client's own experience and begins to distinguish verbal programming and the person.

T: I don't know if I'd tell you that, but I'd ask you to look at something. I'd ask you to look at your own experience and not what some shrink would tell you. If we take these things and say, "Okay, now which would you prefer, depression or happiness?" this is an easy choice. Which would you prefer, putting your finger in the wall socket or having a nice meal? I'm not saying that we live in a world in which "happy" is not preferred over "angry and depressed." But here's the part that's tricky: suppose you have that as a goal and then find that moving toward it—those things of "more happy," "less anger," and "less depressed"—suppose you find that it loops back on itself in such a way that it actually made it quite unlikely, much less likely, that life could assume a level of happiness, anger, and depression that was appropriate to where you really were? You were talking a few moments ago about your sense that maybe these negative emotions and thoughts sometimes give you an important message. Right? Sometimes things are really happening in your life, you know, like a relationship is going into the dumpster, or one of your kids gets sick. "Happy" is probably not the right emotion to tell you that. Emotions can be useful as sort of a guide—at least they tell you about what from the past is now in the present. But if you get too attached to "less angry," "less depression," "more happy," then you've got these emotions less as a guide and you've also got "Maybe I can do some things to 'feel better' right now" … even if that is not helpful.

A shift in the session is occurring here. The therapist is beginning to move from addressing the effectiveness of the client's approach to part of the rationale for a possible alternative approach. As this expands in the next section, acceptance is placed on the table as an alternative. But very little is directly presented. It is still a washing away of the control agenda.

C: You said something about the goal, you know, if this goal moves back on itself. Are you implying that then there is something wrong, that the goal is not appropriate, that the goal is not a good goal, or that the process of getting to the goal isn't working or isn't likely to work? [fusion]

T: Well, there's a paradox. When you're actually in pursuit of the goal, most anybody can recognize that "Oh, yeah, this is better than that." Happy is better than angry, right? And yet, the paradox may be that if you hold it as a goal, it can't work as a goal. You said you ski. If you get afraid on a steep hill, what do you want to do?

C: Oh yeah, you want to lean back.

T: Lean back, right? And then what happens?

C: You fall down.

T: Yeah. You're in deep doo-doo if you lean back, because you take weight off the front of your skis and there's no control. So in the name of getting control, making it safer, you don't have any. Suppose it's like that? Suppose this kind of natural, logical, reasonable, sensible, human thing has a strange loop in it. As you go out after these things, they slip away and somehow it never quite gets handled. Some times are better than other times, and some things seem to work better than others—we've explored lots of those in here. But you know—here you are, seeing a shrink, again.

C: I'm aware of this theory that happiness is in the journey and the going and the doing, and it's true, you know. I'm happy when I'm producing and working on getting things done, and then I get it done and then it's like, well, there's always something else to do, you know. So I can see that kind of problem. You said something last time that was real intriguing to me because I felt like this has always been a problem, my thinking about things in terms of yes or no, black or white, have or have not. I think if I get rid of my depression, what's going to fill its spot is happiness. I know that isn't necessarily the case, but it is what I find myself thinking [defusion]. So maybe not happiness, like not *anything* would be fine and better than this [avoidance]. I mean, I would be very happy to just be kind of a blob. I don't think I'm manic-depressive, but the manic stuff shakes you out as much as being depressed. Being depressed is awful and you can't stand it, but being manic can be intolerable as well [fusion]. So, I would like to not be so angry, but it's not that I'm necessarily looking for more happiness to take its place. It's like I just want to stop it because it hurts [avoidance].

T: Right, right.

C: Both the anger and the depression are painful.

T: Okay. Well, here's what I want to put on the table; you know, we've got more work to do to kind of work this out, this is our first kind of real session together, but, let us put a couple of things on the table. Isn't it suspicious that as much effort as you put into this issue, here you are again talking to a shrink? Don't you think that's suspicious? After all this effort?

C: Something's not working. So I keep looking for somebody who can kick me in the butt and say, you're missing this. You're missing a point, or something. I'm hoping that somebody has got some more insight than I do [avoidance, conceptualized self].

T: Okay, and the way you know they have more insight is there would be—ideally, you'd be happier, less angry, and less depressed, right?

C: Yeah, but happy and insight don't go hand in hand.

T: Yeah, but I mean the kind you are seeking. If it was insight that really made a difference and wasn't just blah, blah, blah.

C: Right, okay, some magic move, the silver bullet, the missing piece [avoidance, fusion].

T: Right, the missing piece. Wherever they got the missing piece, it should make a result, and the result is going to be this result. Right? Happier, less angry, and less depressed.

C: I guess the real miracle I want is to be able to understand why I'm feeling what I'm feeling at any particular time and to be able to control it [avoidance].

There it is: simple, direct, absolutely normal, and word for word, the very core of human suffering. As you can see in the previous statement, the client is not very far from where he started. This is important to notice because a lot of time, in session, has been spent on the uselessness of this goal. But the client continues to have this as his goal and in fact has now finally stated it baldly and without qualification. This is actually quite helpful. There is now no wiggle room left.

Notice that the therapist does not change course because of the client's last statement. The therapist starts to bore in.

T: Yeah, exactly. Precisely. Now here's the thing that I want to put on the table. Suppose that this is part of the problem. Suppose that actually is the sticking point?

C: The controlling? Wanting to control?

T: That I want to be able to understand it so that I can control it. I mean, you've reduced it down now to a real core, which I think is a great move. It's really helpful. Beautiful. Elegant. "This is what I want." And it's a natural human thing to want that. And yet, look at the results it's produced. Consider the possibility that we're in the situation in which all the logical, reasonable, rational, normal things that you know to do tend not to fundamentally remove the issues that you're applying these things to. Your experience actually tells you something like this because you've spent a lot of effort on it, and it's still hanging around. Whereas if you spent that much effort on almost anything outside the skin, I mean it would have been handled long since. Right?

C: But I have; I've done some good things.

T: And maybe that thought kept you going. It would be like somebody falling over a cliff in total darkness who grabbed a branch. The good that's done is "At least I didn't fall to my death." You are stuck on the cliff but you are alive. It turns out, however, if you were to let go, it's only a few feet down anyway and then you'd be free to move around. And so, yeah, "I've saved myself" but at the cost of being stuck. Maybe even the good that's been done has a cost to it.

C: Mm-hmm.

T: The cost that you've actually experienced is that the issue hasn't disappeared. It's still here intensely enough that you want to be in therapy again. What you've done is logical. But here we are.

C: So, what you're telling me is you have something else to offer in its place? Instead of rationality and concentration and analysis, you've got something else that you want me to try? What is it? I'll give it a try! [avoidance]

The Agenda Is the Problem

This is a trap. Topographically, it sounds like he is willing to try something different, but just one minute ago in the session he said with some conviction that his goal was to understand and control his emotions. The problem is not the method—it is the purpose, the agenda. The client does not see that yet, so any answer here that looks like "a thing to try" is sure to fail because it will be used for the same old purpose, and the purpose is the problem.

T: Consider the possibility that your change agenda is part of the problem. Your mind is in there saying, "Okay, now what is it that's the solution? Give me something new to fix this problem." But your mind's hooked up to a formulation that says, "The solution goes over here," right? So if that's the way your mind is set up, anything I would say would fall into that same system. Your mind would say, "Okay, so would that work for my problem?" Well, what do you mean "work"? Work to do what?

And if that's the issue, then we've got to be very tricky. We've got to be sneaky in here because we've got four people in the room—you, me, your mind, and mine. Your mind believes it has figured out what this whole thing is about and what needs to happen during these sessions. It's well-defined to your mind. If that very agenda is part of the problem, then your mind is going to take everything that I say and loop it back around into your change agenda—even things you say—and loop everything back around and try to fit it into that structure.

So part of what we need to do is see whether or not that structure has actually paid off. See if your situation is sort of like this: Life blindfolds you, gives you a bag to carry, and supposedly there are tools in it. It puts you out in the middle of the field and tells you to live your life, and living your life consists of running around. And somewhere—age thirteen, fourteen, whatever—you find yourself having fallen in a hole. And so you feel around and you try to find a way out, and there isn't a clear way out. And so you do what you know how to do: You wait and nothing happens. You call out for help; nothing happens. You finally reach inside the bag, and there's a shovel in there. And so you start digging to see if you can control or get out of the situation you're in. Deal with it; get out of the situation you're in. Except as you dig, it seems as though this hole is getting bigger; it's getting more central. And so you dig some more, and it gets more central. Maybe this situation is more like that. You come in here with a structure of the situation you're in that suggests kind of where you need to go, and yet, part of what we need to do is first face facts. Maybe that structure is part of the problem. Are you with me? Does it connect at all with how things have seemed for you?

C: Yeah. But I'm pretty entrenched in this way of thinking and I want to imagine other ways. I want to think of another way. I just can't [avoidance, fusion].

T: Interesting thought. Thanks Mr. Mind! But suppose that organ between your ears is trying to do its logical, reasonable, rational thing as best it knows how. So it's telling you various solutions. If you try the various solutions, then if that doesn't work, try something else. And then you eventually come in here, essentially asking me to help dig you out. Maybe I've got a shovel, a better shovel, a bigger shovel, a steam shovel, a gold-plated shovel. But in that situation, digging may not be what is necessary. In fact, it actually, paradoxically, sort of cements some things in place. What if it is like that? Bottom line, here we are, still on this issue of feelings that that have been hanging around for years upon years. Yes? I'm not being judgmental in saying that, I'm asking you just to look.

C: I've been doing it wrong all this time?

This is very interesting. The client is hearing what the therapist is saying, but it is going through his verbal filter. He hears all of this as a different way to control his emotions. It is like the client only sees one problem, and that problem is that he feels too much anger and depression. The therapist is trying to put another problem on the table: basically, that the agenda itself is the problem. This can be hard for a client to hear. Superficially it means that the client has been completely wrong for a long time, and the client catches that: ouch!

T: You've been doing it wrong? I'm not saying that. In fact, I'm saying the opposite. You've been doing the rational, logical, reasonable things that people do. I mean you're doing it quite well, in fact, really quite well. And yet, it doesn't seem to have done the trick. And maybe that is because the whole thing is a setup. It's just a mind trick, that maybe this isn't a digging situation—maybe it's another kind of situation.

C: Well, there're lots of answers I think to what the other situation could be. And there's the one that, you know, hey, we are human beings and we are hardwired, or softwired, into being this kind of creature. Thinking—this is our curse. We're unhappy. Because we can think. And yet I don't think that's going to stop [acceptance, defusion].

Some of these words are topographically ACT consistent, but at this stage in therapy, it pays to be cautious of their function. It is unlikely that the client has really let go of his agenda to change his thoughts and feelings in the last minute.

C: The other thing is, if you can do this, I mean, if you've done it. I'm guessing that you know something because you are offering to help.

T: Hmmm.

C: That you have found a different way to be, or see different ways to be. Maybe it's something that you're practicing. And again this something, whatever it is, I don't understand. If you were able to find a way out of this problem, then I should be able to also. So I have this double way of thinking, "Goddamn it, why can't I do it?"—whatever "it" is [fusion].

T: Right.

C: And also, you know [pause], why can't you just show me right now? Why can't you tell me? [avoidance]

T: Right, right. Nice.

C: You know, why are you being over there smug in your chair?

T: Do I seem smug?

C: No, you don't.

T: Yeah.

C: I don't know. So my mind is kind of, right now, ah.... Whew. I'm confused now [defusion, present].

This is great. The pauses and shifts and catching of the mind in flight provide the first real indication that the client is getting less fused with his thoughts. He is starting to tip! The therapist does a good job of rolling with it; the therapist is metaphorically nudging him over.

T: Yeah, cool. Good. Very nice.

Validating Confusion

Socially rewarding confusion is an odd response. But it is meant to socially reinforce clinically relevant movement, which is a key process in ACT. The collection of verbal relations we call "the mind" evolved to problem solve. But our personal history is not a problem to solve. Our experiences are not problems to solve. Our history is to be known. Our experiences are to be experienced. Problem solving just does not belong. When the mind begins to open up, it does so through the gateway of confusion. Confusion is not the means—but it is a marker.

C: And I'm also wondering, can I? I mean if it's a question of letting go, the letting go is scary to me. Can I let go and do or be or see or hear whatever? [defusion, acceptance]

T: Yeah. Good. This is cool. This is cool. Yeah, this thing, you know, it *really is* like there are four people in the room. And I can see *you* see some of what's been happening here. But your mind is sort of going, "Hey, wait a minute! I don't quite understand what's going on here!" and it tries to formulate it back into logic because it's your servant and it's trying to actually be helpful. But it doesn't know how to be helpful to you in this area. Your own life is surely proof of that. It turns out your mind is really not your friend here. It's not your enemy either, but it's definitely not your friend. It tells you that its methods are the only way that you know how to do *anything*. But its not so—your own experience has been whispering that at you for years. There is more to you than your mind.

C: It's like using the wrong tool, like picking up a hammer and wanting to turn the Phillips head with it [defusion; this can be scored as defusion because we have shifted from the literal truth of thoughts to their functional utility].

T: Awesome. Yeah, it's kind of like that. Neat.

This use of a spontaneous and coherent metaphor for both acceptance and defusion is the best sign yet. Something really is happening here. The client senses an opening but can only put it into words metaphorically. The metaphor says a lot. The client senses that a wholly different game is afoot, as different in kind as a hammer and screwdriver. (If the client used two things that performed entirely different functions, the applause meter would be even higher. But this is excellent!)

T: You know when you go into a library, there are stone lions at the entrance, right?

C: New York Public.

T: Exactly, big libraries.

C: Yeah.

T: They have long stone stairways and lions. It goes back to the Greeks or even earlier. The more important the temple, the longer the stairs—sort of a physical metaphor. There is a hard path to enlightenment, but up there you can see a long way. And there are these lions at the bottom of the stairs. The Greeks actually named them. The one on the left was called Paradox and the other one was called Confusion. Part of the structure that is holding you back is very logical, reasonable, rational, and sensible. Minds are really great for dealing with lots of things, but there are some things they're not so great for. And facing that is scary. Do I have some special solution or some inside knowledge or something? I'm not saying that. I've worked with a lot of clients, and I personally intend to stay with what works. I'm not just meaning to flap my gums. But still, bottom line, the *only* thing that matters in here is your experience—yours. It's the only thing that matters. Yet another rap from yet another therapist is not what you need. Is it?

C: No.

T: I mean, I'll be glad to lay one on you if you want one. But I'm with you. Blah, blah, blah won't do it. But *your* experience tells you something. Take a hard look at your experience and see if it's not closer to that person who fell in a hole. There's something kind of funny about how these issues have hung around despite all of your effort. Maybe it's because something else is called for here. Maybe this is a gigantic trick. Like, you don't get out of holes by digging. You create them by digging. You get out of holes with ladders, or something like that.

C: Some people try some very interesting things to get out of holes in all the various areas, like Scientology.

T: Exactly right. There you go.

C: It's amazing how people can get themselves even deeper. I'm very mistrustful of head shrinking and religion.

T: Yeah.

C: And that's because I see people getting into deeper holes or losing themselves completely; I mean, the dirt is over the top [avoidance, conceptualized self; this can be scored on self because the client is in essence saying, "Some people lose themselves, and I am not like that"].

That is a warning. The client is afraid. He is afraid of something goofy, cultish, and so fundamentally different that a person could "lose themselves completely." But even more so, the client is afraid of real change, and he senses that change is afoot. But the therapist does not confront that now—change is coming, and a response that gives the client nothing to push against is called for. It's better to play it small.

T: Right on. So to be real clear, I'm only asking you to look at your experience and to stay with what works for you. I kind of want to look at some stuff and have you look at some things, but this is not El Guru coming down with some holy books or something.

C: Well, shit, what am I paying my money for then? [defusion; this is slightly defused because it pokes gentle fun at wanting to understand everything and have an absolutely correct answer]

T: I don't know, but not that.

C: Okay, well.

Wrap-Up and Homework

T: Well, I'd like you to do two things. In this next week I'd like to see if you'd be willing to stay with a kind of honest look at the stuckness around this issue. And just consider the possibility that you actually have gotten your hands firmly on that shovel, and really what we need to do first is find a way to let go of that—not at first knowing what else to do. Because it's kind of a faith deal, but not faith in what is coming next—faith that comes out of pain. The moves we need to make come out of "I'm fed up" and "I don't know what to do, so what the hell" or just "I've had enough." It isn't something where you can kind of rationally know what the alternatives are and weigh them first. It's more like "I don't know what else to do but I *do* know this digging thing, fundamentally, *this* isn't solving it." That's important. I mean pain is our real ally here. Let's at least do no more of what has ultimately not worked in the past. So, what I'm asking you to do is watch what happens when depression or anger come up, and watch how you want to get your hands on it, you know, watch how you get your hands on a shovel, and see if you can just notice that. Consider the possibility that part of what we need to do is get our hands off it, not at this point knowing what the alternative would be. Not what your mind tells you—your mind will always tell you, "A little more of this, a little different that, a little better that." It's going to try to figure it out logically, but it's the organ that put your hands on that shovel in the first place.

C: Okay.

T: So I don't want you to try to argue with yourself, or anything; just kind of watch it. I don't want you to do anything different. I just want you to just sort of notice how this game plays out. I'm also going to give you a couple of things to take home that are sort of questionnaires and stuff to fill out, but they are just short ones, which I ask you to bring in when you come in [at this point the Willingness Diary is given to him; see Hayes et al., 1999, pp. 142–144]. The main one is this: I'd like you to rate each night the amount of depression and anger you've experienced that day, on a 1 to 10 scale.

C: Okay.

T: And two more things: the amount of struggle or effort to change those emotions through the day, also 1 to 10. And finally, workability: if every day were like that day, how workable overall would your life be? Can you do that? Don't change anything. Just watch. Be mindful. Be honest.

C: Will do.

FINAL COMMENTARY

Overall, this was a nice session. Acceptance and defusion were addressed heavily throughout, and they had the typical effect. It became clearer at the end of the session that the client was becoming less fused with his thoughts. At this point, we think, the client is still attached to the control agenda, but his grip is just a bit looser. The ACT roller-coaster ride has clearly left the station.

There are a few things worth emphasizing about this chapter. First, it shows how ACT concepts and metaphors can be woven into the fabric of normal psychotherapy. Primary ACT texts always say otherwise, but when professionals and especially students first come into contact with ACT, they sometimes seem to believe that concepts are presented logically and metaphors and exercises are laid on top of a largely passive client. That is part of why this book is being done and DVDs are being produced, such as the ACT in Action series (New Harbinger, 2007), because this is very much not the case. ACT is based on an extensive foundation of applied theory, basic principles of cognition, and philosophical assumptions, but those are there for scientific purposes—what a therapist does clinically does not look like a lecture, and convincing the client is largely avoided. Instead, the client's experience is put in the driver's seat, and metaphors and concepts are timed to fit client movement and opportunity. Nothing seems forced in this session—yet the therapist is quite active.

Second, ACT processes are not just the *target* of intervention—they are also the *context* and *means* of intervention. For example, the client throws out several barbs, jabs, pats on the back, false leads, warnings, criticisms, and formulations in this session. Many of these would probably lead to a briar patch of content that would ensnare the unwary therapist. This is largely avoided because instead of trying to address the content of these reactions, they are acknowledged but subtly rolled into ACT-focused issues. Doing this requires that a therapist apply ACT processes to herself and use them as a means of intervention.

That set of features helps define a key aspect of an effective ACT therapeutic relationship. If we use "acceptance" as a code word for the entire ACT model, you could say it this way: in ACT, acceptance is targeted *from* acceptance, *with* acceptance. The transcript segments show that when a fused criticism is sent the therapist's way, undoubtedly resulting in some interpersonal pain and temptation toward verbal defense, the therapist generally takes a defused and accepting stance with the client. The client's comments are noted, but usually no defense is presented. Indeed the therapist often responds with good humor, as if to say (without actually saying), "Yeah, that stings, but I'm cool with that. Look at that great example of your mind doing its thing! No problem. I'm here to serve you."

Another example of the same process occurs when the client describes painful situations. When the client describes how his father told him to take emotion and "stuff it," the therapist says, "Right. Ouch." This says a lot with a little. It says that pain is not going to be avoided here. It says that the therapist understands that it hurt. And that "ouch" also means "Yes, stuffing emotion hurts."

This style of response subtly models and instigates ACT processes. The client would not be able to describe this—it largely flies below the level of awareness—but it has an effect. This approach moves the ACT agenda forward rapidly. It does so in part because the difficult and entangling process of convincing a client or correcting errors can be bypassed, and in part because ACT-consistent responses are supported. There is a tangible sense of movement in this session, and a lot of ground is covered. If the therapist had entered the briar patch that these client reactions could have led to, or had tried to create ACT-consistent movement simply through logical argument, the entire session would have bogged down.

Third, it is worth noting that the therapist repeatedly uses social praise and reinforcement to support ACT processes and to build the therapeutic alliance, where the alliance is defined both in terms of a warm, accepting relationship and in terms of an active, collaborative construction of a therapeutic contract. ACT coevolved with functional analytic psychotherapy (Kohlenberg & Tsai, 1996) and its sensibilities are part of an ACT approach, but they are linked specifically to ACT processes.

This use of reinforcement is deeply functional. ACT therapists praise ACT-consistent content, as when the therapist replied, "Awesome.... Neat," when the client said, "It's like picking up a hammer and wanting to turn the Phillips head with it." The therapist also uses praise when progress is made, even when terms are used that would normally lead to therapeutic rescue. For example, as the client begins to experience the defusion that comes from the breakdown of a control agenda and loses the ability to describe what is going on except to say he is confused, the therapist does not try to explain the moment or bring greater literal clarity, but instead just says, "Yeah, cool. Good. Very nice." Confusion is absolutely perfect, and no change is warranted. This same pattern is also seen earlier when praise is used unexpectedly to reinforce emotional exploration and honesty, and therefore acceptance and a present-moment focus, when content is raised that the client might normally believe would become the target for change. For example, when the client says, "I hate me.... I hate everyone," the therapist unexpectedly says, "Right. Nice. Very nice," and even when the client says he has been suicidal the therapist says, "Okay."

In the end, this session nicely lays the groundwork for future ACT work. The control agenda is now firmly the focus for change, and it is clear that learning how to do something new will be more experiential than logical.

At the end of each chapter, we will present a breakdown of time spent on various processes in the session (see figure 2.1). Figure 2.2 is our sense, from scoring client responses, of the strength of ACT processes. The ratings are based on the entire original transcript, so they may not correspond precisely to the segments selected for the book, but in general you will be able to see the flow of topical emphasis and the changes seen in the client.

Figure 2.1 Time spent addressing ACT processes in session one

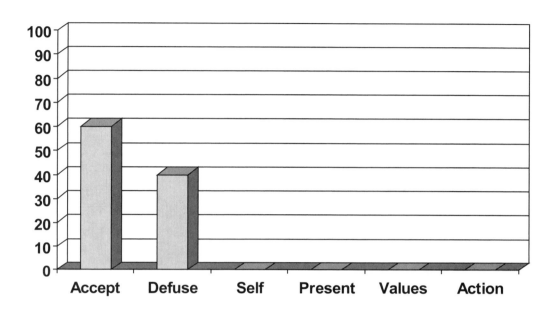

Figure 2.2 Status of client's ACT processes by the end of session one

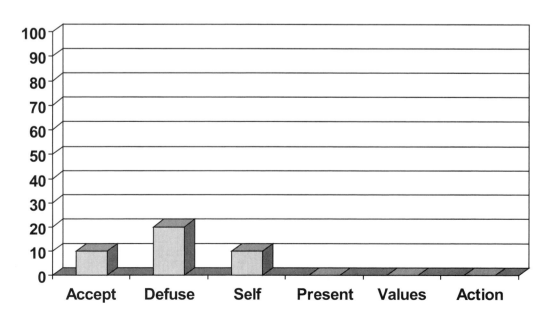

CHAPTER 3

Problems with Control and the Beginning of Self as Context

The last session focused on decreasing the client's initial hold on his control agenda. He believed that he was pretty successful at controlling his depression by sleeping, exercising, and taking medication. He was aware that these were not full solutions, but the immediate reinforcers had been effective at maintaining behavior even if the full long-term benefits were not there. He had been less successful at controlling his anger, which is seemingly what he thought the therapist would teach him how to do. Instead the therapist flipped things around and asked the client to examine how these moves had worked in general. The therapist began to focus on defusion and acceptance and sent the client home with homework targeted toward struggle and overall workability, not just depression and anger.

It is pretty unlikely that the gains from the previous session will all still be present as the second session begins. The contexts that support acceptance and defusion are fairly weak outside of therapy until real gains in areas of vitality and valued action show the client the benefits. Television, friends, family, and other health professionals generally suggest that health is the absence of psychological pain. These contexts support the same avoidance behaviors the client came to therapy with and treat language and cognition in the same literal fashion as the client. ACT works to create a new, strong social context that treats thoughts and feelings as ordinary events that do not need to be changed, thus allowing the client to function the ways he is, without needing to change the ways he thinks or feels. When the client experiences some of the successes that are produced by acceptance and defusion processes, these processes will begin to be maintained even when the cultural context is not supportive. The tiny cracks in the system will be targeted once again, and the second time around, things can often move more quickly.

In this session the therapist seeks to consolidate these gains, beginning with the homework assignment.

SESSION TWO

T: Okay. I'd like to kind of reach down into your day-to-day world and get a picture of what things are like for you. I sent you home last week with this, so I'd like to go back to it and see what is happening. I asked you to think about three scales. The first scale is the amount of depression and anger you experienced; let's put it on a 1 to 10 scale, where 1 is nothing and 10 is apocalyptic intensity, as intense as you know how to be. The next question has to do with how much effort is involved in regulating, manipulating, avoiding, controlling, and changing that level of negative emotional stuff. I'm not sure it's just emotional because you've got kind of these critical thoughts that bother you too and I'm not sure exactly, yet, how to characterize it. But let's just say "negative emotions" as a way to start. So, how much struggle is there—and how much focus, attention, and manipulation are there—from 1 to 10? Is there an incident or a day or a time when the amount is more in the moderate range than the low range, or above? Anything come up over the last week that you recall?

The classic ACT move is to go from the content to the relationship to the context. The therapist is trying to help the client see how much effort he is putting into changing these emotions versus the amount of change that is occurring. It is usually a safe bet that the more effort that is going into controlling these emotions, the more out of control they are. This process usually results in a decrease in life satisfaction because the person ends up spending great amounts of time and energy controlling something that can't be controlled readily and meanwhile he is not doing things that are meaningful.

C: Hmmm. The back of my mind is working [defusion, self as context; learning to look at mental processes in flight is a defusion move that also decreases the attachment to the self]. This is not a great example. This person does something that annoys me because I think he should know better. There's a brief flare, which is how I would characterize most of my anger. It goes down pretty quick. So I would rate that particular spot of anger as maybe a 4 to 5, and my degree of effort in containing it was probably less than the amount of anger that it is, maybe a 2 or a 3, and not really lasting long at all.

T: Okay. The last scale is workability, which is kind of like, if your life was like this continuously, how workable a way of living would that be? If you take this pattern and you project it out, is this something that leads you in the direction that you'd want to go in?

C: Yes and no. It's something that I've been working on all my life. The best way that I know how to handle negative emotion is to let it flare up; then it dies down because you can't sustain any intense emotion for very long. I let it die down and then put an emotional damper on it because it's getting in the way [avoidance, fusion]. If I need to examine this later, I will. I will try to work out a solution to why this happened and how I can prevent it in the future. So later, when I have time, I will deal with this and fix it [avoidance]. And that, in the long term, has not worked, and that's one of the reasons I'm here [acceptance]. It is because those flare-ups are injurious, but I have worked so hard all my life at dealing with it that it's gotten me where I am, and I'm happy about where I am in terms of productivity and whatnot [conceptualized self; this is scored because avoidance is built into his self-concept].

In ACT the focus moves from strategies aimed at controlling thoughts, feelings, and bodily sensations to *workability* (workability involves judging action on whether it helps to move the client in a valued direction or not—there is no right or wrong, just what works). The client's response suggests several different possible targets. He is not willing to experience these emotions that are occurring (e.g., "I put an emotional damper on it"), so avoidance could be targeted. There is a need for defusion in that the client experiences thoughts and emotions as dangerous ("because it's [emotions] getting in the way at the moment"). Finally, there is a need for self as context work in that he experiences these private events as having the ability to affect his behavior and define who he is (e.g., "I have worked so hard all my life at dealing with it [emotions], that it's gotten me where I am"). Overall, his response shows a low level of psychological flexibility, and he himself rates it as poor in workability.

Examining the Workability of Control

The clinician then begins to look at how these features interrelate.

T: Okay [the therapist is waiting for more on how well it would work for the client to live his life like this].

C: In the long term, no, because it doesn't feel right at some gut level, that it's sort of squashing things rather than expanding things or something [defusion, acceptance].

T: Okay. Good.

C: It looks like it's not a long-term answer [acceptance]. One of the other things that I tell myself is that I know that there's a light at the end of the tunnel and I don't have to put up with this forever. One way or another, I'm going to get out of this situation. Knowing that there is a light at the end of the tunnel has helped me through a lot of things. This isn't going to last forever. I can survive it [avoidance].

T: Right.

C: But, again, it's like that's a bandage over these feelings, about which I would like to be better able to say, "Hey, it's okay," you know [acceptance]. These feelings are pretty high-powered stuff. I know they're not hurting anyone else because I don't let them out, but they're hurting me [avoidance]. So I want to be able to deal with them better.

T: Okay. Of those three things, sort of intense negative emotion, control efforts, and workability, what do you think goes with what? You've been looking at that over the week in the homework. What have you noticed? In particular, which of these things are hanging together, correlating, part of the same system, and so on? Do you think that workability goes more with lower or higher levels of negative emotionality or does it go more with lower or higher levels of effort at control? What is your sense on that, instinctively?

C: Well, my instinct is that workability relates to how hard I try to deal with them as opposed to the emotion itself. The emotion is somewhat separate [defusion]. I can't control it [acceptance].

This is a very important moment in this early stage of ACT. The client is beginning to notice the struggle-unworkability relation, and sprinkled throughout his answers are indications of much more willingness to look beyond his control strategies for answers. The therapist is doing a nice job at getting at the function of language rather than the content of it. The therapist is not offering or suggesting another way to target these thoughts and seems to be keeping an open mind to whatever the client's experience says. That is always a bit of a risk, but the payoff is that the client's experience is the guide here, not the clinician's opinion, and if ACT theory is worthwhile, it will be corroborated by the client's experiences.

T: Yeah.

C: What I do to it and how successful that is seems to be governed by something else. It's not just the emotion. I don't know what that is [defusion, acceptance].

T: So if the control effort is high, how are things going workability-wise?

C: Not very well.

T: Yeah.

C: If I have to try that hard, then I'm shutting down everything else [acceptance].

T: Yeah [pause]. In here over the few sessions we've had, you've used a lot of words like "squashing things," "When things get extreme, I try to control," "These things are just wasting my time," or "I feel like I have to wash away the bad thoughts." A lot of metaphors in there: "squashing," "washing away," that all have to do with …

C: Getting rid of.

T: "Getting rid of." Yeah. Exactly. I think part of what we need to do in here is to look at how *that* works—how it's been working for you. You say, "It seems to be governed by something else." If there's a system here that's not workable, and yet it's persisting, then there's got to be some glue that holds it together, something sticky, something tricky. Otherwise we would just quickly dismantle the system, do something else. That's not so easy because it tends to be very tricky. Or something. I think it must be hard to deal with, hard to dismantle—not hard in the sense of effort; hard in the sense of tricky.

Note how the therapist is not being very direct. The therapist is vague about the issues and the problem, and there is a stumbling, almost mumbling quality to this section. That is done on purpose. Anything that is said to the client will go directly through his verbal filter. It then becomes a rule that the client will follow in the service of some purpose, which is likely now, still, to be a control agenda. Both tightly held rules and the client's control agenda are treatment targets, so it is good not to fuel either. The therapist is washing the control agenda out from under the client's feet. By emphasizing that this is hard, the therapist is asking for the client to continue to lean into these issues and explore them for himself. By deliberately being somewhat incoherent, the therapist is "playing small" and is giving the client permission for difficulty. This in turn puts the responsibility on the client but without setting a high bar of performance.

C: Well, I think the way you learn to get along in the world is by watching other people. Role models can tell you what they do, offer you suggestions, offer you feedback about what you're doing, whatever. You get information that way, and you also get information by just guessing what it is. "Oh, they must not be mad" just because they're not showing it. "They must not be upset, so it must not be that big a deal."

T: Right.

C: "If they can get by, then so should I. Therefore, I'm wrong, and they have something that I don't" [conceptualized self, defusion; this is tricky to score, to a degree, because it is being said almost in a third-person perspective. It seems defused for that reason and may even reflect a beginning crack in a system of attachment to a conceptualized self. But it is possible this is just an attempt by the client to rescue the therapist from the therapist's bumbling]. I think that's a source of a lot of my self-imposed regulations about how I should be feeling and how I should be [defusion; he can see the process as separate from the content].

T: Does that go on now? Do you find yourself doing that?

C: Oh, all the time. I care about what other people think way too much [defusion, values]. And I know that I do that, but it still governs practically everything I do. "How is it going to look if I do that?" "What are people going to think if I do that?" "How do I cover my ass on this one?" "How can I get what I want but make it look like it's what they want?" [defusion; the client is beginning to notice the process of cognition instead of just living inside cognitive products].

T: Do you think people around you would suspect that about you?

C: For sure [acceptance; this is acceptance because he was willing to admit to something that might evoke guilt or self-judgment]. I think that people who really know me, parents and good friends and stuff, are probably aware that I can be chameleon-like [acceptance, values; there may be a fragment of values here because the client is implying that this is not what he wants to be about]. Probably fewer people know it than I think know it.

T: I don't know you well enough to really say this, but in terms of how you carry yourself and your style, the immediate presentation is one of "I'm competent and I'm going to do it how I like it, and you better adjust to it." As I'm saying that, it sounds almost as if I'm saying you are hostile in tone, and I don't mean it that way—but maybe a bit rebellious.

C: For sure. Yes. I can see that. I know that there are people who perceive me as being brave and getting things done, because that's the way I want to be, and it works sometimes. But if I'm challenged, boy, I retreat real quickly [acceptance, self as context; self is scored because there is a sense of looking at the act, not literally buying into the act].

T: Yeah. Okay, that's cool. Probably people who don't know you well put you in one place, and then as they get to know you, they see you as sort of more of a marshmallow gorilla than an actual gorilla. Is that fair?

C: I do sort of put on a show [acceptance, self as context].

This is good work, and the client is clearly making progress within an ACT model. You can feel the lower levels of defensiveness and rigidity. The client seems more open to looking at the workability of patterns of action without heavy judgment and self-criticism.

Examining Control Strategies

Now the therapist will try to bring that sense of openness into a larger issue and to "drive a nail into the wall" in the sense of claiming some small bit of experiential progress and having enough confidence in its experiential basis to put it into words. There is a pattern to this in ACT: first create progress; then you can risk a formulation. It almost never goes in the other direction, sequentially, in effective ACT work.

The metaphor of driving a nail into the wall is apt because when progress based on experience is made, describing that progress allows the therapist to return to it easily later and to hang new ideas and new steps on the nail of that previous progress.

T: Last time we were talking about this sense of being stuck. Where you've gone here really does fit in with it. It's worth just kind of putting a little point on it as to what this thing is about. What is all the digging about? See if this isn't right: part of what that effort is about is getting control of the world inside your skin—your thoughts, feelings, memories, predispositions, and so on, and if we could just sort of get those in line, then things would be okay. That is kind of what our minds tell us. It says to evaluate them, and there are certain ones you like and certain ones you don't like. So I've got to get rid of the bad ones. But the problem with that is that there's a fair amount of evidence from a lot of different areas that if you try to go frontally after the world inside the skin, it loops back around on you.

There's this guy at Harvard, Dan Wegner, who does research in which he brings people in and he tells them something *not* to think about. And then he has them talk aloud as they do other things. Well, sure enough, if you tell them not to think about it, then that thought goes down for a bit and then way up. That's been shown also with emotions. If you have people put their hands in cold water and you say, "Now whatever you do, don't let yourself feel any pain there" (versus, you know, "I really want you to notice how your hand feels, and if it's hurting, really notice that") and then you look at what happens. It's more painful to try not to have the pain. Furthermore, later on, they give them a little vibration that is barely negative, and the people who have been suppressing the pain earlier now will rate that as quite painful. Other people will rate it as a vibration.

So pushing things down has this kind of sensitization thing where you're looking for something that's going to intrude in some way. You're getting yourself in a defensive place, and things look more hostile than they would otherwise look. They look scarier. Kind of a metaphor for that would be like if I could hook you up to a polygraph that can't be fooled, and while I watch the readout, I tell you, "Don't get nervous." Now to motivate you here, I'm going to hold a gun to your head and if you get nervous, I'm going to shoot you. So don't get nervous. In circumstances like that, the very effort not to be nervous, because bad things will then happen, is enough to make you nervous. So, for example, when your mind really gets critical, I'm guessing, you get critical about how critical you are. Do you not?

C: Mm-hmm.

The beginning of this is good, but it goes a bit too far. ACT needs to be experiential. The therapist's dialogue is technically ACT consistent, but the therapist is probably overestimating how much to trust the earlier openings and is presenting too much material and too much in a literal way. Much of this likely went straight through the verbal filter. It would be pretty easy to form a rule from this such as, "If I do not struggle with my emotions, they will be weaker." It might have been therapeutically more useful to stop halfway through and to work on acceptance in a more experiential way. For example, the therapist could actually play out the polygraph metaphor or could do one of Wegner's experiential exercises. Still, slight technical errors like this (which probably come from the clinician's excitement over seeing clear progress) are usually not lethal in ACT.

T: Just consider the possibility that part of why anger, depression, criticalness, and so on, sticks is that it's stuck into a loop of trying to do something about itself that paradoxically amplifies it. Or it even doesn't amplify it—it sort of grinds it in, glues it up, makes it stick. What would you do if you didn't do what you always do?

C: Well, I know there are lots of things that I could try that I haven't.

T: Like what?

C: Do a mantra. "I'm not mad, I'm not mad, I'm not mad," or some other distracting-type thing like singing [avoidance]. I could stop whatever it was that I was doing, except that sometimes it is me that's doing whatever it is that's making me mad. I could just stop. I mean I'd have to do the physical correlation because supposedly you could tell your mind to stop: "Stop thinking that." Train it to think, "Oh, I'm on that merry-go-round again. I'm going to get off." You have to force yourself to think something else [avoidance, fusion]. But then you get into all that, if you try to stop yourself from thinking about it, then you'll come back and gnaw at it like a scab or something [pause]. So I don't know what else to do, to be honest with you [silence] [defusion].

Notice that the client is going through his usual, logical attempts at controlling his thoughts and emotions. When asked about alternative response options, he lists a huge number of control strategies. It shows how ingrained and sticky this control agenda is. Also note that at the end of his statement, he pauses and realizes that this is the same thing, and then he stops talking. That pattern of halting, self-correction, and silence is a very clear sign that defusion and acceptance is occurring. It is a signal that the client sees the futility of avoidance and strength of entanglement in the moment. It reflects a crack in the verbal system. Much in the same way as a person will just stop talking to someone who they don't like, people will sometimes do the same thing with their own chattering monkey minds after they have had enough of them.

> T: So here's the thing that I want you to notice. And this is exactly where I wanted to go. Things that you listed, you know, like chant your brains out, mantra yourself into bliss or something …

> C: Are temporary fixes.

> T: Yeah, and the other thing is, they're driven toward a purpose. They have a goal. What's the goal?

> C: To get away.

If ACT is really more effective when done experientially, then this is a much better spot for the client. It feels like it just hit him that no one can control this process. He gets this experientially rather than factually. But, not to be too harsh on our earlier comments, it is worth noting that getting chatty and literal earlier probably did not have a huge cost and might even have given the client a brief rest from the more effective boring in that the clinician is doing. The clinician catches it and backs up a bit and immediately begins relying more on the client's experience. And here the client very clearly contacts the inherent problem and formulates it in no uncertain terms. This is clear progress.

> T: Exactly right. What I want to put on the table is the possibility that your experience is valid. It is not your fault that this is not working. It can't work because the system itself is set up in such a way that it can't work—like the gun to the head sitting down at the polygraph. If I've got a good enough polygraph—and you do, you've got your own nervous system—and I've got a good enough gun—and you do, it's your own self-esteem and sense of life progress—it doesn't matter what you do once you're in that situation. You're already toast. There isn't a way to make that arrangement work. Is there? This isn't a matter of a technique or method: "Well, I'll get in the seat and I'll get the polygraph and I'll put the gun to my head and then instead of doing this I'll do that." No. I mean, the system is bad. Are you with me on that?

> C: Mm-hmm.

> T: We have this fantasy that there's some guru somewhere that can get away with this kind of thing ("and then the swami controlled all of his

emotions"), but I've never met that swami. If you know one, introduce me and we shall see. Here's what I'm saying: consider the possibility that the method doesn't add anything—that it's the system, the agenda, the purpose that matters. It's kind of like, if digging is the problem, how you dig doesn't matter. Whether it's a teaspoon or a steam shovel, it's the same thing. It's the digging that's the problem; it's not the implement being used. It's the agenda that's the problem, not the control method. Do you know what I mean?

C: Mm-hmm.

T: We've got to face the agenda itself, head on. So when I say, "What's the alternative?" look at that list that you came up with. They're different tools but are they the same agenda? So suppose the agenda *is* the problem.

C: So what's the opposite of that, I mean, if you're trying to get away from your feelings or squash your feelings or whatever, then what are you going to do? Embrace your feelings? Please, yes! [fusion; you would have to hear the tape to know that the client is being sarcastic when he said, "Please, yes!"].

Cognitive Fusion

This is another example of high levels of verbal fusion. Verbal fusion causes private events to be experienced as literal, meaningful, or something to be threatened by. This client is very worried—almost petrified—about experiencing his feelings. The thought of not working to decrease these feelings is very scary to the client. You may recall he said that fairly clearly in the previous session and even warned the therapist about it.

T: But even then, you know there are lots of folks out there that try to do *that*. But even then, what I want to know is … in the service of what?

C: The same thing—to get rid of them. It's like going through the side door but you still go in there [defusion; despite the client's sarcasm, another part of himself sees the game].

T: You still go in there. Beautiful. It's the agenda that's the problem and not the technical details. This is a funny kind of bit of knowledge, if it is so, because you notice you can't use it in the service of a normal agenda. If you say something like "Okay, well, I'll just embrace my feelings" well, for what purpose? To get rid of them? In the world outside the skin, there's a rule I think that kind of describes how things work, which is pretty reliable, and this is what language evolved for: "If you don't want something, figure out how to get rid of it, and get rid of it." Ninety-five percent of the time it works great. It works great in creating the room we are in so that the rain won't come in on us. There's a light here, so it is not dark. We've progressed enormously in being able to regulate health, move around at hundreds of miles an hour, call people up and talk to them on the other side of the planet. I mean we can do incredible things that are a matter of manipulating and controlling our environment. But, also, we're the only species that kills themselves. We are the only one that struggles with mortality. The only one that gets depressed, anxious, and so on, even when things are going great on the outside. That rule works great out in the world, but the problem is, we don't know when to stop doing it, because doing it is what our minds evolved to do.

C: The way that we deal with the external world is to be able to describe it, to understand it. Okay, so if we apply that to our mental processes and we say, "That isn't working here," does that mean that we cannot describe our emotions or that the labels that we are using are wrong? Or just don't apply? I mean, do we have to back all the way up and say, "We don't know what's going on; we can't do anything about it"? I mean, I think this psychology goes around and around. We can't accept that; we've got to keep trying.

This is a very good example of how ingrained this process of understanding and control is. The therapist says to consider the possibility that deliberate control does not work on private events so maybe we should stop trying to control them, and the client hears, "Those tools don't work to control, so we should try even harder to understand how to control them." There is more work to be done. In fact, this mirrors the difficulty that many therapists experience when trying to learn ACT, because it does not fit into most psychological models that exist.

Language and Control

T: Those are good questions. But they're twisted questions. You know, when we describe things in the external world, that's also part of a larger thing: it's to understand it so we can manipulate it, so that we can change it.

C: Right.

T: Language evolved so we could make things be different, right? We've got to figure out the external world. But the world inside the skin? I don't know how to cordon off language in such a way that you won't talk about what's going on. But consider the possibility that the simple agenda, figuring out how to get rid of it when applied inside the skin, just doesn't work, that there it's something more like *If you're not willing to have it, you've got it.*

C: So the correlation is, if you're willing to have it, if you accept it, then it becomes not a problem [avoidance].

T: Neat. Depends on what the purpose is and what you mean by "not a problem."

C: That's too much like the side-door thing.

T: Could be, couldn't it? Let us look and see if that doesn't fit. What does your experience tell you about your own internal life? It could actually be true that if you're not willing to have it, you've got it.

The therapist could jump a little more on defusion at this point. The therapist could simply thank the client's mind, for example. We suspect this did not happen because the therapist was trying to get to "If you're not willing to have it, you've got it." The client is so verbally entangled that he is hearing everything that the therapist says through a "control agenda" filter—even though he now pauses and notes the crack in the system ("That's too much like the side-door thing"), showing that we now have the alternatives in the room.

Beginning to Accept Private Events

C: It depends.

T: We need to look at the long term because we can't trust the short ones. You're in here. So that's suspicious.

C: Right.

T: How did that happen?

C: Well, we've kind of been coming at this thing from all these different angles for these three times now, and I agree. Sometimes I think my distraction stuff is working very well, but long-term? I don't know that there's anything else to do. I don't know very many people who do anything differently than I do [fusion].

T: Yeah, I know.

C: So, you know, maybe I can just learn to live with the doubts and the bad times and just go on, you know? But I don't want to admit that. I don't really like human beings and I don't want to admit that we can't get beyond this pathetic state that we're in [conceptualized self]. Sometimes I think, well, either we have a lot of evolving to do or we won't get there and we'll blow ourselves up first [avoidance, not present].

T: Yeah. It's hard to look at. And even this moment.

C: In my own personal life I haven't ever really challenged myself in a way that I'd like to be able to die and say that I had lived [values]. I'm not afraid of death, I mean, God, I've tasted it a couple of times; it's scary as hell. But even scarier is to open a door in your mind and look at what's in there and go "ew" [conceptualized self, values; it is a bit of a stretch to put in values here, but the sense in hearing this is that this comment is painful, not just because of content, but because life is not being lived].

T: Yeah.

C: I may not be able to change that [fusion].

Linking Acceptance to Values

Talking about things that he would normally not talk about is a sign that he is becoming more accepting of his private events. This client, for example, has started talking about what is important to him without even being asked. That is a clear sign that his defenses are down due to acceptance and defusion. We hurt most in the areas we value, and when we put values on hold while we fight, it usually creates even greater pain than we started with. As he begins to accept his emotions, he turns naturally to that even larger pain: the pain of a life not being lived.

T: Interesting thought.

C: That's what I'm kind of looking at here. I want to be a better person for going through this type of thing. I want to live a better life [values].

T: Cool. Let's move toward that.

C: I'm not sure that I can. But I don't have to look too far in the future as to what happens if I don't. I'll probably go on as I have been going for years, and then in a few more years I'll try again. I'll find another therapist and see what his or her thing is, his or her way, and I guess the goal would be to be getting rid of pain or whatever. I don't know [defusion, values; again values shows up with the connotation that this is a life not being lived].

T: [Pause] You just touched on something here a few seconds ago. It looked like you were talking about opening a door into something you really care about. I was just watching your eyes, and it looked like you just cracked the door open. I don't know. Right here. Now. Am I fantasizing?

This focus on the present moment and values is, in a way, ahead of the style of ACT that this therapist is pursuing, but when these opportunities present themselves, it is often useful to follow them. In ACT, the therapist can move in from any of the six areas on the hexaflex and loop back to where they were with little difficulty. With experience, you can relate any topic to any area in the hexaflex at almost any moment in therapy.

C: I told you what was most important to me as a human being, which is not something that I tell very many people [acceptance, values].

T: I could see it. Just for a second something kind of went across your face as if there was something important in there.

C: I mean, that's what I want [pause]. That's my stated and internal goal in life. It was to know whether there's hope for human beings [values]. Are we the creatures of value, or are the gifts that we have that make us human wasted on us?

T: Let's find out.

C: That is a scary proposition [acceptance, present]. I think there are a lot of people that don't look at whatever it is. It's not about money. With some people, I think they find it in a marital relationship. But for me that isn't there, that's not the challenge. My kids are certainly part of it. But I feel like I am in here to work on me; it's finding something in me that is honorable. I'm not sure what it is. I've always had this feeling that I'm hiding from something in myself [values].

T: Good. And what if finding that requires getting in touch with your feelings? What if some of those answers were in the very painful things you've pushed away? Suppose the main thing that would help you here is your own pain. You've got to kind of look inside yourself and see if you're at a place where you hurt enough, you're tired enough, or exasperated enough, you're sick of it enough to show up. Even though you don't know what you're doing, you don't know what I'm talking about exactly, and the whole thing might just be psychobabble bullshit, and what good is it? Even with the thought that "Maybe I'm being manipulated and I don't know what's going to happen." Even with all that, the fact is, this is painful. "I've run this thing out. I don't know what to do. Whatever it is, it's not this." That's our biggest ally right now. It's just being fed up and sick and tired, and if we're going to try something different, fundamentally different, we're going to kind of follow the pain inside. If it's something fundamentally different, then that will likely be scary, confusing, whatever. We have to hang on to this not having knowledge of what the alternative is, because right now anything that seemed logical would just loop back into the same verbal system. Just call a spade a spade. Am I happy with how my life is going or not?

C: Oh man, I'm not.

There is an opening that could be pursued that is being lost here. Ironically, this is not bad ACT work. It probably will work. But it may be the long way around. The client connects with the deep desire to be about something and the pain that comes from that. The therapist points to the process of avoidance and rightly suggests that in his pain, the client might find his values but then the therapist did not immediately go there. The therapist probably does not go there because he or she is targeting a different process that seems more important at this time. Later we will see that the clinician pursues self as context and probably believes that this context should be established before fully opening this door. Nevertheless, if the therapist had done a mindfulness exercise about what is most deeply desired, the whole system might have cracked open right then and there. To do that, the clinician would need to go beyond his or her original plan and begin to explore the values inside the client's pain.

Back to Acceptance of Private Events

T: Those are pretty important little animals out there, who aren't humans. If they had all this, they'd be as happy as they know how to be. We have all this and we're still not happy. Because that last little 5 percent is the world inside the skin, and it just doesn't seem to work that way. It works the exact opposite way: if you're not willing to have it and you run away, you're in it. Conversely, you can't use that information for anything without dropping the agenda because if you say, "Okay, well then I'm going to feel whatever comes up," the purpose of it is the same thing—control.

C: Yeah. I can't possibly imagine another way of working it [fusion].

T: Right, and so all we need right now is *not* that, because that would be another example of your mind trying to do it. Let's not imagine another way to do it.

C: Zowie. Let's not find another distraction.

T: Exactly. Your mind is not ready to let go of this agenda because it's wired into your mind. Yet it's not working. Hang on to that, and that's not psychobabble. You don't have to have any faith in that at all; in fact, I encourage you to not believe a word I'm saying. It's not going to help you to believe it anyway. But there is something you can trust, which is your own experience. I bet there is something in you saying, "I'm ready to move ahead from here." Trust that. If you can't trust that, I don't know what you can trust; I mean, let your own experience tell you.

C: I do trust that. That doesn't mean I'm not scared to go ahead. That's why I'm here. I know that I could go down farther, that I could hit the bottom, I could lose it, and I can see that that could happen with my business, and I don't want that to happen [fusion, avoidance]. I can tell myself that it's not working and know that it's true. It isn't. I can say, "Make it work," but you know, it's very "blech" [acceptance, values; the tone on the tape makes it clear that he is fed up with "making it work" and is ready to move on—thus these labels].

T: Yeah, exactly. Good. If you're tired enough of trying to make it work, that's cool. That's your main ally.

C: I can see that I have to remind myself of that. If it gets unpleasant or if I get scared, if I'm losing, you ought to feel like you have a grip on yourself, reality or whatever [conceptualized self].

Creating a Context for Acceptance

Now we begin to see where the clinician has been going: a transcendent sense of self. The clinician undoubtedly believes that this element is crucial to true acceptance work.

T: Somehow what we need to do is let go of something that you don't quite know how to let go of. Before we try to do anything else, we need to create a context in which that's possible. Consider the possibility that we've got this sort of thin overlay of language that's only been around one hundred thousand years—not very long in geological time. Writing, and all the rest of modern language, is only about four thousand years old. Our ability to figure out how to get rid of things is quite recent. We've only really been evolving culturally a few thousand years as a verbal species. But language is sitting on top of some primitive functions that go back as long as there's been life on the planet. So it's not reasonable to expect us to turn and do something other than evaluate and manipulate and control, which is all about what minds know how to do. If your thoughts or feelings look like they're going to harm you, then you engage programming that's millions and millions of years old that's all about "Get me out of here."

So what we have to do before we do anything else is create a context in which it's possible to face monsters without having our lives on the line. It is sort of like this: Let's say your mind is like a computer, and we've got two computers here side by side that are exactly the same. They're loaded up with the same software, same data, and so on. I type in a little string of words and hit enter and I get a readout on the screen. Because the data and the programs are the same, the readout is pretty likely to be the same, right? So imagine we've got two computers, one here, one there, and they're exactly the same, and the same input is put in, and we push the key on both. Okay? Same readout comes out on the screen, very reliable.

Situation number one: The operator over here is very into what's on that screen, like, metaphorically sitting right up on it. She's almost forgetting that she's watching a screen, like when you go to the movies and you forget that you're watching the movie, you're so into it.

Situation number two: The operator in front of the machine is aware that there's a distinction—metaphorically, the operator is sitting back, a little bit away. Let's say the output is "Life's not worth living" or "Deep down, people are really no good" or "Deep down, there's something wrong with me." Okay? Critical thought. If that comes up for this person (the one sitting really close to the screen), this is bad news. This is something that has to change. Paradoxically, the degree to which they believe it affects the degree to which they have to change it. You with me?

C: Mm-hmm.

T: This person over here [person sitting farther away in situation number two] is sitting back and he sees that output, "Deep down, there's something wrong with me" on the screen. Is there anything that has to change? No, it is just some words that popped up. He might say to a friend, "Gee, come over here and look at this. I typed this in, and this is what I got." Are you with me?

C: Mm-hmm.

T: My point is this. If *you* are your mental machinery, there isn't anything you can do except try to regulate the machinery. Because it means what it says it means. So when you think bad things about yourself, you've got to do something about that. Or if you feel bad things, you've got to do something about that. But if there's the distinction between you and your mental machinery, why do you necessarily have to do anything about it? Maybe it's possible to have a little bit of space there, a little bit of blue sky, a little bit of fresh air.

C: For sure, well, that's why I know that I'm not a depressed person; it's my biochemistry that makes me depressed, so I take drugs. I don't have to deal with that, it's not who I am [acceptance, self as context; the scoring is a bit difficult however—see below].

T: Yeah, actually I think that's one of the most helpful things about a disease model is that it instantly does certain things like that. Sometimes at a cost, but you know.

The client's previous response is a bit ambiguous. He states that he is not his feelings—but adds that they are caused by his biochemistry. Whether or not we agree scientifically, functionally this might be helpful. It helps to create a distinction between the client's concept of self and his emotions, which is a step toward a more open and less attached psychological posture.

C: If you're saying that I am not my mental machinery, if who I am is not necessarily what I think, or how I behave … um, if I can't control those behaviors, then they will affect who I am. They will get me in trouble [fusion]. I am ultimately responsible for those behaviors. If I need help controlling them, then I go to the doctor and make him give me antidepressant medication. That has worked, for the most part.

This is a small step forward and a small step back. On the one hand, he senses the possibility of a distinction between himself and his emotions and thoughts. But then, on the other, he moves this into the area of actions and their costs, which is a different issue, and does so in a way that mixes feelings and actions. It seems likely that he fears that not controlling these emotions will ultimately get him into trouble because actions and emotions are so clearly tied together, and, further, he has his identity tied to controlling these emotions.

The practice of acceptance can be difficult for some clients when defusion and self as context are not well in place. It is like asking someone to stand in front of a loaded gun. A fused person will experience emotions and thoughts as if they are a gun that is real and dangerous, whereas a defused person who experiences her private events as just thoughts and feelings will experience them more like a toy squirt gun and will more willingly stand in front of them without needless defense.

Another way that we will describe this to a client is by saying something like this: "I feel that the way you experience your thoughts and feelings is something like this. In the first example, you are driving and you encounter a large tree that has fallen across the road, and there is no way that you can get past it. The tree is totally in the way. So you must stop and deal with it; it is a real problem. In the second example, you drive past a man who yells at you, "Stop—there is a tree blocking the road ahead." In this case you have a choice to stop or continue. Maybe there really is a tree ahead, or maybe this guy gets a kick out of making people late. The only way you will ever know is to keep rolling along and see how things go. You usually treat your thoughts and feelings as real trees in the road that you must stop and deal with on their own terms. Maybe they are just weird guys yelling warnings at you, and other than noticing them, no particular action may be required."

Defusion and Self as Context

The therapist continues to try to illustrate this distinction between the client and the client's private events, thus fostering defusion and self as context.

T: Well, you will be held responsible for what you do, for sure. But we're talking about things here that aren't necessarily outside the skin at all. I mean, they lead to things that might be outside the skin, and that's where the cost would be.

C: Right.

T: But the struggle starts way earlier, does it not?

C: Right, so does it matter that my mental machinery and I are two separate things? [defusion, self as context] I don't judge what I think, or my feelings; they're there and they rule me. I don't want them to. I want to control them [avoidance].

T: Right. Well, but paradoxically the place in which they rule you may be the place in which you try to have control. This is the negative emotion. [The therapist holds out a piece of paper perpendicular to the floor and moves it toward the client in such a way that he puts up his hand to stop its progress.] All right, now I'm going to try to get it to touch you, and don't let that happen; make sure it doesn't get anywhere near you. [The therapist pushes while the client pushes back, moving the paper in various directions to keep it from touching his body. They continue for several seconds with considerable effort being expended.] Now I want to ask you something. How much is this thing controlling your behavior?

C: A lot.

T: A lot. Right. Now, I'm going to throw this thing in your lap, okay? Put your hands to the side. You don't have to do anything; your lap will catch it, okay? Notice that you might want to put your hands out, but don't. [The therapist tosses a sheet of paper on the client's lap, then pauses and tosses another sheet and then another.] How much are these things controlling you now?

C: Not at all.

T: So, there's a paradox here. Suppose these sheets are your thoughts and feelings. Your mind says, "I can't have these things control me." Right? But what if controlling them is to be controlled *by* them? Because if you can't have them control you, that means they're very, very important. Something shows up that's not supposed to be there; this is danger time. So your hand goes up, and you start struggling. Is that control? Aren't they controlling you?

C: But where are they coming from, if not from me? Aren't I bad because they're coming out of me? [conceptualized self]

Problems with Control and the Beginning of Self as Context   **69**

This is an amazing response, if you think about it, but it is entirely coherent with ACT theory. It shows how fusion with thoughts and feelings leads to fusion with a conceptualized self, which then makes acceptance impossible. Leaps like this—from "Aren't they controlling you?" to "But aren't I bad to have them?"—provide frequent support in sessions for an ACT model if you just step back and watch how these leaps from one topic to another pop up precisely in the way the model predicts. And this is part of why the clinician probably took the "long way around"—wanting to do the defusion and self as context work that would allow acceptance before getting back to the pain inside a life not being lived.

T: Mary had a little …

C: Lamb.

T: Where did that come from?

C: I was taught it.

T: Presumably. Do you remember when you first learned it?

C: No.

T: Yeah, it's just part of the programming, right? Okay, now I'm going to say the same words again and I want you to make absolutely certain sure and be positive that not one bit of your response has anything to do with lamb. All right? Get ready. Mary had a little …

C: Fish.

T: Okay, did you do it?

C: Yes.

T: How did you know to say yes?

C: Thought processes. You know, it's an animal, but it's not … I can't say this … can't say … [pause; chuckles] … yeah.

T: Right. You can't say it because then you touch …

C: Lamb.

T: So lambs are in there. It's "fish—not lamb" not just "fish." But that means it's related to lamb! I'm going to say something again, and watch your mind processes. Make sure what comes up is not what usually comes up. It's not related to it, doesn't touch, doesn't have any contact with it whatsoever [pause]. I'm not a good person; deep down I'm really …

C: Bad. . . . There's got to be something to replace that with! I mean, if you're not going to do it, you've got to have something else.

T: If you try to replace it, you only increase it. Here's the thing: I'm with you in the sense that *being* a bad person is not what you want, but that is not what is happening. These are thoughts. These are feelings. Do you remember how old you were when you first thought that you were bad?

C: Really, really young. Really young.

T: You can't have the ability to evaluate things and apply them to everything else and not apply them to yourself. Find something in this room that you can't criticize [they both look around]. The cheesy picture, you like this picture? You like the frame? The flaking gold paint? They probably spent a *lot* of money on those pictures! I bet you that one was at least $12.95. They probably got it at K-Mart. You're pretty good at evaluating things, right? Is there *anything* in here you can't criticize and judge [they both look around]. [whispering] Why are *you* going to get off scot-free? How would *that* be?

    So what do you put on top of it? My guess is you put achievement on top of it. You're smart, successful, put some effort into school. Right? You put Mr. Smarty Pants on top of it, no? But here's the thing. "I'm bad … No, really I'm good. See here, look what I can do." … Doesn't it stick you even more to "I'm bad?" Doesn't it kind of creep up: "I'm a fraud"?

C: Mm-hmm, that's good … hmmm. . . . We were talking about these two people on their computers and how there was the concept that you are or are not your machinery … mental machinery.

T: Right.

C: And I wasn't … I still don't know if you're trying to say that you see a self as separate from that or not [self as context].

The client just asked a question. If the therapist had not been afraid of supporting the programming that got the client into this place, the therapist could have answered, "Yes, there is a self that is separate from your programming." At this moment that could have led to "If I don't follow my programming, then it will become less intrusive and bothersome"—still essentially a control reaction. Instead the therapist tries to find a less direct way to answer.

T: Watch your mind. Watch it right now. Watch how it works. By programming. If you are it, then we're in real trouble, because number one, you've got all kinds of crap in your head. If you can't get rid of "Mary had a little lamb," how are you going to get rid of "I'm bad"? Look at all of what you've done … all the Mr. Smarty Pants things you've done; the machine doesn't know how to stop doing what it does. In that metaphor, you know, the operator does not have personal investment in what's on the readout screen because there's a distinction, but over here there's no distinction [between the two computer screens]. There is personal investment, and so you've got to change it. This operator over here doesn't have to change it [person who is back from the computer screen]. What difference does it make? It's words on a screen. Where did you get your self-critical thoughts, for example? How old were you when they showed up?

C: I don't know, three or four, something like that.

T: Do you know where they come from?

C: I can guess. But it's all happening when you're starting to learn who you are, developing your language skills, applying labels to things, getting along with other people, and having to create boundaries. You're learning "yes" and you're learning "no," what's okay and what's not okay, and you're so young and impressionable that the "not okays" come down harder than they would when you're older. So you take these lessons to heart. Or you don't and you become a psychopath or something.

This last sentence is interesting, common, and telling. People fear if they accept their feelings and thoughts and especially if they distinguish these from themselves they will become psychopaths. This is part of the glue holding the system together—the conceptualized self is leading to nonacceptance. To go further, the therapist will need to establish another sense of self. All that can be done in this session has been done.

T: We've got to find a place where it's safe to be you and to turn and face these monsters. That's kind of what I was trying to put out there, and I think we'll work on that next time. If we can find a place where you can stand, where *you're* not at stake—who you are is not at stake—then it might be possible to get in there and muck around and look at the slimy lizards that are running around in your head and history. Okay. There's some dangling ends there, but I'm not going to try and tie them up because we've burned enough time here. I will see you next week.

FINAL COMMENTARY

Overall this is a good session. One of the things worth noting is that a lot of classic ACT material is covered, even well-known metaphors and exercises, but the session does not feel forced. It has a flow and a notable sense of progress.

If there is a worry, it is that the therapist at times seemed to assume too much. At times the therapist went ahead too fast, seeming to have a sense of the session that at times did not permit the therapist to chase leads, so the client may have sensed that the therapist was not 100 percent present in the session or in focus. Still, this is an effective piece of work.

Looking ahead, the therapist has committed to a particular plan. That is not always wise, and we can expect that this client will push back a bit.

Figure 3.1 Time spent addressing ACT processes in session two

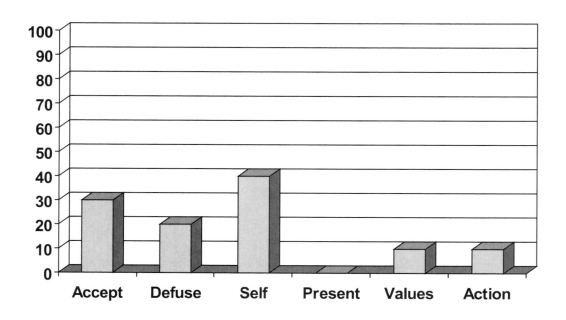

Figure 3.2 Status of client's ACT processes by the end of session two

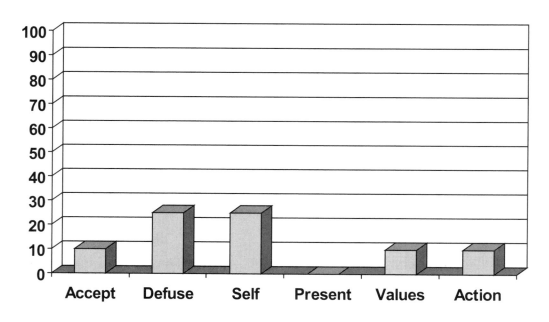

CHAPTER 4

Self as Context

In the previous session, the therapist tried to help the client see if attempts at controlling private events have been useful or harmful in the long run. It became increasingly apparent that control strategies were not as useful as the client assumed they were. Indeed, the client began to see that that struggle itself was associated with a sense of his life not working. Values and the pain of not living life emerged naturally, but the therapist decided just to take a peek there and then open up the need for defusion and for contact with a transcendent sense of self.

This session aims to foster the processes that were touched on in the previous session by helping the client connect with the idea that he and his thoughts are not one, and that the conceptualization that the client has of himself is separate from himself.

SESSION THREE

T: So how are you doing?

C: I didn't do my homework because whenever I started to struggle with my feelings, or whatever, it wasn't convenient to be writing [inaction]. At other times when I could be writing, there didn't seem to be much to recall, and it didn't seem to be very relevant. I thought, "Well, if what we are doing is looking at a new way of doing something, that doesn't necessarily mean that you have to throw out everything else you have already learned." And perhaps we could leave that exercise and just continue on with whatever it is you wanted to present as an additional means of coping [avoidance].

Avoidance of Homework

This is the second time in a row that the client has not done his homework. The main concern is not the data; it is that there is something getting in the way of the client keeping a commitment. We would assume that making a difference in the client's depression or anger would motivate him to complete the homework, but that is not the case. There is likely something that is emotionally difficult about doing the homework that he is avoiding, and this is probably not the only area in his life that he does this. Thus, avoidance and the processes that foster it should be addressed. The other process that can be related to not completing homework is values. Linking homework and all therapy-related behaviors to the client's values can cause these actions to have stronger reinforcing functions.

> T: Hmmm. Tricky business this homework. Besides it being hard to do because of time, what else was in the way of doing it?

> C: It didn't seem worth my time. The idea of placing a number on the means I was using before, and them being completely ineffective. I know that is your goal. You want to make it more easy or acceptable to embrace a new way of trying something or dealing with something.

This is an example of cognitive fusion. The therapist tried to help the client come into contact with what his experience actually says about the effectiveness of his control strategies, but the client has again taken it in a different, more social direction, in which the therapist has a predetermined goal that goes beyond his experience. Further, it seems as though the client believes that this is a part of a process to get him to control his emotions in a different way. This kind of thing is not uncommon, especially when doors have been opened in previous sessions but not fully walked through. It is a kind of "morning after" effect in which the mind struggles to keep from being dethroned and raises fears of being part of a crazy movement, turning into a psychopath, being dominated by a therapist, and so on (all of which we have already seen in these sessions).

> T: Well, you're several steps out ahead of me.

> C: Well, I read a journal article on ACT, you know [avoidance, fusion; this is a distraction, which is a kind of avoidance. It also would move the issue into one of theory, thus the fusion score].

> T: Interesting. My purpose was more to see how it is than to have it be a particular way. We all have investments in whatever our thoughts are. The whole thing that we're working on here is trying to, at least in part, put those investments in on the basis of what works rather than on what's reasonable. That includes me. And who says I'm so smart? I view myself as a hired hand. I work for you. It doesn't mean that I'm willing to take your thoughts or mine as being literally true. It does mean that you're the boss in here in an important way, and the bottom line is your bottom

line. Take the measures we were looking at. They are all your bottom line: how much suffering you've done and how much effort has gone on and whether or not whatever is happening there is moving you ahead toward what you really want or backward. Those are pretty basic things … that don't have to have numbers. But I do like numbers.

This is a functional response to an avoidance move. The client does not want to continue talking about the homework because it is making him frustrated or generally making him feel bad about not doing it. Furthermore, he is bumping the topic toward a kind of social compliance issue—the therapist and ACT theories rather than the client's experience. The therapist does not bite and stays on topic. It is a functional way of saying, "I know you don't like talking about this, and I am okay with that" and "Your experience is the measure here, not ACT theories." Of course it could also be experienced as invalidating, and the therapist is tracking that and will come back to this issue of the article later.

C: I don't like numbers [fusion, avoidance].

T: Well, they make it easier for me to know if there's change.

C: It seems like putting apples with oranges. I can't trust my assessment of that stuff, and it's not convenient to do it at the time. I can't just leap from what I'm doing.

T: Hmmm. I asked you to do it once, at the end of the day, actually.

All of this is also functionally avoidant. The therapist's last response is okay, but we know it will not really go anywhere because the client knows this full well. Another way to respond to this situation would be to work with him to contact what is getting in the way and then challenge him to confront it in the service of his values. For example, another response could be "I get that it is not convenient, *and* what might you gain by working with me on this?"

C: I won't remember at the end of the day. And I don't want to remember. It's like, why dredge it up again? [avoidance] It wasn't fun or useful or anything else at the time. I don't know why I'm so resistant to doing that; I really don't know [acceptance]. I couldn't tell you. Although it doesn't seem very relevant; it pisses me off.

T: Well, that's okay that you're resistant. I think that's fine. I would advise that the both of us in here take that as grist for the mill.

C: Right after I saw you the last time, I was at work when one of my waitresses called up—she's one of the ones that I'm having the most trouble with—and she asked this stupid question that she shouldn't have had to ask because I left complete instructions about what she was supposed to do on her shift. I felt this "swoosh" and thought, "I want to strangle her!" And I'm saying, "Be calm, be cool; it'll eventually subside. There's no point in getting mad. It's obviously a miscommunication; she didn't understand what I wanted her to do." It's like, all right, why be mad? [fusion, not present, avoidance] It's probably my fault that she didn't understand.

T: Okay.

C: If I try to put it into your task, I was probably an 8 on the mad scale and an 8 on the effort scale. My effort is always equal to the feeling. I guess it must have been a little bit more because I'm able to push it down and stop it [avoidance], dissipate the emotion so that reason can come back into play because the reason is where things happen [fusion]. Emotion is not a productive state. It's enjoyable or it's destructive in my opinion— that's it. And when it's destructive, then it needs to be controlled or it can cause damage [fusion, avoidance].

T: Yeah. Last time actually, we came up on your models and it's ...

C: My family—they're not very good models. You think adults have all the answers and they've managed to control the beasts within them, and actually you realize when you grow up that at best they've caged the beasts but they're still there.

T: Probably caged them at a cost, too.

C: For sure.

T: If you don't stomp the negative ones down, they're going to ...

C: I've let them out a couple of times to see what would happen. I've experimented with throwing things around [avoidance]. You break things, and people look at you like you're an idiot and then you have to pay for the stuff you've broken. And beyond that, you injure or damage people's trust in you; they want to be able to count on you to not be something that's weird.

Back to Emotions

The linkage of action to emotions is very common for clients, especially in the case of anger. It is a sign of cognitive fusion and self as content in ACT. This indicates that more work needs to be done to help the client experience that he is not his emotions or his thoughts. If the client can't get to a defused place, then he will continue to fear his own thoughts and feelings and work to control them. Defusion fosters acceptance.

This whole section could be discouraging to a therapist who expects ACT to be a smooth process. It is quite common for progress to be up and down. In fact, a "good session" (like the last one) very often is followed initially by a presentation like this. Usually, however, if progress was ever made, it can be reconstructed fairly quickly.

The discussion of models was not fully presented in the transcript sections we looked at in the last session, by the way, but you can tell from context what was examined.

T: But the throwing is not an emotion; that's an action, right?

C: That's true.

T: Actions can create serious problems if they're not appropriate to the situation. Anger is the most difficult one because it seemingly links up with action so tightly. And we almost talk about it as if it's an action.

C: Do you think it's possible to experience anger without experiencing physiological reactions to the anger? Can you divorce the two or teach yourself to?

T: I don't know, but physiological reactions aren't behavior either.

C: No, but they're scary; they're uncomfortable; who wants them? [avoidance, fusion] Wham, wham, wham, or you're getting cold or your eyes are crossing or whatever.

T: I don't want to conclude anything here, I'm just asking: how much do you know about that when you are feeling feelings, period, just feeling them without running from them or regulating them, and so on? Put aside the issue of behavior; I think it's distinct. What I'm asking is, how unpleasant is anxiety, fear, anger, and so on, if you're not adding to it by efforts to regulate it?

C: I find it very unpleasant because my center is my stomach, and it just starts turning, and I will have diarrhea whether I'm too excited or too upset.

T: So positive emotions are also costly?

C: Yes.

The Control Agenda and Sense of Self

T: And yet, am I wrong on this? We were talking about this last time, and I think you said you are afraid of emotions. Maybe "afraid" is not what you said.

C: Leery.

T: Leery. And what you seemed to say almost sounded like, "I kind of know I need to go there. God knows I don't want to, and it sounds like so much crap to me."

C: For sure, I think that's close to what was happening.

T: Okay. So it sounds like you are of two minds about emotions. Would it be possible to take your ambivalence with you? You don't have to put it away; you don't have to be clear in your mind about it [pause]. What I'm asking is, is it okay to be ambivalent?

C: Sure. It's also possible to not be [avoidance]. I can relate it to things that I've done or tried. I was really scared, dragging my feet the whole way, knowing that I had to at the same time. So, I gotta, I just gotta let go of the branch and drop, whatever.

T: Well, I want to go back and pick up a little strand from the beginning of the session. You have the Internet and you did what people with the Internet do: you looked up the stuff written about ACT. And now there're lots of words in your head—things to be right and wrong about. We'll have to deal with that. So I cop to the fact that I do have an angle I want to pursue here—we went over that in our intake session—*and* it's more important to do what you've hired me to do than to be right about writings or theory or something other than what really works for you.

C: That's good, otherwise I'd fire you.

T: So there was that strand when you came today that sounded like I'm trying to make you think something, make you believe something, make you …

C: Persuade me.

T: That's okay [pause]. I don't want to persuade you. Just consider the possibility that your mind is not your friend here—nor your enemy. It's evolved for a different purpose. It's not who you are. It's a tool you use, and it's blabbing to you constantly and claiming to be you. Claiming to know everything. Claiming to be so smart. This is how minds are. All minds—mine too. What's the exact opposite of persuasion? It's something more like showing up *with* this morning-to-night chatter. What I'm more interested in than persuading is to see if we can show up with our minds. Take an attitude more like a dispassionate observer who is willing to just sort of sit and watch what goes on in here, and also what's gone on in your life, and just call a spade a spade. With that sense of, if you see something, then you saw it, and if you felt something, then you felt it. Not adding or subtracting anything; it's sort of just watching the raw data. I don't think that's persuasion. It's something more just like …

C: The viewpoint?

T: Yeah, the viewpoint is not an intellectual viewpoint. The viewpoint is you sitting there looking at your life. That's a viewpoint. I don't mean like my opinion is. Because that's all mind stuff.

C: Well, that's easy, that's easy; I can buy that. I can agree with you immediately that my mind is often not my friend. That I want to tell it to shut up and I want to control it [avoidance]. And I can step aside and look at me and go, "something is wrong."

In the section above we really get the sense that the client is still very fused with his mind. There is some talk here that might lead you to believe that the client is becoming more defused and possibly more willing to leave his thoughts and feelings alone, but it is thoroughly mixed with fusion and avoidance. The fusion can be detected by the way that the client talks about these private events. He still talks as though they are real and important. It seems more like he is saying, "Yes, if I do that, then they will go away." If he were more defused, then they would appear as less of an issue.

T: Right.

C: But that doesn't mean I can't sever the feeling, I mean, the gut going along with the mind. So it's the physical manifestations of what's going on in my mind that I really want to stop [avoidance].

T: That's your hook.

C: Yes.

T: Hmmm. And where can you stand that you would not get hooked? Imagine that there's this chessboard. It's out in all directions, and there are pieces on it and there are two teams. Say there are white ones and black ones, and they're fighting each other. And they're sort of working out as a team. The black team and the white team fight each other. Right? Now in this metaphor, these pieces are your memories, your thoughts, your bodily sensations, what your stomach does, your pull to behave with predispositions, memories, bad experiences, good experiences, nice thoughts, good memories, calm moments, and so on. It's just all the stuff. And indeed, they kind of ally with each other. Some hang out over here and some hang out together over there. So a thought like "I'm bad" or "Life sucks" or whatever probably hangs out with moments when you've been depressed, angry, hurt, anxious, and so on. Or gruesome memories or scary memories or things you've done that you're not proud of, and so on. Conversely, you know, warm fuzzy feelings kind of hang out with other warm fuzzy things.

All right, your normal move is to—nominate some of those pieces as who you are, or who you want to be—the team that you want to have win. And most people nominate the good ones. So you go off and you try to do something about the bad ones. Okay. Metaphorically it's sort of like jumping up on the back of one of the queens and riding off to do battle with all of your private monsters.

A couple of things happen when you do that. One is that the monsters get more salient and central. Which they would, because you're focusing on them and if you are not willing to have them, you do. Doing battle against them shows they're very important. Number two, although the goal is usually to sort of push them away (and get them off at least in a dark, dusty corner so you won't have to see them, or ideally even push them off the board, checkmate the other team, and win), in fact, I've met precious few people for whom that's happened. Usually what happens is, at best, they get kind of obscured but you still know that they're there. Like, think of a really traumatic memory that you've got.

C: Okay.

T: Find something that really hurt or frightened you. That memory, if it's a black piece on the board, unlike a real game of chess, isn't it true that that piece has not fully been removed from the board? Can you even conceive of a universe in which that memory won't continue to be part of your life?

C: No, these thoughts are there somewhere.

T: Okay, so we ride off to do battle against them, except it doesn't seem to work very well. Plus, whole great portions of you are your own enemy. If whole great portions of you are your own enemy, there's something wrong with you.

C: Well, I wouldn't put it that way. I mean, in terms of your metaphor yes, that's what you say, but I don't believe that.

T: Okay, but at a higher level: if you're in that posture, where you're sort of somehow trying to battle with your own monsters, you're in a posture in which the enemy is you.

C: Okay, gotcha, you're right. I follow what you're saying. Although, your friend, your therapist, your mother would say, well, you can't help that. That happened when you were in sixth grade and you did what you knew how to do then and you don't need to feel ashamed, you don't need to be embarrassed, you can let it rest. And of course, you can't [acceptance].

T: Right. So this is exactly …

C: So it's not working.

T: This is the enculturation we get, which basically says, "Well, just put that out of your mind, honey"—explain it away. This is kind of like, here's this black piece, and it's really quite unpleasant, and it's associated with other things that are unpleasant, like how your body reacts when you even think of it. It's like your stomach—the black piece comes over and stands next to it, you know. Here is how we usually battle: we take this piece called "It wasn't my fault," and we'll throw it at the black pieces and see what happens. Well, I don't know if your mind is like mine, but my mind says something like this when I throw one like that out: I'll say, "It's not my fault." And I'll hear back an echo something like …

C: "Yes, but … you should have, you could have."

T: "You could have." Exactly. Okay, so there's a white team and a black team. "I'm perfect" is over here, and over here is the thought "There's nothing about me that's the tiniest bit worthwhile." If this is 100 percent true, what happens to this one? This is absolutely positively 100 percent no reservation, permanently 100 percent true; what happens to that one?

C: Then that one can't be.

Acceptance and Transcendence

The overarching move that the therapist is making is to try to increase a more transcendent sense of self and to show how we nominate elements of our experience to *be* us. The contextual, transcendent sense of self seems particularly needed for this client because he is highly threatened by his own experiences. The client believes that if his thoughts or feelings grow too much then he will behave in ways that will hurt him, or that the private events themselves will harm him. When someone is very afraid of her own experience, it is a sign that she sees herself as a conceptualized object.

T: At all, can't even be thought—it literally disappears, right? It's dead. Now, if you're sitting on the back of the white queen, that means this guy over here is your blood enemy. Your life is on the line to the point that if the thought that you are fighting is 100 percent absolutely positively true, the white queen disappears. These polarities can't stop. They don't know how to stop fighting with each other. From the point of view of each side of the polarity, I better fight because my life is on the line. If a tiger came in here and slowly ate you one gulp at a time, my guess is you'd have a hard time just being absolutely calm about that. Because we're tapping into some very primitive programming that goes back to an earthworm level of existence. So where I go with all that is, if you *are* those thoughts, you *can't* stop being in the war that's in your head. At that level you have too much invested in it. We spent a little bit of time sort of saying, can you win the war? That's what we did for a couple of sessions. But what I'm saying right now is this: even though you can't win it, you can't stop fighting *if* you believe you are these thoughts, these emotions.

C: Mm-hmm.

T: You just spent a couple of weeks saying that fighting only gets you deeper into the quicksand; it doesn't get you out. Yet you can't stop. So, in this metaphor, if you are not the pieces, who are you?

C: [Pause] Got me.

T: Within the metaphor. Who could you be? What could you be?

C: The hand.

T: Yeah, the answer presents itself, except the hands are invested in winning too. They're the ones that manipulate the moves, manipulate the pieces. They do this with the intent to box in the other team.

C: The table. I don't know.

T: Suppose you really were more like the table?

C: If I were the table I could give a shit about what's happening on top.

T: But you're very much in contact with it. In fact more so than the pieces. The table is the only thing in that whole image, the table meaning the chessboard that is the table on which it's played. You have a checkerboard table—it's the only thing in the metaphor that's in contact with everything.

The therapist does something neat here. The client is pretty aligned with the idea that he needs to control his thoughts and feelings. So instead of leaving the door open to the possibility that taking the stance of the board would decrease the power of the pieces, the therapist says that the board is the only thing in contact with all the pieces. The therapist is almost telling the client that he will come into greater contact with his emotions from approaching it this way. This should foster acceptance, defusion, and awareness of an ongoing sense of self.

C: All right, then. That's not how I saw it in my mind, but then I choose not to be the table [avoidance].

The client picks up on this aspect of what the therapist is saying. This is not a problem. It is good to know where the client really is. If the client still experiences his thoughts and feelings as real and dangerous, then more defusion work needs to be done.

T: Because?

C: Because optimally I want to disassociate myself completely from those silly little pieces. I want to do something else [avoidance].

T: Yeah. And that is what you've been doing, yes?

C: I try to do that.

T: Consider the possibility that doing that comes out of a place in which you've been relating to pieces from the other team. They're your enemies, right? But who knows these reactions? Are they the table's enemies? Say this is a chessboard [picks up a magazine and puts it on the floor]. Suppose I put something really gross in here, like this [blows his nose into a tissue and puts in on the magazine]. My guess is that the table finds it as easy to hold that snotty rag as this pen [puts the pen on the magazine].

C: I'm lost.

T: It can hold what's put on it, and the whole thing can move. The one thing it doesn't get to do is suddenly come out from who it is to start moving these things around. Suppose it's something like that? Now you get to hold all your experiences, and you get to move in a direction. You get to make choices, you can go places, you can do stuff. And you have your experiences to experience. But you don't get to put that traumatic memory of yours back here or take that one off the board without going from who you are to who you aren't. And up here the war is *important*.

C: They're always going to be there, and somehow you've got to learn to hold them in a way that doesn't burn your hands [avoidance].

T: Follow out that metaphor. The white pieces can't hold the black pieces.

C: And vice versa.

T: And vice versa. Exactly. Now, that's important. Good thoughts—so-called—lead you into this polarity as easily as bad thoughts. And haven't you experienced that? "I'm good" can lead to fighting just as much as "I'm bad." From either side, the other side is life threatening, dangerous, incomprehensible, undesirable, scary. Normally, we don't think about how to get rid of good thoughts, but actually, you don't know how to 100 percent eliminate those either.

C: Exactly.

T: Enough blah, blah, blah; this is all just a metaphor after all. I'm not trying to make a logical argument. I'm just trying to create a useful picture. But I'd like to do something a little more experiential. It's an eyes-closed kind of deal. How willing are you to do an eyes-closed exercise?

Going Experiential

This is a good move by the therapist. There is no point in trying to teach the client that he is correct or accurate in his metaphor. As soon as things start getting very verbal or "heady," then it is time to shift gears. When the therapist starts trying to explain what the client was supposed to experience, it is time to move on. This will be one of the first experiential processes for this client—it will be important to see how it goes.

C: Sure.

T: And what I'd like to do is to take this metaphor out into the world of experience and just see what it's like out there. I might periodically ask you something and I'd ask you to respond or I might not. So you don't need to tell me what's happening, although you can if it seems real important for me to know some bit, but in general you don't need to. Just follow my voice. I'm not hypnotizing you. I'm not trying to relax you. We're just trying to go and get some raw data. And then we'll come back and talk about it.

C: Okay. I'm ready.

The therapist then leads the client through the observer exercise (Hayes et al., 1999, p. 193). There is no point in repeating that material here because therapists who are serious about doing ACT should have this initial ACT book, and the content of the transcript is extremely close to the written material there.

In this exercise, the therapist begins by having the client come into contact with different sensations, including hearing, what it is like to sit in a chair, what it feels like to breathe, and so on. The therapist helps the client notice that there is a part of himself that is noticing that he is noticing these things. This is called the *ongoing sense of awareness* or *observer self*. The therapist then leads the client back through time and guides the client to remember different times in his life, such as a week ago, a year ago, young adulthood, teen years, and childhood. Then, during each of these memories, the client is helped to notice that this same sense of self is present.

Finally, various domains are examined—roles, emotions, bodily sensations, and thoughts—and in each case, the distinction is made between what is being observed and the person doing the observing. The utility of this exercise is that it creates a space from which it is safe for the client to experience any private event without damage being done to the self. About 95 percent of clients will respond very well to the exercise, and in about 25 percent of those cases, the exercise creates very noticeable and immediate change. That is not the case here.

T: Thoughts?

C: I didn't like it.

T: Okay. Do you know what it was associated with when you didn't like it?

C: I was bored. I felt like you were trying to persuade me with something. You were trying really hard, and I already got it and I thought, "We can stop this now" [not present, fusion].

T: Hmmm …

C: That's what I thought. It was like, what's the point? Yes, there is a "me"; there is something there behind all these things.

T: The part of you that just said that, is that the part of you that is aware of what's going on?

C: [Pause] No.

T: So, cool. Okay, so we make a connection, and then your mind comes in and says, "Okay, I got it." Sort of evaluates it, puts it in words. And then the same mind says "Let's get on to something else; enough already." Right? And that's fine. Still, as it's doing that, is there a part of you that is just aware of *that*? Is there more to you than evaluation?

C: Okay, so, now I want to know, is there something about that exercise that I can use? [conceptualized self, fusion, avoidance]

This is where having a good understanding of these functional processes really becomes necessary. The client is responding in a way that was not expected and not common. But because the therapist is familiar with the processes of this therapy, the therapist can still continue doing the work and roll with the punches. The client is responding in a very fused way. He has the feeling of being frustrated with the exercise because he does not see benefit from it. He probably also has the thought that "This is not worth my time" or perhaps even more (because we have seen it several times already) "You are trying to persuade me" or even "You are trying to control me" and is responding to that.

T: It depends on what you're going to try to do with it. You said earlier, a couple times, that there are certain kinds of things that you don't have much room for. You said something like, "I'm dang sure I don't want those things." I've used the metaphor of a chessboard holding all of it. The board-level part of you holds your bad memories as easily as your good memories. But at the piece level, that's a whole different thing. That's a war zone. And the war can't stop. It doesn't know how to stop. And as you just said, your immediate reaction was something like "I don't want that." So part of what I would ask you is, is it really true that *you* don't want that? Or is it that *your mind* doesn't want that. Can you connect with that part of you that stands back behind this persona, that part of you really committed to not having whatever you have?

C: When you first introduced it as a concept, which is not a new concept, a zillion thoughts went through my mind. What is that separate entity, that "me," what is that thing, you know? And is it something that can be shaped or improved, or is it just meant to be there with all of the things that happen around that core: the physical things, the thoughts, all that kind of stuff? [conceptualized self] If those are just occurrences to that central core, then who's calling the shots? If you as a person are wanting, you're striving and educating and whatever, if those concepts don't mean anything to that central entity, then the whole thing falls apart, and I'm just itching to know what you're trying to get at [avoidance; scored this way because we are guessing that the client is still trying to link the issue to a control agenda]. If the whole purpose of trying to focus on this center, this "you" that's there through experiences and everything else, and this is separate even from your body, but it's not—I mean it is and it isn't—then what the hell are we talking about? What can I gain out of this in terms of why I'm here talking to you? I mean is it supposed to make me feel better in some way to know that I'm still going to be there through thick and thin. Well, yeah, right.

T: The purpose isn't to make you feel better. The purpose I had was to see what is so. If at this deepest level, you haven't been fundamentally changed in terms of your basic core humanity, through all of what you've been through, how likely is it that you're going to be fundamentally changed through the next thirty years?

C: Define fundamentally changed [fusion].

The client is trying to draw the therapist into a mind-level discussion about what is "fundamentally changed" and what is not. Those types of discussions are smart in some situations, but often they strengthen fusion. Even discussions about ACT topics like fusion and acceptance, when done in a really technical way, are not all that helpful to foster these ACT processes. You will see in the response how the therapist avoids being sucked into this discussion.

Pulling Together the Session

T: Well, I can only do it experientially. When you go back and you find that strand of awareness. You find the teenager who was behind those eyes. You find the child before that.

C: That's you; that's an awareness.

T: That's right. And I'm not saying that this is everything that's important about people. I don't mean that at all.

C: Okay.

T: Here's what I'm doing: You don't know how to win this war, and it's not comfortable to live inside a war zone. And I'm guessing that's part of why you're here. I'm asking you to look and see if there's a part of you that's not in the war zone, even though it's 100 percent aware of the war. There is a place from which to stand and do something other than win the war. Will that mean that the war stops? I don't think so. And who said it had to stop? The part that's troublesome about the war business is that usually we have the idea that we're going to win the war and then life will start. Have you ever caught yourself sort of thinking, "My life will start sometime later"?

C: For sure. All the time.

T: Well, suppose this is it. This *is* your life. It's already started. The question is, are you going to live in it? Well, you need a place from which to live if you can't do it by first winning the war and then living. Once you're up on that "piece" level, you cannot stop fighting. It's not only that the war goes on, which it will, but that your personal success and failure is invested in it. Is it not? So it's not only going on, your in the middle of it. And you've got really important things at stake.

C: Mm-hmm.

T: How are you going to mask this? Is there any way that you could have peace of mind living inside a war in which you have tremendous investment in how it turns out? I mean, you've got to track it and watch it, tend to it, work angles, you know? What else do you expect of yourself? Of course you're going to do that. This is the computer thing. Of course, you're going to try to reprogram it. If your mind is telling you that you're horrible or life's horrible, or whatever, you're going to be tapping on those keys. There isn't anything else that you can do. So I'm just trying to find a place from which it's possible to do something different. The chess game just goes on and on and on. I don't know. You tell me—what it's like inside your head? This is not a belief system; I'm not trying to persuade you in a sense that you need to think a certain thing. Not at all. Absolutely not at all. You've got a strong mind, though, whew. It's almost like your mind is like a mental bully or something. Not of me, I don't mean that. I just mean I can sort of feel its bite. It's probably part of what scares you when it gets on someone else; it almost doesn't know when to stop. Right?

C: Yeah.

T: It's like you could literally tear the person's head off. But there's also a person in this room. Is there not?

C: It's interesting to think about that. I guess I feel to some extent that my mind is overpowering me. Like it says it's me [self as context].

T: Yeah.

C: But I don't really know what I'm saying even when I say that [defusion].

T: Cool. Good [pause]. We have to talk very metaphorically because your mind is listening and it will turn it all around into words. Part of what we're trying to talk about is beyond words. So we have to make some room for that sense of confusion. There's one other thing you said that created a dangling end for me. I wanted to put a point on it [pulls magazine with tissue and pen forward again]. This is the chessboard; this is a piece. That's one thing. Here's another thing [slides the magazine across the floor with the pen and tissue coming along for the ride]. Come on everybody, here we go. So I'm not just talking about navel watching or sitting around and chatting or something.

C: I didn't get that at all before. You can take the chessboard and move it.

T: Yeah. Good. Let's just let that rumble around. It's responsive to something you said earlier that you were disturbed about. Sooner or later we'll tie the loose ends up. Are there any other dangling ends that you feel need to be tied just from what we've done?

C: No. I'll probably think of stuff later.

FINAL COMMENTARY

This is a good example (warts and all) of a relatively structured session. Having committed to a course of action in the previous session, the therapist pursued it here. You can see that the clinician is not completely free to move, on the one hand. On the other, certain material was covered that otherwise might never have been covered.

The value of structured sessions cannot always be seen in the moment. It is one of the ironies of ACT work that very, very often you have to proceed on the basis of faith in the model, grounded in process and outcome evidence. Probably there is no example in which this is clearer than in ACT research. Regularly, ACT interventions do not look more effective at post-test. Sometimes they look worse. Then at follow-up, the value of the work emerges.

This is a scary fact of life for ACT clinicians and researchers, and you see it here. The therapist has planted seeds in this session. The client largely did not applaud. He even let out a few raspberries. It is only over time that we will see if this investment of time was worth it.

Figure 4.1 Time spent addressing ACT processes in session three

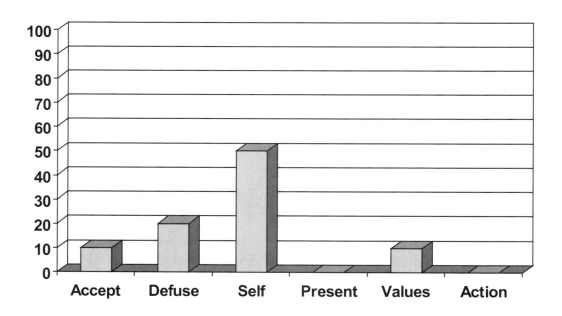

Figure 4.2 Status of client's ACT processes by the end of session three

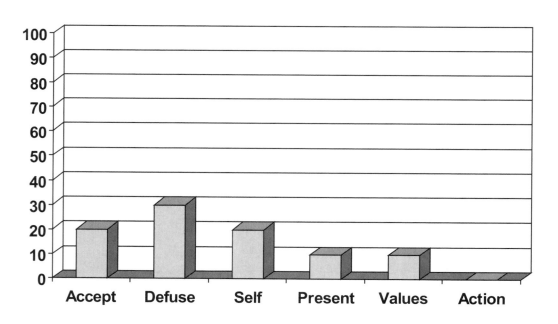

CHAPTER 5

Learning to Be Present and to See Self as Context

The previous session presented the concept of self as context and explored it in a brief exercise. There were moments in the previous session when it seemed as though the client was seeing himself the way he usually saw himself, as his cognitive content, and he would briefly catch that there was more to it than that. But then there were moments when the client was fused completely with the content. He seemed to be pushing back against the therapist, which has been a theme and which is usually some type of an avoidance move. It also seemed as though he was confused and frightened by the formlessness of his own sense of consciousness.

The therapist is early in the treatment and will need to continue to chop away at the verbal processes that are maintaining this way of living.

SESSION FOUR

T: How are you doing?

C: I'm doing fair to shitty, you know? It feels like my emotions are all over the place. I had a medication change, which I think is part of it.

T: Oh, really? Before you go, we'll get that written down, just to keep track.

C: I sometimes feel like a basket case for no reason. I am having really bad headaches—they feel like migraines. My joints and nerves feel like I have a real low-grade fever. You know how you have body aches when you're sick? It feels like that just a little bit. So, basically, that is a pain, and I'm waiting for it to stop. I also have something going on with one of my feet; it hurts. I might have hurt it while hiking with my kids. I need to walk and I need to hike and when I can't, I'm a hurting puppy. I'm also thinking, "What the hell am I doing, coming and spending time with this person?" and, it's like, what's this, the fifth session I think?

T: I think fourth, other than the intake session. What did we carve out—ten?

C: Yeah, sort of a preliminary-type thing.

T: So at ten we'll stop and look again.

C: So what do you think about what we're doing and how we're doing it?

T: I think you're very slippery. You've got a very strong mind that beats you up. It's pretty quick. We're going to have to figure out a way to work around it. It's not trying to hurt you; it's actually trying to help, but we've got to find a way to not have it completely dominate. Where are you?

C: Just hanging on. I'm trying not to think about anything too much. I try to think about what we've talked about and, you know, bounce it off my mind and see if anything else lights up on the pinball machine. I tend to see things as yes or no, black or white, all or nothing. I know I want for things to be that way because it's easy to peg things. It's more comfortable to know where you stand all the time. And intellectually I know that nothing is that way, but I guess that's another struggle that's going on in me all the time. Life is always a struggle, and sometimes you kind of just want to lay it aside, smell the roses, which can be fun, too. I mean, I can do that. But I was raised to keep working. Keep pushing. So, I'm sort of pissed at the circumstances that I find myself in [fusion, avoidance].

T: How would you describe those circumstances in a sentence?

C: Being driven, I guess, but if I wasn't, where would I be? Working in the place I own, I guess. I wouldn't know what to do with myself. But I like driving myself because I like results. I like learning and I know that there's way more out there than I'll ever be able to get my fingers on. It's hard to let up even though it's tiring.

T: Is there anything bouncing off what we were working on last time?

C: Well, a couple of things. You said there's somebody there. There's a "you" there that's been there all this time. I'm real intrigued by who that "you" is and what kind of capabilities that "you" has. I can catch it for moments. Could it be working for me to help me feel better? But I don't think so. It seems like a neutral "you" that just is there [self as context]. You said, "You don't have to believe what I'm telling you," but there's either believing, an intellectual understanding, or suspension of belief, where you're playing. Let's pick one [fusion].

Using Language to Blow Up Language

At this point the therapist has to take the session in a direction and chooses an odd one.

T: Let's look at that just a little bit, just kind of some intellectual play. Which is risky business with a quick-minded person like you, but let's do it anyway. Language is a funny business. It has some funny effects. Try this out: try to describe something in which what you describe is 100 percent in the moment—in the present.

C: You can't. Your nose is there on your face, but it's changed already in the amount of time that I'm describing it.

T: Okay, now, as you look at things, at the instant that you see them, is your experience of seeing them in the present?

C: [Pause] Yes, but only for a nanosecond.

T: Yeah. But it's there, right? The instant that you see them is in the present. Right?

C: Right.

T: So you experience things in the present, right? Not in the past or the future. But if you say something, the thing you're talking about is always somewhere else, sometime else. The "now" that you're talking about is about this much behind the "now" that you said it. So here's the problem: Imagine that we've got a continuum like this, and over here is belief and over here is disbelief. Now imagine that there's another continuum that rides this way. And it goes from "in the present" to "out of the present"—in quotes. It's in quotes because we can't actually get out of the present. But you know, when you go off in your mind and you're thinking about stuff, what you're going to do next Tuesday, or what your mother did when you were five, it's like, of course, you're alive that moment, but what you're thinking about is not in the moment. You're off into the verbal past and the verbal future. [If engaged in this type of verbal activity, the client is likely not present with what is occurring in life—he is in his mind. Discussion of "right" and "wrong" or "belief" and "disbelief" automatically takes the person out of the present. Being present involves detaching from that content and being aware of the process of thinking. See figure 5.1 for a visual description of this concept.]

C: Right.

T: Here's the continuum, and here's another continuum. Suppose in order to get over here—which is here and now, present—you have to step off, kind of slide off that continuum altogether. We could be over here saying, "I don't believe that," or over here saying, "I do," but both of them have this same characteristic, which is a belief and disbelief that's entirely a verbal event. No "now" there at all.

The therapist is taking a gamble here. This client is very verbal; very "mindy." The therapist decides to walk right into that, knowing full well the danger. This same approach was taken at the beginning of therapy when the therapist put trying to control private events against how well the person is living life. It is not clear, even in the long run, that this was a very powerful move. What the therapist is doing is an interesting way of pitting two processes against each other. It helps highlight that it is the process of believing or not believing thoughts that is the issue rather than whether a specific thought should be believed or not. It is not the content but the process that is the problem. But going in this direction will feed fusion initially, for sure. If it is going to work, it will work only later. To put it another way, the therapist is trying to fight fire with fire, and for a while it is sure to be hot (in the form of confusion, back chatter, and so on).

Figure 5.1 Distinction between cognitive entanglement and being present

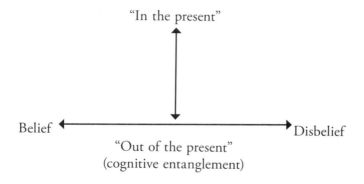

C: How is this going to help me?

T: Help you do what?

C: Feel good.

T: [Pause] Let's look at that phrase, "feel good." "Feel good" has two things in it: "feel" and then an evaluation, right? And the way that we would normally do it, we want to feel good, with the emphasis on the evaluation—the word "good." We want to feel *good* again. The problem is, the ability to evaluate pretty much also means you don't want to feel bad things. The problem with that is, there are lots of things to feel that are bad. There are bad memories, bad bodily sensations. Here your body is sort of doing various things for you this morning and mostly you are calling them "not good." So, if you're going to feel, you're going to feel both good and bad. Where I'm going with that is, the part of you that can step off the continuum may indeed help you feel good, but it won't be feel *good*; it will be something more like, *feel* good.

C: [Pause] Okay.

T: Do a good job of feeling—which is different than feeling only the feelings that your mind tells you are good. Which is kind of a harsh place to put yourself. If you can only feel the ones that are good, how do you know what's around the corner? I mean, you might get into this feeling-emotion area, and the next thing you know, you might be feeling something bad. This is not safe. So if you can only allow yourself to feel *good*, you can't afford to *feel* at all. Are you with me?

C: Mm-hmm.

T: So, I think, yeah, I can help you *feel* good. I can help you *feel* … good. We're not quite to the part we need to do this, but just as a game in here for the next few times, would you be willing to watch for feelings, thoughts, evaluations, and if we can catch them, say what they are, like "I feel this. I think this. I evaluate it this way." Because what language does, it will take those things and put them in the objects and then forget to tell you that it did that. "Feel good" is an example. There's an evaluation in there. But it looks as if you're just feeling something; you're not evaluating anything—as if the evaluation is in the event evaluated. So even though it's kind of artificial, I'd like to work on this for the next couple of times and ask you just to call feelings feelings, thoughts thoughts, and evaluations evaluations. Just name them, so we're clear what it is we're dealing with. Because they'll blend themselves into the object [holding up a coffee cup]. If we say, "This is a lousy cup," it is as if the "lousy" is *in* the cup. But wait a minute. If all living creatures were gone from the planet, the cup is still there. What happened to "lousy"?

C: Right. It's gone.

T: It's not there.

C: [Pause] Oh man. I'm sort of getting a feeling like I've been hit, you know? You're talking about being in the moment. But the minute you assign a value to something, you're not in that moment anymore. I don't know— you put a label on something and decide whether that's good or bad based on your memories. Can you avoid doing that? If you can't, can you ever see it for what it is? I know that I'm doing evaluation all the time. I'm thinking about this morning, being outside, "God it's gorgeous outside; it's beautiful." I'm starting to think about work and I could feel myself getting worked up and it's like, "I know that this is not productive. I don't want to be doing this." I don't have to be doing this, but my mind is down in the rut and it's like, "Okay, how can I change this?" [defusion]

The client is in that weird place where his mind is not totally making sense to him. He still feels like these are bad experiences that should be avoided, but he is also aware that the moves that he uses to control these feelings do not work. The process is becoming clearer. He feels like he should struggle, but he can tell that fighting with these things only makes them worse. His mind is almost gasping for air. If you are going to use fire to fight fire (language to limit language; "mindy" talk to "blow minds"), this is about what you could hope for—not an "aha" moment filled with understanding, but an "oh dear" moment filled with confusion and not knowing what do to next.

Defusion and Getting Present

T: Good.

C: I want to be enjoying walking, smelling the flowers, watching the kids, all this kind of stuff. But then I come back to "I should be able to control this," and then you're into this "I should" space and evaluation and labeling myself.

T: That's exactly right.

C: I've been going around in circles [defusion].

T: That's beautiful. It's neat. We need to work in here on doing something other than going and letting Mr. Mind just completely dominate on the one hand or trying to rein him in like a disciplinarian or something. Because I don't know how to do it. If you do, I'd be interested, but you know, it's like a very disobedient child. It's just blabbing from morning until night. You can yell at them and argue with them, but even that doesn't shut them up. So there's got to be something else that we can do.

Do you want to do just a quick little exercise? Not a very long one. It's right on this point. Are you willing to?

C: Oh, sure.

The therapist conducts an experiential defusion exercise with the client: the leaves-on-the-stream exercise (Hayes et al., 1999, pp. 158–162). It involves having the client close his eyes and shift his attention to the present moment, to things like his breathing and what it feels like to sit in the chair. Once the client is centered, he is instructed to picture himself sitting on the side of a river and watching leaves float by on a stream. He is asked to place his thoughts on the leaves and to watch them float by—one thought after another.

Whenever someone does this exercise, she will inevitably get sucked into one of the thoughts and the exercise will have stopped—the river will be gone and the person will be somewhere else, dealing literally with a thought. The task will have ended. The client is asked to notice when this happened and to see the different ways of experiencing thoughts, and to let the exercise start up again. The focus is not to relax the client but to help her see the difference between seeing a thought as a thought and buying into it. This exercise helps the client see how her thinking shapes the world she lives in.

Debriefing the Leaves on the Stream

C: I had this jerking back and forth between the person on the bank and putting the thoughts on the leaves and letting them go.

T: Good.

C: There was some outside stimulus of some kind, and I would like to put that on a leaf but I can't. It's like bam, bam, bam, bam, back and forth.

T: Okay.

C: It's not just quiet and peaceful like it should be [avoidance].

T: Did you get it flowing for a little bit?

C: For sure, a little flowing and then boom, back to thinking and I'm gone.

T: What happened the second before you went back to thinking? Take me through a sequence. It's starting to flow, and then you do something. You think something. Did you not?

C: I don't know. I mean, I've been doing that exercise for years. I've tried to let everything just be outside of you, but you can't maintain that kind of awareness for very long [avoidance; superficially this sounds like the point of the exercise, but functionally he is trying to not have the thoughts].

T: Well, check this out and see if this is what happened: You get a thought in there, and it's starting to go by, and at some point you get hooked. You might reflect on the structure of the exercise, for example. But that thought doesn't get on the leaf.

C: There are too many thoughts; they're too fast.

T: That would be an example. But if we could just slow down that one instant, when you think that it is not being looked *at*—it is being looked *from*. Is that something like what happens?

C: Yeah.

T: Okay. You can have a thought that is out here, one that you can notice, or there is another way you can experience a thought. The other way is more like you're *looking from something* rather than *looking at it*. At the moment that you are noticing that, you are having a thought; just at the moment that you catch it, put that one out there and just let that one flow by.

C: Gotcha.

Getting Present with Thoughts

T: Okay. Let's do this again for a few moments. So let's get back up on the bank and a nice warm sun, shade from the tree, and we've got the brook in front of us. Just allow a thought, whatever thought shows up, to be on the leaf. If you find yourself thinking self-reflectively about what you're doing, put that on the leaf, gently.

C: I'm not getting any leaves at all, just chatter, chatter, chatter, chatter, chatter.

T: As the chatter comes up, can you get it out?

C: Barely.

T: What's some of the chatter? Give me an example.

C: Oh, I feel upset. I want to write this on the leaf. ... I have a picture in my mind of how my hand is doing it. ... Isn't that funny. ... Backing up, okay. ... Feeling overwhelmed ... this constant criticism of how I'm doing ... what I'm supposed to be doing [fusion, not present].

T: Good. Put that on a leaf.

C: Okay. I see it. Wouldn't it be nice if I could do this all the time? I have mental pictures of things, aside from what I'm thinking about … what I'm seeing inside my head … and thinking about everything under the sun … how my lids feel when they're down instead of up … a constant barrage of observation and evaluation. I'm putting each one out there [pause]. Is this how I should be? [avoidance]

T: Cool. That's great. You can come back now. That last one hooked you, no? Check this out. Look and see. When you think, categorize, analyze, interpret, plan, evaluate, and so on, when you "language" about or think about things, all of that is happening in the present. It's happening right now in the same way that your heart's beating. You're breathing in and out, right? If you go into its literal content, you get pulled away from just seeing it. We don't have a good language for that; it's something like buying a thought—operating from it. But it doesn't mean believing it. If you resist it—like disbelieve it, criticize it—it has the exact same effect. Anything on this continuum, belief and disbelief, has the same effect. Check this out; see if this isn't something like what you were doing when noticing your thoughts. At the point at which you were operating on a literal basis of thought, the flow was gone. I mean you're into thoughtland, and the moment is categorized and evaluated. At the point at which you can see it as an unfolding process, you can flow for a while. Is that a fact?

C: I don't understand what you're saying. Are you saying that as you conceptualize something, it's just there, but if you analyze it, it's suddenly more huge and occupying more space? I don't understand.

T: Just look around the room. You see things, right? At the instant that you see them, it's in the present, right? And it doesn't have that quality of just kind of getting pulled in; it's just kind of a flow of individual events.

C: Mm-hmm. For sure.

T: As you look around the room, does it have the quality of a cacophony or arguments in your head or like that?

C: No.

T: Right. It's lots of different things when you look around, but it just kind of flows along. When you get into your thoughts at one level it's like that. You're seeing the visual stuff outside, but you also see thoughts inside. But that's the tiny part of the experience for most people, most of the time. Most of it's more like this kind of sense making. It doesn't flow, it kind of goes … boom, boom, boom, boom. It's herky-jerky; it's not in the present; it's somewhere else, sometime else. Figure it out. Evaluate it. Do it or not. Believe it or disbelieve it. Are you with me?

Learning to Be Present and to See Self as Context   **101**

C: Okay, yeah.

T: Okay, so what I want to get to is, were there any times in that exercise that for just some moments the thoughts were just going by?

C: Yes. For sure.

T: Okay. And could I ask this: when you were doing that, when you were looking *at* the thoughts, could you still understand them, yes, even though you weren't looking from them? You weren't buying them; you weren't arguing with them; you weren't believing them in a literal sense.

C: Mm-hmm, mm-hmm. Yeah.

T: Okay. So that's what I'm trying to get to. What pulls us out of this kind of observer place—where you can see thoughts the same way you can see objects in the room—to a place in which you can't tell the difference between a thought and yourself? It's kind of like if you had plastic bubbles that would fit down over your head, and if I put a red one on and I look at the white wall, then the red paper on the white wall might look exactly the same, it all looks like one thing. And then if I put a blue one on, it would look different. You know, the red paper now is visible and the wall just looks blue. It's like that. Like when you take a thought and sort of buy it, you don't see it anymore. You see everything else *from* that filter.

C: That expression of seeing "from it" doesn't quite fit yet. I'm not sure where you're coming from there. But I know there is a difference between just letting thoughts happen and seeing them and then grabbing onto one and chewing on it [acceptance, defusion].

T: Right.

C: And what makes that happen? I don't know, but I'm guessing it's because that thought triggers your mind to ask, "Why did I have that thought," you know? Or "What does that say about me?" or "What should I be doing about that thought?" It triggered a memory, an experience, something like that. I think your mind is given to this, if not trained and directed. It's always relating, relating, relating, and trying to build on it [defusion].

T: Right on.

C: Take it and do something with it.

T: Right.

C: Not, just let it happen.

The client is able to label the process of thinking—to see it as something different from himself. This is one of the beginning processes of defusion. It is not yet clear if the process of acceptance is building, which is an important aspect of real defusion. Is he more willing to have the thoughts as thoughts?

T: Exactly. Exactly. Manipulate, analyze, categorize, change, figure out, understand, exactly. And all of that requires some literal language. You have to sort of buy the thought, you know, and take it seriously, in terms of its literal content. But then it's not just a process. Not "Now I'm having this thought; now I'm having that thought." Not something in the present. Instead we are back in the war. What are you thinking, and can you marshal evidence for it and against it? In problem-solving situations there's nothing wrong with that. I mean, that's what it's for. That's what it evolved for. But peace of mind? Forget it.

You will see that the therapist does this a lot throughout this book. The therapist takes what the client offers and rolls it into the area that the therapist is trying to cover. The client actually says, "Take it and do something with it," suggesting that the thoughts themselves might be "done with" in a different way. And the client says, "Not, just let it happen," which is probably a mix of "not letting the normal war happen" and "not letting the thought happen." The therapist acts as if it is much more the former.

This is a different approach to directly working with the client's normal verbal system. For example, the client might say, "But I don't get that." Instead of saying, "What part don't you get?" the therapist might say, "Cool, we are making progress" and roll confusion into a useful area. This just occurred in the previous dialogue. The client treats in a mixed way what the therapist is talking about, and the therapist just rolls it into something useful. Instead of saying, "That is the opposite of what I was talking about," the therapist validates the client and gently transforms what the client is saying into what the therapist is targeting. If you are not following, look at the previous dialogue and see how the therapist does it.

This move comes right out of the RFT literature. Because verbal relations are historical, they cannot be effectively or directly eliminated. In relative terms, they can weaken over time as other responses strengthen, but that is a slow process, and reacquisition procedures show that once learned, behaviors never get to zero strength. But it is not difficult to expand a relational network. Responses that are at high strength can be used to train new relations that are therapeutically useful, expanding the relational network where it is helpful. This is done by embracing existing verbal relations and slightly reframing them to build new relations. In that way, even harmful cognitions can be used to increase the strength of helpful ones without directly challenging or taking other steps to weaken existing verbal relations.

Challenging the Limits of Language

C: Right.

T: But most of its purposes originally were outside the skin. You know, "How do I get warm in the winter." Things like that. But now we've got advanced enough that we've got it inside the skin and it's "Am I happy?" and "Do I belong here?" It includes all kinds of things that just don't have any business being involved in that. But you can't keep it cordoned off. Minds are like a smart-aleck kid that just will not shut up. Is there anything in your experience that your mind isn't happy to inform you of? What's right and wrong, good, bad, proper, improper. I mean, it knows everything. Mr. Smarty Pants. I'll give you an example. Do you know how to touch your nose?

C: Sure.

T: Let me see. Okay. Glad to see that because I need to know how to do that, okay? So, tell me how to touch my nose.

C: Well, one way you can touch your nose it to take one of your appendages and put it in the vicinity of your nose and establish contact.

T: Okay, which one?

C: Whichever one you like.

T: Okay, I'm going to do this one over here.

C: Okay.

T: Okay, how do I do that?

C: Well, you're going to have to put yourself in contact with your brain, and it's going to fire off things to your muscles that will make you lift your arm and extend probably just one finger, and put that finger in contact with your nose.

T: Okay. Now, how do I do that?

C: You have to tell your brain to do it.

T: Okay [pause]. It's not working.

C: Your brain isn't working?

T: I'm telling my brain.

C: Tell your arm to lift.

T: Arm, I want you to lift. … I'm sorry, it's not working.

C: [Chuckling] Maybe you ought to think about not touching your nose right now.

T: Are you sure you know how to do this?

C: I know how to make it work for me, but I can't make it work for you.

T: Why not?

C: Because it's something that you have to deal with inside yourself. I can't get inside your skin.

T: Are you sure you know how to touch your nose?

C: For sure. I know how to make it work for me.

T: So how do I do it?

C: Keep practicing; practice makes perfect.

T: Do you see the problem? You know that stroke victims actually do that? You've got a sixty-two-year-old lady who's trying to recover from a stroke, and they literally shout things like "Move, damn you!" My point on all that is, minds will come up behind and claim everything: how to relate to people, how to be happy, how to have a meaningful relationship. Sometimes it's just minds claiming credit for stuff that you've learned other ways. You know, like your body knows how to do more than your mind does.

C: Every once in a while there will be a situation that will happen, and it's like, "I don't know what to do about this," but somewhere inside me there's a feeling of "Just wait, this will work out," and it does. Sometimes I jump the gun and make it happen in some other way, but oftentimes there will be a voice inside of me that says, "Don't take action on this; wait for something else to happen." And that's happened with little things, big things, whatever. And it made me wonder about how do I have that knowledge inside me? And why am I in some cases willing to trust it and not in others? Could all kinds of things be happening that if I wasn't so damn preoccupied with trying to control and know everything, then maybe I wouldn't have to put out so much effort? [acceptance] And then you consider that there's all these portions of the brain that nobody has any idea what they're doing. But they're there. But I don't know any more than I did five minutes ago [fusion].

The client is seeing a connection. He is noticing that there is more to *knowing* than *verbal, analytical, evaluative knowing*. He's seen that repeatedly in his life, but his mind does not get it. But as soon as he notices that, his more dominant repertoire reemerges. That is why that statement ends in a funny way. We assume he is noticing that this is not making normal verbal sense to him—he understands what the therapist is talking about, but in a more verbal way, he can't figure it out. We will know he is doing better when he is able to sit with not knowing what is going to happen next or not completely understanding what the therapist is saying. Silence and action will give us a guide, but we are not there yet.

> T: Well, your mind probably doesn't, but I'm working for you and not your mind. I'm looking for weak spots here to see if I can get around it, because this is not something that a mind can understand. We're talking about the limits of conscious stuff and seeing if we can find a place in which some of the stuff can be moved off, thereby making some room to do some other things. But they can't work if Mr. Mind is in there trying to do everything. The only way that we can work on this is with language, but your mind also loves that. It's listening, and of course it's trying to figure this out, everything that I am saying, which is fine, but what I'm trying to talk about is something that is off that continuum of belief, disbelief, evaluation, figuring out, and so on. So it's a tricky business. Even if we're able to really make some progress here, your mind will come back behind and say, "Oh, I understand; now it's clear to me what the point is." And even if what it says is true, it's functionally false because you can't do it that way. It's like, "Oh, I know how to hit a baseball." And even if we have the mathematical formula showing the curve the ball follows, if you try to hit it that way, you can't hit it. So it's functionally false, even if it's literally true. So, part of what we're doing here is just trying to figure out a way to put your mind in its place without "minding" it into its place.

ACT is an experiential type of therapy. We want the client to learn things through coming into contact with them. The client is confused right now. So instead of saving him, the therapist is purposefully keeping him confused. The therapist's answer is not very clear on purpose. It is like saying to the client, "I see that you are confused and that your mind is not sure what to do with this stuff, but I don't need to save you from it because it is not dangerous, and, in fact, it is a good sign." After some additional defusion work, the session draws to a close as the therapist gives the client a couple of homework assignments (this time deliberately without ratings to see if compliance will be higher).

> T: Would you mind doing two things? First, at least two times, for about five minutes, do that sitting-on-the-side-of-the-stream deal at home. Just get quiet and just watch your mind go. It may be very noisy. See if, as things come up, you can gently put them out there and just keep doing it. And if you lose it, when you notice you've lost it, then notice that's a thought

and put it out there and see if you can note what hooked you moments before.

C: For sure. I can do that. I'd like to see how it works if I try again actually [acceptance].

T: The other thing I'd like to ask you to do is something a little different. You'll need twenty minutes to do this. There are only a couple of rules, but one is, once you start, don't stop, and go for twenty minutes. Get yourself in a place that's quiet and think of something sad or traumatic that's happened to you, especially something you haven't processed much or haven't worked out very much. Get out a piece of paper and write everything that comes to mind. Just let it flow. Write anything that comes to mind. Notice what your body is doing, write emotions, other thoughts, go wherever it occurs for you to go, and as you go, I want a part of you to just kind of watch this happen. Just let it flow and take advantage of it, especially if this is something you haven't gone into much before. You don't have to bring the paper in; you can rip it up, tear it up, burn it afterward, but just go through it and experience it as part of your history. While trying to get into the depths of whatever is there as much as you can, simply watch what shows up in the areas of thoughts, feelings, and sensations. I don't mean watching in order to defend yourself; I don't mean to disassociate. I mean, just notice yourself experiencing what comes up as you do that. The exact opposite—stand back so you can *see* it.

C: Gotcha.

FINAL COMMENTARY

The focus of this session was on self as context and defusion. The therapist was trying to help the client see that he is separate from his mind and to give him some skills to begin to see thinking in flight without disappearing into thought.

The client is clearly a very verbal and "mindy" person: he tries to figure everything out and make sense of it. This makes talk therapy difficult. The therapist is trying to counter this by using exercises and metaphors, but the client is still taking every metaphor and exercise and trying to figure out what it means and what the point is. His initial response is almost always judgmental.

This can be difficult and frustrating for an ACT therapist. The best thing that a therapist can do is try to stay away from arguing and discussion and stay as experiential as possible. This will hopefully decrease cognitive fusion in the long run and open up space to do additional work.

Figure 5.2 Time spent addressing ACT processes in session four

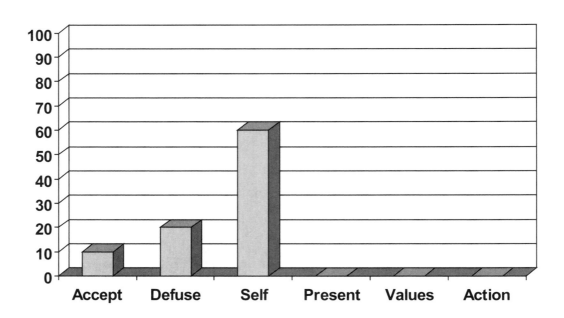

Figure 5.3 Status of client's ACT processes by the end of session four

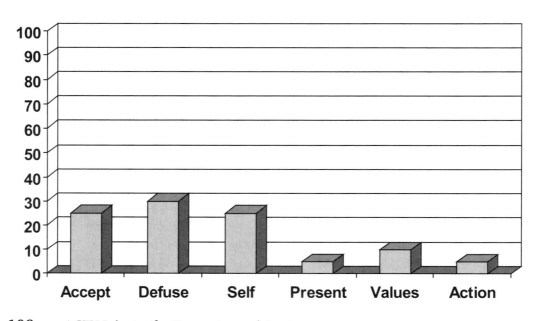

CHAPTER 6

Applying Acceptance, Defusion, and Self as Context in Imaginal Exposure

The focus of the last session was to support self-as-context processes and to build defusion. Some progress is being made, but the client tries hard to understand these concepts at a conceptual level, which is making everything more difficult.

In this session the therapist presents these concepts experientially. The therapist checks in with the client and fairly quickly begins an experiential exercise aimed at bringing together the work done so far in acceptance, defusion, and self as context. You will see that the client is still trying mightily to figure things out. He is barely willing to sit with uncertainty.

In this struggle, this client provides nice examples of why ACT is done experientially. It is pretty obvious that explaining the point of the exercises and helping the client figure out their meanings would only support the verbal system that says, "We must figure things out before they can work." A clear sign of progress will be when the client begins to move forward without verbal knowing. He needs to let his experience teach him.

SESSION FIVE

C: I did do my homework, which was to free-associate and write down about a previous painful or traumatic event [committed action].

T: Yeah, for twenty minutes.

C: For twenty minutes. I also did the other exercise were you have the thoughts go floating past and watch them as they go floating past. They were hard. I was as disgusted as I always am with my attempts to try to control my thoughts, which is what I end up doing in these types of exercises [acceptance].

T: Is that the point?

C: I tried not to control them, but that is what my mind always went back to [acceptance]. I chose to write about my last divorce because I never really sat down and thought about it [acceptance]. But that's not really how human beings do those things. I mean, if they're flat on their back and all they can do is think about it or obsess on it, yes, that's one thing. But usually your mind is working behind the scenes, and you see somebody that reminds you and somehow it triggers your mind, and there you are on a new topic. I couldn't focus on it. Maybe a tenth of what I wrote was about the divorce and not being with my kids all the time, and the rest was about peripheral things. I'd lost focus during the meditation assignment [not present]. So I just tried to meditate in a way that I had picked up from books. I let my thoughts go or whatever. I imagined myself in a calm spot or imagined there's nothingness in front of me. But I can't do that for more than a tenth of a second or something. The jabber-jabber starts up again.

There are a couple of interesting things in the client's comments above. First, he is starting to get a little more on board with some of these ACT processes. He can see his thoughts as separate events and it seems that he is less attached to them, but he still seems to want them to go away at some level. He is still working under a control agenda and is not totally accepting of their presence.

It is also interesting how he pulled information about meditation into the ACT exercise. The therapist wanted the client to experience his thoughts as only thoughts and be able to discriminate between these types of experiences. The client took the exercise (and meditation itself) as a method of silencing the mind.

This is an old theme with this client. But the therapist is about to take a very different tack, as we shall see.

Being Small

T: On the traumatic thing, have you actually looked at what you've written? When you went on tangents, did they turn out to be related?

C: For sure.

T: That exercise is not another way to control your thoughts. The exercise is just watching your thoughts. And even what does not seem related in some sense is related.

C: But they take over [defusion].

T: [Pause] I have sort of had a sense in the past two weeks or so that I'm not sure that I'm on board with you. Maybe I'm missing something. I may need your help here. There is a kind of fogginess about the whole situation, and usually when that happens, it is because I'm off on something that isn't relevant or I'm not being sensitive enough to what is going on. Sometimes it's because something isn't being said. And sometimes it is neither of those—it's just because the problem itself is foggy.

C: Well, if I understand what you mean by "There's a fogginess of some sort present," then I would agree that I lose why I'm here or what my goal is and what your goal is here or if it's a good thing to be here. But that is not unusual, in a way. I have never finished a course of therapy with anyone. I'm not sure you do therapy that way—start at A and get to Z and then you're done—but also I find myself pushing off of any therapy. I also have a hard time dealing with my doubts. I'm not all in. I keep coming back to the words of this psychiatrist who was only too happy to prescribe me some medication. I thought he was full of shit. And yet there's this doubt—do I need medication? Is there something else going on? I don't know—I'm glad I have the drugs on one level. And my mind tells me I need the drugs. I start thinking my chemistry is out of whack and then I switch drugs. Who knows? I don't know anymore. I don't know anything anymore [defusion].

T: What is this experience of not knowing like?

C: A part of me wants to hold on to something. I need a rock, a root, or something that is going to lead me up to the surface of the water and I can say, "Okay, now I know the answer to that" or "I can put that in a cubbyhole." I really like to put things away, not have them popping out again; I don't like that. It's hard [the content sounds like avoidance, but the fact that he is admitting it seems like acceptance]. This is a pattern of mine—I try and figure things out, but at some level I know life isn't like that, so I live in this vague place that I can't change [defusion]. I see that. So I want to see what this guy has to offer. But then I want to be able to resolve in my mind what that shrink said about therapy—that therapy isn't of much value. Still I enjoy talking to somebody about this stuff because I can't with anybody else.

T: Yeah.

C: That in itself is therapeutic. Whether it's worth the money, I don't know. So I'm still open, and whatever we talk about gives me food for thought. That is how I've come to terms with things in the past. That's the way I've brought peace to myself. So you're helping me think. I think I'm making progress. And yet, that's not what this ACT stuff is all about.

T: Hmmm. You have an active mind. That's for sure. You think about everything. That's all right.

C: Well, it has to be all right.

T: Yeah, exactly; how would you stop it?

C: So this foggy thing, you said it was just like that, or something that's not being said, or. … I'm not sure what the third thing was.

T: I don't have as good a handle on your situation. I do feel the vagueness in here. Usually, I see an angle that is fairly clear, and it keeps me clear about what we need to do. If we look in terms of depression, according to the depression scores we've been collecting, you're not depressed. Not close. In terms of anger control, it's episodic and more of a peak kind of problem. Anxiety—that's a bit clearer. You are very cognitive—it seems as though you kind of retreat into your head. You can be very much captivated by worries and what is going on inside to the point where other things might be excluded. The other thing that I feel in here is that it seems as though you've lost your sense of direction in your life. A while back we touched on that, and I remember it was painful [pause]. You see the fogginess of what I'm seeing right now? So I just want to sort of stop and say, "Help me out here and get me in line," or whatever. Why do you think you're really here? If you could change one thing, what would it be?

C: Well, if I were to change the most important thing, it would be to quiet the clamoring within. The clamoring often has to do with deep fears and self-criticism—"Am I okay?" I guess. Does everybody else spend as much time picking at all these things and relating how they stand with respect to other people, and worrying? It seems to be just under the surface. I'm trying as hard as I can at almost everything. I'm working and I'm not getting where I want to or where I was told I was supposed to be. I'm mad. I feel cheated. I'm mad at myself, I'm disappointed, I'm tired, and it's like I'm reaching the end of my rope. I don't know what the rope is. I don't know what's going on. I'm just floundering—but floundering very energetically and anxiously and angrily. I don't feel despair—I just feel a sort of confusion and disappointment and irritation.

This is a very interesting move by the clinician. In essence, the therapist is becoming small and asking for help. This client is both highly concerned about what others think and yet deeply resentful of social control of any kind. Later in the session he will show some of the history that has led to that, and we can understand a bit more of how this came to be. By getting with that thought of "I don't know what to do," the clinician is giving the client the space to step forward. Probably in part because of the previous work done, the client is stepping forward powerfully. This is a very good indication that acceptance and defusion are, in fact, more in place and that the pot stirring in the form of exposure and mindfulness exercises is opening up doors. Defusion can be detected when the client speaks about his thoughts and feelings as something separate from him. It is also obvious (because the client is less attached to controlling his thoughts and more open with what he is feeling) that the process of acceptance is growing stronger. He is saying things about how control attempts don't work in the long run and he is tired of trying. All of these are very good signs with this difficult client. Substantively, it is also clearer that the core problem is a kind of ruminative, anxious, self-critical pattern deeply related to self-acceptance and to values. This pattern is much of what the client has meant all along by "depression." The therapist has probably known this for a while (recall the therapist's assessment that the client's depression does not really fit that label), but even now the therapist is more interested in the client seeing what is happening than in categorizing it as a diagnosable syndrome.

The Direction Needed

T: Where do you think you need to go?

C: I guess it's a whole bunch of things lumped up together, but most of what I want is peace of mind, to know that I'm okay: "I'm producing enough, I'm good enough, I'm kind enough, I'm smart enough, I'm healthy enough, people love me." I don't know. It seems this struggle is always present. I'm bored with it. I wonder if other clients would say this. It is possible that the focus on letting go of the struggle is making me hate the struggle. But I think not. I've hated it forever.

T: And when you're struggling, what would you say you're struggling with most of all?

C: I know enough to know that the answers are not there; nobody is going to tell me, "You're okay; you've reached it; you're fine," whatever. I would not believe it anyway. It's like I don't know what I want or how just to be me. And the struggle is constantly there.

T: Would it be fair to say that what you struggle with more than most other things are evaluations of yourself?

C: For sure.

T: Just now, just sitting here, looking at an average day, how intense do you think your negative self-evaluations are? If you were to put them on a 1 to 10 scale—10 is about as critical as you know how to be, pretty much constantly, to 1, in which it is not a problem at all—where is your average day?

C: It varies. Sometimes I'm sailing. Maybe this is chemical, I don't know, but there are days and weeks and months when every little thing that happens is an 8 or a 9 or a 10. And it's pretty terrible. I feel like it is not appropriate to feel this amount of anger for this long. This amount of self-criticism. I will misplace something—I can't find my cell phone. I know I had it, and it's been missing for a couple of days. Those are the things that wake me up in the middle of the night, and it's like, "Oh, where is it?!" My brain starts working, and it's like, "Where's my goddamn cell phone?" I say to myself I'm not going to worry about it. I'm going to go back to sleep. Then I'm up worrying and harassing myself. Why do I do this to myself? It's stupid [not present, fusion].

T: And what is the emotion underneath?

C: It's an anxiety thing. It's something anxiety will trigger. There is a constant scramble to try to overcome it or do better or whatever. Now, it's getting into fatigue and sort of generally all messing up into a big ball. I don't like myself; I don't like being that way. Not liking myself and that gut feeling of anxiety—I'm bad—is probably the root of everything, the constant message. Oddly, it gets me to try even harder. I'm sure some of my business success comes from that. But I don't need to be doing that. It's the old head-beating-against-the-wall routine.

T: The basic message?

C: Get it together. You are just not good enough.

T: Do you have an example of one that really gets you rockin' or gets you hooked? Give me a core one.

C: Most of the time when I get hooked into something like that is when it's a power thing. I want something to be a certain way, and something prevents it from being that way. I know this is related. Just recently I talked to the owner of the space next door about renting the space to expand the store. I'd prefer he just sell it, but he said no to that right away. Anyway, he had some preliminary numbers, but then I realized I'd be stuck with a couple of expenses I had not planned on, so I tried to change the numbers to reflect that. Well, he is not a wimp. He came right back with a counteroffer and said, "Well, you said, blah, blah, blah, so those original numbers seem right to me." It was a good argument actually. It is not the actual outcome that is an issue for me. It is that next thing, you know—I'm feeling awfully anxious. And I'm thinking, "This is making me really uncomfortable." And right behind that is "Who cares anyway?" And I'm thinking, "Okay, it's okay; if it doesn't work out, you can always go back to the situation you have now. It will be hard but not impossible." But there was this feeling of "I've been pushed to the wall; somebody else has power over me." It was not a big deal, but my sense is that it is somehow related to what we are working on. There is this sick feeling in my stomach, and I feel like my prestige is at stake, my credibility is at stake, and somehow even though nothing bad happened, I feel badly about myself. I always have to be in control. I'm tired of living this way. Can't we just go with the flow a little bit more? Then my mind says, "No, we can't because you have to know everything that's going to happen; you have got to be prepared." Sigh. Does this make sense?

T: Yes. Want to do some exploring around this example? Your gut-level sense is that it's an example of something, so it seems like we should lean into it.

C: It's an example of power and fear and anxiety and not knowing. It's what's hardest.

There is a sense in this segment of things coming together. The therapist continues to lay low, but as the client steps forward, the therapist captures the gains by getting a well-worked-out example on the table that somehow is deeply connected to the client's struggles. That in itself is major progress. But now the clinician is going to try to leverage that by a long experiential exercise.

The therapist is about to launch into the tin-can-monster exercise (Hayes et al., 1999, pp. 171–174). This exercise has multiple purposes. It helps foster acceptance because it allows for structured but deep contact with a feared experience in a safe context in which acceptance skills can be used. The therapist helps the client come deeply in contact with a variety of thoughts, feelings, and memories in a context where it's okay to experience emotions, where there's no indication given to the client of any danger or need to escape. Acceptance is fostered in part because of the way that the therapist reacts to material that the client presents. The therapist reacts without judgment or evaluation—everything is acceptable. This exercise also fosters defusion because thoughts are treated as just events, not, in principle, anything that has to change. It fosters a transcendent sense of self as the "observer you" is appealed to as the basis of behavioral observations. And, finally, it is an exposure exercise in which new responses to old, avoided events can be established. Acceptance, defusion, and self all empower this kind of exposure.

From an ACT perspective, exposure is not so much a reduction in arousal as it is a broadening of psychological flexibility. The point is not to stop feeling anxious; the point is to have many, many things at hand that one could do. This process is facilitated by breaking up difficulties into elements because the elements are not as functionally dominant.

This exercise goes on for the rest of the session. We decided to leave most of the exercise in the book because it is a good example of the give and take of an actual therapy session even when doing structured exercises. It is useful that the exercise does not flow as described in Hayes et al. (1999). In this case, the client sometimes gets hooked, and the exercise stumbles. This happens all the time clinically—few clients are like the ones that are imagined in books. It is useful to see how an experienced ACT therapist responds to these difficult situations. This is a very experiential dance where the therapist keeps the client in the experience while teaching acceptance, defusion, and self as context. You will see that the client tries to pull out of the exercise and tries to figure out the point of it, in effect attempting his usual move of highly fused avoidance strategies. The therapist does a nice job of keeping the client in contact with the exercise.

Imaginal Exposure to Private Events

T: What I'd like to suggest is that we do an exercise that will go into that. Back up a little bit. So an event occurs, and you react to it. Your reaction to the event objectively may be quite strong. One possibility is that the event that occurred is not just *that* event but it's everything that is co-occurring with the event. It has to do with your history, your memories, your background—all the things that you have. It's kind of like this monster shows up with a core made of one thing and limbs made of something else altogether. The total gestalt, the total picture, looks big, even overwhelming. But the elements may be quite different. I'd like to do a little bit of an exploration; the main purpose of it is to just see how the mind works but also to just sort of see what shows up with regard to this particular example. What I'm going to ask you to do is to close your eyes, and we'll get in touch with the feeling associated with that conversation with the person owning the space next door. And then we'll go looking for things that show up in association with it. It's kind of like there is sort of this big monster that walks in the door, and instead of looking at everything at once, we will focus down on the hand and we're going to look at the foot, things like that, with the purpose of, number one, seeing what it is, and number two, seeing how much flexibility you have. If you have to respond to it in the normal ways—being entangled with it, trying to change it—my guess is that it will work the ways it's always worked. But maybe there are other things to do, and maybe when you do those things, they will work another way.

C: Before you do that, I think I can see I really have mixed feelings about even renting space instead of buying it. And any sort of power over me is something that I try to avoid at all costs. It makes me nervous because I try to anticipate what that power wants, what problems are going to be presented, how it's going to cost me, is it going to make my life difficult. So I try to avoid the situation. Here I am, inviting something in that I know I'm going to have trouble with.

T: Right.

C: So I'm pretty aware of what these anxieties are that are popping up around the situation.

T: Okay.

C: My dad has a theory that people get themselves as busy and involved in things as they possibly can, until they're almost losing it, and they stay there, and it creates this kind of instability that is not a good thing. I keep telling myself I want to simplify my life, and yet, obviously, I don't really want to or I'd find a way to spend less money or something [conceptualized self].

T: Right.

C: Based on that, if you want to continue this exercise, we can look at monster parts [acceptance].

T: Yeah, all of what you just said is something you can bring right in. Get yourself comfortable. Close your eyes if you can do that. And just start out by getting centered in the way we have before. Just notice the sounds that are in the room. … Feel the air moving around; there's actually a little breeze in here [continues with the usual centering dialogue]. Now in the exercise I'll ask you some questions, and you can just answer out loud. As you do, try to just stay with what you're saying. We don't need to engage in a conversation, and I don't want to get pulled into that. Don't open your eyes. Just sort of answer in a couple of words.

       I want you to start out by getting in touch with that conversation and the feelings that are associated with talking to the owner next door and having him push back. When you can get in touch with the general feeling of what showed up in that conversation, let me know.

C: Gotcha. It was fear.

T: Now, go ahead and get in touch with the feeling. We don't have to label it here. I wanted to ask you if you're in touch with it now. Have you got it? I want to ask you about your body. Take a moment to watch your body. See if you can find one specific bodily sensation that shows up in association with that feeling. Don't overthink this—just look and see if anything pops up.

C: There's sort of a tightening.

T: Good. Where do you feel it?

C: Mostly in my stomach.

T: Super. Okay, I want you to focus just on that. See if you can kind of feel exactly where in your body that is. It's probably a sensation you've had at other times, and so, kind of see if you can draw where the dividing line is for this particular sensation and see if you can notice any of the kind of attributes it has.

C: You mean describe it?

T: No, you don't have to describe it; just notice it. I don't think I need to know these. But what I want you to do is see if you first feel that sensation. Do you have it? [client nods] Okay. Now see if you can sort of have a sense of being willing to have that particular sensation in your stomach. It would be as if you could just sort of welcome that feeling like you'd welcome a child [pause]. Is there anything in this sensation that you can't have?

C: That I can't have?

T: That you can't have.

C: That does not compute.

T: Is there anything in there that you have to change? Like get rid of, diminish. Is there anything in that that you are treating as your enemy?

C: Yes. Pain.

T: Physical pain?

C: Yes. It's in my stomach. It's burning, it's churning, whatever. Results in diarrhea, and I don't want it [avoidance].

T: Okay. I want you just to focus on the sensation and not the thoughts—thoughts like, "it will lead to diarrhea"—we will get to those later. We're trying to do one thing at a time.

C: Okay, so the sensation in and of itself.

T: Yes.

C: But it's a manifestation of something happening [fusion].

T: And even that's a thought. Thank your mind for it and let it know we'll get to that later. See if you can stay with the sensation—just that sensation, the sensation in your stomach. Is this sensation, as a sensation, something you have to struggle with?

C: I can't struggle with this sensation. Right?

T: People try. And that's your choice. I am asking you—even if it doesn't make sense to you—see if you can drop the tug-of-war rope with that sensation just for this moment. Later on you can change and let that sensation be your enemy if you want. Right now, see if you can just look at that sensation and let go of a defense against it. You might watch what happens with your hands for example. I've found that when people defend, they very often can feel it in there. It's almost as if they literally take up and do battle, and I see your hands tensing. Okay, good. Are you able to let it be there for this moment?

C: Okay.

T: Good. Put that sensation aside and go back and get in touch with the original feeling. And when you've got it, let me know.

C: Okay.

T: Okay, now watch your body again and see if there's anything else that shows up.

C: Well, there's sort of a general tightness, sort of a muscular tightness in my chest and in my arms.

T: Okay. So focus on that and see exactly where it is and what you're feeling. Try to get in touch with exactly what those sensations are. Where do these sensations begin and end? Go inside and notice them [pause]. And once again, can you sort of carve out a little more space for you to have your shoulders and arms feel like that when they feel like that?

C: Yes.

T: Your mind may want to turn this into an evaluation, like "I won't like it" or something else. Just let your mind know that we'll get to that later. It will have ample opportunity for all its reactions. But just focus on the sensation itself. Is there anything in there that demands that you struggle, or can you open up a little more space just to have it?

Applying Acceptance, Defusion, and Self as Context in Imaginal Exposure   **119**

C: I'm not being successful with that.

T: Okay, tell me what happens.

C: I feel like my mind is beating on its door saying, "No, no, no. Let me out. We have to control this! This shouldn't be doing that! We've got to stop it because it's going to lead to something else." How can this sensation be divorced from thinking about it? The two are too tightly linked, and if I just let it be there, then I'm not fixing it [avoidance, fusion].

T: Good. Thank your mind for all those thoughts. Those are very interesting thoughts. And we will get to those thoughts. Meanwhile we've got this sensation. In fact this sensation is probably associated with some of the things that your mind is telling you to do but not in the literal way it supposes. Just a guess, but your arms and shoulders probably feel tight because those are muscles you use to defend yourself, or to attack, one or the other. I can see the tension. But in any case, here it is, however it got here. So if your mind starts to fight its way in, just see if you can pat it on the head, kind of like a child that can't keep quiet, and say, "You know, we'll have time to get to you a little later. Just be patient," and meanwhile, go back to that sensation. See if you can drop a little more of the struggle with it. Allow this sensation to be. You don't have to take charge of making it be a particular way. You might actually watch your hands and see if you can almost physically drop any struggle with the arms and hands. Let me know when you have the sense of dropping the struggle a bit.

C: [Pause] Okay.

T: Okay. And now try to go a little deeper into dropping the struggle and let me know when you are able to do that.

C: [Pause] Okay.

T: Good. Now put that one aside and go back and get in touch with the original one. Let me know when you've got it.

C: The original what?

T: The original feeling associated with the talk with the owner next door. Can you get in touch with that feeling?

C: Okay.

T: Once again, just watch your body, but this time you don't have to tell me any sensations. As you notice each one, I want you to just kind of pat it on the head. Just tip your hat and acknowledge it. It is not like you have to like it; it is just as if you're walking down the street and you see people you know. You're not going to like every one of them, but you can still be polite and acknowledge each one. Acknowledge each sensation that comes up that's associated with the original feeling. With each one, as you kind of acknowledge it, see if you can let go—watch your hands and your arms—see if you can let go of the need to control the particular ones that you see. Your body is not your enemy, and bodily sensations are not something that you have to fight with. Just feel them. Okay, put all those aside and go back and get in touch with the original feeling and let me know when you've got it again.

C: It's harder to get the feeling, but it's sort of there.

T: Okay. Take your time. It does get harder to go back as we go through this [pause]. Now watch to see if there are any emotions that come up as you feel that feeling, and if so, let me know.

In this segment we continue to see the client taking a couple of steps forward and then a step back. There is nothing wrong with that pattern. It does not mean the client has failed or is going backward.

Emotions

C: Oh man, there are lots of them.

T: Just give me one, whichever one is the first in line.

C: Sort of a resignation.

T: Tell me more about it. I need to understand it as an emotion.

C: I see these feelings again, they're "Why can't you do better than to react in this way?" …

T: That's a thought.

C: Okay.

T: Stay with the feeling.

C: Okay, so the feeling is disappointment.

T: Okay. Good. So see if you can just focus on disappointment and what it feels like to feel disappointed. Once again, your mind is very powerful and likes to pull you off into another kind of play. So if it tries to crowd in, just let it know that we'll be with it next, but we're going to spend some time here on disappointment.

C: Okay.

T: Is there anything in that emotion, just considered as an emotion, that is inherently damaging, dangerous, harmful, destructive to you? Is it inherently bad to feel disappointed? I don't mean is it pleasant; I'm not asking that. I realize that this is a so-called negative emotion.

C: It's not dangerous [defusion].

T: Okay. So see if you can spend some time creating the emotion of disappointment. I want you to go into what it feels like to feel disappointed, and this time do it nondefensively—really feeling good and disappointed.

C: I'm embarrassed to do that.

T: Okay. Give me just a little more.

C: My mind laughs at me pretending to be disappointed [defusion, self as context; this is self as context because he talked about himself as separate from his mind].

T: Okay. I'm not asking you to pretend; I'm asking you to feel it by choice. When you were going through this, you found disappointment there. That wasn't pretend. That was real. Now what I'm asking you to do, in addition, is to choose it. I don't mean to evaluate it a particular way or to like it or anything like that. All I mean is to willingly feel that disappointment—without defense.

C: Is there a difference between allowing yourself to feel it and willingly feeling it? [fusion, avoidance]

T: It is like the difference between twiddling your thumbs and opening your arms, like the difference between "Oh, well, I guess I can't do anything about this" and "Come on in!" Is there anything in that emotion that demands that your posture be one of "Oh well, here it comes again, and I can't do anything about it" or "I've got to get rid of it but I don't know how"? Can you actually shift it over to something more like "Disappointment is an emotion that is here and it is here to be felt"?

C: No man. I can't do that [avoidance, fusion].

T: Is that you or your mind talking?

C: I can't let that feeling be there. It's like sliding off it, like bouncing off.

T: Okay.

C: It's not working.

T: Okay. Notice your mind working here.

C: All the other stuff comes with it, and I don't know how to leave it off.

T: As much as possible, stay with the emotion. It is not what it says it is. Try to stay with what you experience directly. The *feeling* is something like *feeling* sandpaper, *feeling* an apple, *feeling* water. The feeling is an emotion; it brings with it other things, but those we will get to later. I just want you to focus on the emotion. Is disappointment *as a feeling* inherently dangerous to you? What stands between you and simply feeling it?

C: You can't have emotions without a source and a process. Why am I feeling this? [fusion]

T: There it goes again. And that's okay. Just notice that your mind is doing its thing here. Let's go back and get in touch with the original event. Remind yourself of being in front of that guy and then what came up. Got it?

C: Mm-hmm.

T: Do you?

C: Yeah.

T: Okay, now watch your emotional side again this time to see if there's anything else that shows up other than disappointment.

C: Anxiety.

T: Good.

C: And with it, the attendant physical swirlings around.

T: Where do you feel those?

C: In my stomach.

T: Okay, see if you can sort of focus on the emotional part; I know the bodily part will come right along with it. And once again, this is an emotion that's pushed you around a lot, is it not?

C: For sure.

T: Okay. I want you to see if you can try to open just a little bit, starting from where you are, just a little more; you don't have to hit some absolute level, but just a little more willingness to feel what it feels like to feel

Applying Acceptance, Defusion, and Self as Context in Imaginal Exposure   **123**

anxious, without doing anything else with it. Just kind of like, "Hello Mr. Anxiety." "Here you are and you're just like that." "I know you well, old fella." What I'm trying to do is see if you can just get a little more space in which it's okay to feel anxious when you feel anxious. I don't mean that you like it, but that you're not going to posture as though it's your enemy or that it is lethal in some way or inherently damaging to you. It's just anxiety. True? And who is in charge here? You may not know how to control anxiety, but you do know how to do this, at least to some small degree, because I'm asking you to do nothing other than what you did to begin with: feel anxiety.

C: Okay. I can do it for a few moments [acceptance].

This is good work. The client keeps slipping away, but the therapist is successfully redirecting.

Thoughts

T: Good. See if it isn't true that you can shift your posture with anxiety and see if you can let go of any struggle with it. Then put that one away and see if you can get back in touch with that original thing, that meeting. Now you don't have to say it out loud, but just briefly watch what other emotions show up. As each one comes up, try to see if you can make room for it without having to change it or buy into it, do what it says, or resist it. Try something more like waving at it, patting it on the head, acknowledging it. Just let them kind of parade by. We have two more domains to go into. Put all those emotions to the side, and I want to go into a more difficult area, your thoughts. Your mind finally gets a chance to come out and play. As you say the thought, see if you can say it and look at it a little bit like what we were working on last time; that's kind of just like words but on a leaf floating by. Don't do this to diminish it or get it to go away; that's not the purpose. The purpose is to see it as a thought, without adding or subtracting from the actual direct experience of having a thought.

C: Should I visualize it as written in English?

T: Sure ... or in picture and images. However it occurs to you. In some small way I'm asking you to see it, to look at it rather than through it. It is like that colored-glass-ball metaphor that we were using, having it out there in front of you instead of putting it on your head. It will show up on your head, but take it off and then put it out there and then kind of look at it. Get in touch with the original thing you were struggling with. Get in touch with how you felt with that owner. And then watch what Mr. Mind has to say.

C: It goes into defense mode. You want me to say the thoughts or just watch them?

T: Sure. Say the thoughts.

C: They're really fast.

T: Okay, grab one.

C: First thought that I can grab is my thoughts are more personal than my feelings are; I'm wondering how they're going to be perceived out here in the room [conceptualized self].

T: Okay, cool. So thank your mind for that one.

C: Hmmm.

T: Exactly.

C: The mind is perverse. It is trying to do exactly the opposite of what you asked it to do [defusion].

T: Cool.

C: It tries to hide—oh, let's do the meditation exercise now and try just to make our mind a blank slate.

T: That's cool. No need to hide. Let's see the thought.

C: I'm thinking very half-formed thoughts about this girl and who she is, what it would be like if I asked her for a date.

T: Okay. So notice that that happened; it's kind of like the computer metaphor: we tap on the keys and here's the readout. Nothing wrong with that readout. It's just your history showing up.

C: And I know that my mind has that option. It feels very smug about storing what you say and then being able to chew on it, work it, spit it out, judge it [defusion].

T: Right.

C: And I'm thinking back on the exercises that we've been doing and how they weren't pleasant, and my mind doesn't like that.

T: It does not like being dethroned. Who would?

C: Okay, now I'm thinking about what time it is, whether I get to go yet. [This could be a sign of avoidance, but in context it felt as though he was slightly humorously noticing his thoughts of avoidance. In that case it is acceptance and defusion.]

T: Okay, good. Funny. Now let's remember where we started. Go back to the meeting. Go back to what it was like.

C: I get a picture in my mind. I remember the expression on his face and I'm trying to guess what he's feeling. I'm wondering if we're avoiding a conflict or if a conflict is starting. I'm thinking, "Why do I need to do to protect myself" and "What do I really want?"

T: Okay, let's do them one at a time. As you do this, see if you can step back just a little bit and watch your mind roll out; this is what your mind does, yes? See if you can just watch it, the way you might watch a television show. Not to get away from it—I'm not asking you to disassociate or defend yourself, or zone out. I'm asking you just to think the thoughts as a person who's aware of the thoughts that you think.

The Spontaneous Emergence of Self as Context

In an ACT model, all of the processes are interrelated. The spontaneous emergence of self as context provides an interesting example of that process in flight.

C: I'm envisioning the conversation and the visions and images that I had in my head, but suddenly there is another part of me that's laughing [self as context]. There is a part of me that is aware of what I'm trying to think about. It is like that self that you talked about in an earlier exercise. I'm watching.

T: Right.

C: Then I think, "Who is that person? Who is laughing?" I can't figure it out. That still is an unintelligible concept that keeps bothering me [fusion, conceptualized self].

T: If you try to grab that part of you and figure it out, it will slip away.

C: I see the game. Hide the fear; hide the feelings of inadequacy; heck, hide the real inadequacies.

T: Okay. Be careful here. Your thoughts about yourself are not yourself. You can't grab this more spiritual part of you and look *at* it; it is the place you look *from*. So watch your mind looping back to try to figure this out. And as you do that, I want you to notice also that you're here noticing that.

You're not that thing you are noticing; you're the person noticing it. You don't have to believe that; this is not a belief thing, but just notice that when you notice it, *you* notice it. There's a distinction between *what* you notice and *that* you notice it.

C: I catch it, and then it slips away. It feels like a hall of mirrors.

T: Yeah. So just touch it and let it slip away, but knowing that you touched it.

C: I keep kind of backing up and noticing this and noticing that, like I'm falling backward.

Memories

T: Perfect. Beautiful. Exactly. You've got it. You don't have to grab it and hold it; just get a sidelong glance at it. You are here, conscious and alive. There is more to you than the word machine. What is most important here is to watch what your mind does. Can you simply drop the rope? Can you drop the struggle with having to have your mind go in a particular way? And behind all that, here you are. This talking machine that you've got with you all day long, that you have gotten very entangled with and you have struggled with and tried to discipline, it's even claiming to *be* you. How bold is that? Instead, take a little leap. Let go a little. Whatever you can do, see if you can then do just a little more. And a little more. Let go of trying to do anything about it—just watch. Your mind is not your enemy. And it's not your friend. It's just running its mouth. Okay. These thoughts that show up, is there anything in there that you can't have—that is inherently damaging to you? [Client shakes his head no.] Okay. Nice. Stay with it. Just watch your mind a little more, seeing if you can just kind of quietly let it run on without having to push it or pull it or follow it or resist it; just watch it. And now, I want to go to one last domain. First, I want you to put all those thoughts to the side and go back and get in touch with that conversation and then kind of wrap yourself around the feelings that show up in association with that meeting. When you've got it, let me know.

C: I have it.

T: I want you to picture all your memories as snapshots—multisensory snapshots—that are in a file drawer, starting from now, back to your very first memories. While staying in touch with that feeling, I want you to flip back through that file drawer and just keep flipping back and if you pause over a picture for some reason, even if it does not seem logically related, pull the picture out and tell me what's on it.

C: [Pause] My father leaning in the doorway of my bedroom talking to me.

T: Okay, good. How old are you?

C: A teenager—maybe sixteen or seventeen.

T: What is going on?

C: Dad's lecturing me.

T: About what?

C: He's telling me how I'm supposed to do it. He did that a lot.

T: Very good. Stay with this. How do you feel as you're being lectured to?

C: I feel small, irritated, not understood, unappreciated …

T: Good. See if you can open up to that experience and what it felt like [pause]. What is Dad saying?

C: He is angry. He's justifying himself. He had a fight with Mom and he senses my dubiousness and censorship of what he's done. He wants me to understand and he wants to persuade me of his opinion. He is telling me why Mom is wrong.

T: Watch the tension in your hands.

C: Yes. Okay [relaxes his hands].

T: See if you can just let go of that a little bit. Kind of let go into that memory and let go of some of the defenses that you had then. As he's doing this, are there parts of what's coming up for you that are scary enough, intense enough, horrible enough, or confused enough that you're having a hard time staying in the moment? You're not really listening to your dad. Is there a sense of trauma in there? Pain? I want you to see if you can go where that is, and even though it may not make sense here, or even though you may find some resistance, see if you can go where that pain is. If your mind comes crowding in, let it say whatever it has to say but stay with whatever you're doing. Get with what the teenager was feeling. You didn't know when you were that old that you could feel things like this and not have it harm you. It was too scary. So see if you can sort of stand with that teenager now by opening up to what that teenager was feeling.

C: It feels exactly like the things I feel now. It's a sense of powerlessness and anger at being talked at instead of talked with [acceptance]. I'm not sure why I felt that.

T: Good. Let go of any kind of critical quality that you bring into this; see if you can drop that. Stand with the teenager—kind of stand with him without attachment to judgment. Be receptive to what it was actually like—to feel in the middle. Is that fair?

C: Yes.

T: To feel powerlessness. To feel conflicted. What else?

C: Not being considered.

T: Beautiful. So let's not do that. Let's consider what *he* was feeling. That was hard watching your parents fight.

C: For sure. It was hard.

T: Now put that memory away and get in touch with that meeting and how you felt. Then flip even farther back in the file drawer. Take your time, get in touch, and then go back. Take your time. See if you pause over any picture.

C: I was a kid, and we lived in a house that had a tree that allowed access to the roof over the patio, and I thought it was really cool to go and be up there by myself because nobody could see me.

T: Okay.

C: I liked to be alone. I went up there when I was pissed or felt unjustly punished or something like that.

T: Well, let's just go into the memory; let's not interpret it. It's come to mind so in some way it must be relevant. We can think of how it's relevant later. See if you can actually catch a clear memory of climbing that tree.

C: Oh, I can easily see climbing the tree and being on the roof, what if felt like, the color, what I could see from there, what I was wearing, all that kind of stuff.

T: Go into that memory and see if you can look out over the landscape that you could see from there. In your mind's eye, let's just go there, let's be there now. How old are you?

C: Maybe nine.

T: In your mind's eye, I want you to look down at your hands and see how small they are, look at what you are wearing. In your mind's eye, you might reach up and feel how your hair is.

C: Greasy.

Applying Acceptance, Defusion, and Self as Context in Imaginal Exposure   **129**

T: Okay. What time of year is it?

C: Summer.

T: Okay. You like being up there?

C: For sure. The leaves on the tree are big, and there are wrinkles in the tree. I took the same route up there every time.

T: Let's get back up on the roof and stay with the specific one so that we're not interpreting it too much or summarizing but we're actually there. What are you feeling up there?

C: [Suddenly shifting in tone] I'm not feeling anything up there. I'm back. I'm feeling nervous here [fusion, avoidance].

T: When did you lose it?

C: As soon as you asked me to feel how I was feeling up there.

T: Okay. Let's do it a slightly different way. In your mind's eye, I want *you* to go to that patio except you're forty-five years old. You're the age you are now. And go up that tree and sit on that roof. You up there?

C: Yeah.

T: Good. Now, magically you look back and there is this kid climbing up that tree. Somehow or another, there's this kid coming up on the roof. And you realize, although the kid doesn't know it, you realize that, incredibly enough, it's you when you were nine. Look at how he is carrying himself. He doesn't know who you are, but somehow it is okay that you are there. As you see him, what do you see?

C: He's afraid. He has it all covered up though. He has a swagger—his hair, his clothes. But he is hurting.

T: Okay. As you look at him, can you see what he wants from the adults around him? What does he want?

C: He doesn't trust adults.

T: Okay. And what does he want?

C: He wants not to be questioned or instructed about what he's been doing climbing the tree or being on the roof or whatever.

T: Yeah. Is there anything else he wants?

C: He needs to know that it's okay. He's wary. He's waiting for me to yell at him or lecture him. He's defensive.

T: Yeah. What's he doing up on the roof?

C: Standing up, sitting down, crunching around, walking over to the edge, titillating himself with his fear a little bit by being close to the edge.

T: What's he really doing up on the roof?

C: What is he really doing up on the roof?

T: Well, he's doing those activities, but what is that about? Why is he up there?

C: He's thinking rebellious thoughts, escapist thoughts. He's getting away from the pressure.

T: The pressure?

C: To perform. To pretend everything is okay—Mom and Dad and their drinking and drugging and their fights.

T: What does he want?

C: This is hard.

T: I'd like to bring the kid right in front of you. If you could have him in this actual situation, what would you say?

C: What could you possibly tell a child that they'd retain or believe or … [avoidance].

T: Ouch. If you have to stand there and intellectualize, then tell him that. Look him in the eye and intellectualize.

C: I don't want to do that. I don't [uncomfortable pause]. I don't know.

T: There is more to do for him, and we will come back to this later. Take a last look at the nine-year-old, and we will leave that roof. Down to the patio, and then magically we're back here. And when you are ready to be here, open your eyes [pause]. Why don't we take a minute to debrief. I know it is late. If we had more time, I would have stayed up there for a while more. I don't know about the connection between those two memories, but you might think about it. How did you feel?

C: I'm seeing something. I can almost hear the voices. I can see that stance: "You stupid idiot." Very critical. All at the same time realizing that that kind of stance with yourself doesn't solve anything [acceptance].

T: Does that sound like anybody by the way? Who said that kind of thing to you?

Applying Acceptance, Defusion, and Self as Context in Imaginal Exposure   **131**

C: Mom. All the time.

T: So you came by it honestly. Look at what that kid wanted. And then look at what happens when you buy into self-criticism. There's something kind of harsh. It's like slapping the kid around saying, "Cut it out. What's the matter with you?" But you don't have to do that anymore. We can find a kinder place to stand. Is there anything else from that exercise that you want to put on the table before you run out of here? I'm sorry it's so late.... That clock is just brutal.

C: There's a feeling of sadness and pity for the kid [acceptance].

T: Tell me just a little bit more about that.

C: There's a feeling of a desire for strokes, permission from somewhere to just let go and be okay and stop trying to be someone else [acceptance]. To be okay to be me.

T: You're the only one that can do that. And you can't do it just by saying it. You can do it, but it's very twisty as to how to do it. It is exactly what we are working on. Do you see that?

C: Yeah.

T: And it can be done. But you can't just take this thing frontally. Because the next thing you know, you're wagging your finger at yourself criticizing yourself for not being accepting or for continuing to try to control thoughts. And there you are, same old, same old. It's very twisty as to how to do that.

C: I don't think I can make this space that you're talking about between my feelings and my thoughts.

T: You did.

C: I want more drugs. [This was said with slight humor, but it is mixed and hard to score. It could be that he felt some sadness at not being able to get over the hump with the nine-year-old.]

T: Okay, we'll stop there.

FINAL COMMENTARY

This was a very different session than the previous four. It was much more experiential, which is fitting with how verbally entangled the client is. The client seemed to be engaged with the exercise. That alone is a good indication of acceptance as he would not have been willing to do something like this during some of the earlier sessions. He was still pretty avoidant during much of the exercise, but the therapist did a good job of keeping him in the exercise and taught acceptance. It seems as though the client became more accepting by the end of the session, but there was still some avoidance. He sort of slipped back and forth from acceptance to avoidance. Hopefully this can be built on in the following sessions.

The exercise also built on the defusion and self-as-context processes. The client was able to experience his thoughts, feelings, and memories as something separate from himself. He was also able to come into contact with the sense that his self that has been present throughout his entire life is stable.

We think this was probably the most successful session thus far in terms of fostering the ACT processes. But the hugely painful, nagging, dangling end is how he abandoned the nine-year-old with intellectual talk at the end. We could tell that the therapist felt out of time, but frankly, more time might not have solved it. There is simply more work to do.

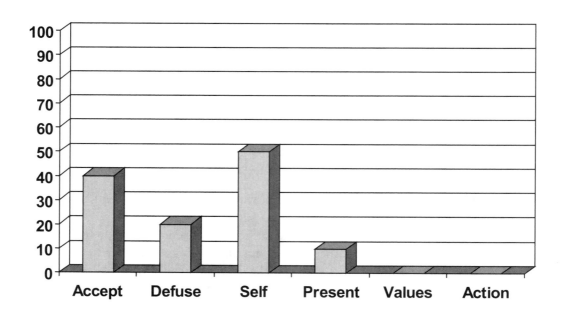

Figure 6.1 Time spent addressing ACT
processes in session five

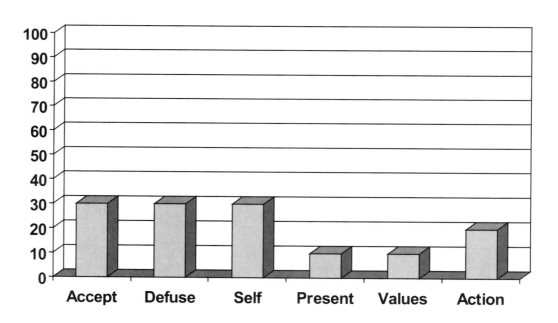

Figure 6.2 Status of client's ACT
processes by the end of session five

ACT Verbatim for Depression and Anxiety

CHAPTER 7

Choice and Values

It was not fully evident perhaps from the transcript, but the last session was quite emotional. As the therapist took the client back to visit the nine-year-old, the client cried in session for the first time. This was something quite different.

The client called before this next session saying he did not want to come. The therapist talked to him briefly, and the client suddenly said he would come.

A "morning after" effect is not uncommon, especially for someone quite experientially avoidant. A lot has gone on the table by now. We can see the basic dynamic quite clearly. The client is a driven, hyperrational person, very successful at work but not very successful with his relationships. He is judgmental of others and himself and socially withdrawn and anxious. He lives inside a very noisy head, and emotions of any kind (other than anger) are hard to acknowledge. Much of this he originally called "depression," but really it is not depression in the sense the term is used in mental health fields. He pushes back against the therapist and any interaction that feels controlling, but in the five sessions so far, he has grown a lot. This is evidenced by more than mere verbal behavior; he sees the issue of emotional avoidance and senses how he gets entangled with thoughts.

From an ACT point of view, this is a case that could resolve quickly. By "resolve" we do not mean "be fixed." Lives are not "fixed." The kind of resolution we need is one in which the client abandons fusion with his story, and his conceptualized self, and learns to walk into pain and chatter in a defused, accepting, and mindful way in the service of chosen values. Once there, his life would initially look very similar to its current state, but the functions would have changed and doors would begin to open in his life. This process of growth would be lifelong, and there would be no need for the therapist to walk that path with the client. What is important here is to get the client on that road in such a way that life itself can become the teacher.

You can do ACT as a form of long-term therapy, but it is remarkable how short ACT can be and still be effective. Gains often continue during follow-up. ACT methods are weakly supported by our feel-good culture, but they pay off directly. Thus, we only need continue therapy long enough to get and strengthen the key repertoire-broadening actions enough that the consequences of those actions begin to change.

But this client is not there yet. He still needs more work on values. The therapist is going to go there in this session while doing a lot to keep the client's analytical mind at bay as this work is being done. Then the client will need more exposure and in vivo work on acceptance and defusion, especially on the ground. With that in place, he may be ready to let life be the teacher.

SESSION SIX

T: So you didn't want to come in?

C: No.

T: You said, "Get me out of here." What was going on?

C: Oh, we are coming off a one-day weekend, and it was a very busy day, and I was pooped and I didn't have the energy to work. But then on the call I thought, "This is BS," so here I am [committed action].

T: Do you think last week had anything to do with it?

C: Last week when I was here, I had just finished a difficult day at work. I was surprised how much things were getting to me, and when I got home, I thought about things and I was like, "Oh, that explains it." When I was crying in here, it wasn't because of what we were talking about, or what I was thinking about. I was just wound up. I felt pushed; it's like, "Okay, I don't want to do this" and I'm like, "No, don't make me," and then the tears just came. So that's what was happening.

T: Really?

C: It's like having a sore and then you scrape it; it's like the sensations are that much harder or deeper or whatever. The subject wasn't pleasant—but the reaction was out of whack.

T: Out of whack kind of relative to what?

C: To what's normal for me to feel.

T: Maybe that's good. Maybe we are into new territory.

C: It was different to sit in a room with a dude and cry. I don't think I've ever done that before in my life.

T: How often do you cry?

C: That's a good question. I'm a guy: I don't cry very often. But I have felt closer to it in the last few weeks. I don't know why. But I am noticing that there have been times when I've been angry and that might actually go together [acceptance].

T: What do you think is the role of an emotional expression like crying?

C: I don't really know. Most of the time they seem to be just something that's kind of along for the ride; they're there. They can be titillating. I mean, while you're feeling titillated, it's kind of like, "Ah." Most of the time to me they feel like a distraction, or a bother. "Oh, I'm feeling something now and isn't that interesting." I mean I don't think that's right [fusion]. I don't think that's the way that most modern humans are, or should be. I think most people know what to do with their emotions [fusion]. You know, I think we could cultivate our emotions and enjoy them more, or use them more or whatever, more than we do. Most people teach themselves to put emotions aside because they create problems. I'm not sure that is wise, but I don't know what else to do.

This client is feeling the sand slip away from beneath his feet. He says, "I think we could cultivate them and enjoy them more," and at the same time he seems fused and avoidant.

T: Right. I'm not sure we need to understand emotions intellectually.

C: I don't think we can.

T: My experience has been that the point at which you begin to clear away the domination of the word machine over how things go, that's when emotions start rumbling around, not even necessarily trying to make you do anything. But you do learn, if you watch them, you can learn when they show up, what happens when you let them run the show. It seems to me emotions are basically just the past in the present. A situation shows up, and what we bring to it is ourselves with our history. Most of what we tell each other about how to talk about that is in emotional terms.

C: But emotions are present in infants.

T: Sure. But then emotions get more and more complex as we learn to speak. Some of our emotions are things that are controlled by very direct things, probably like when a tiger walks into the room and you're afraid. A lot of it's not like that. I mean, if you're like me, a lot of my emotions don't seem to have anything to do with the obvious external environment. Somebody else could be sitting right next to me and be feeling something completely different.

C: For sure.

T: One of the things you said on the way out the door last time was "I don't know how to do what you're asking me to do." Something like that. But what I wanted to ask is "Would it be okay if what shows up is some fairly raw form of emotion? Would that be okay?" You kind of said, when we first started working together, that one of the things you wanted to do was figure out what the heck this emotion stuff is about anyway. Would it be okay if part of what it's about is kind of like a fish swimming in water, things show up and you just function in and with those things? As opposed to something like "Now I understand, I'm feeling this, and feeling this means that, and because it came from here and there it means that I should do this or that." Emotions are often not categorical, logical, linear, or sequential. They're often mixed. They're often muddled. So what I'm asking is, how willing are you to swim around in murky waters, where you don't have great clarity?

C: That's really hard for me. I don't like doing that [avoidance].

T: Yeah.

C: I've spent all my adult life trying to rationalize my way out. It's scary [fusion].

T: Yeah. Not unlike that nine-year-old. Do you have any idea what you're afraid might happen?

C: It's something to do with losing control. What exactly of, I don't know.

T: Now, what would happen if you did lose control? What would you be like?

C: Well, in a worst-case scenario: My business would fall apart. I'd lose everything I've built. I have my kids half the time and I guess I could lose them too. They depend on me.

T: Okay. Just completely blow your stack and …

C: Yeah. I'd lose credibility as a father and an employer, and I really want people to like me and work well for me. I wouldn't want them to be talking about me and feeling sorry for me and avoiding me. It would be embarrassing to be that dad who loses his kids completely. Stuff like that.

T: So if you lost control, you'd be a mad, unlikable, the object of pity and derision. Something like that?

C: Mm-hmm.

T: Kind of hard to tell what would happen if you opened up in a more accepting and mindful way. You don't know.

C: There's also this strong voice in the background. It's a motherly, authoritarian-type voice saying, "Losing control doesn't solve anything." But then I feel this desire to just cut loose, to deny responsibility, to just let it all out, to barf out all these emotions, and it would be stupid and ugly; also it wouldn't solve anything because it never has in the past [fusion, conceptualized self].

T: Yeah.

C: I mean, there's a momentary or short-lived relief, like, "Oh, it's out." But then it all builds back up again, and you have to deal with the consequences.

T: Yeah. Still, trying not to "lose control" and stuffing emotion has consequences too, doesn't it?

There is an interesting point in therapy where the therapist has to make a decision about how to respond to a very important statement. The client says that he is afraid of "losing control." ACT agrees with traditional CBT that the need for control is an important and valid therapeutic issue for clients. But it differs from CBT in how it is addressed. In a more traditional CBT-type approach, you would work to increase this feeling of control over anxiety. In ACT, the therapist would work to step aside from emotional and cognitive control in exchange for control of your life direction.

You can see how this client has avoided emotions for so long that he is not even sure why he is afraid of them. As he steps back, he begins to see that there are other options.

Values

C: Sometimes I think, "Oh, somebody has heard me, and they've understood," and a little later, "Zowie, nothing has changed," you know.

T: Does it feel like that in here sometimes—last week, for example?

C: Maybe.

T: I think we need to be careful not to idealize this. Emotions are not ends in themselves. It's more like staying open to them allows you to keep a direction. Suppose you're standing here, and it would work for you to go there. Between there and here there's a swamp, and it goes as far as you can see that way and as far as you can see that way. You walk along it and you don't see your way across. Eventually, if it's important enough for you to go in that direction, you walk into the swamp or you don't. And if you don't, well, then you're here. It's kind of like that. Feelings are things that show up on a journey. And that's what dignifies them; it's because they're about something.

C: Nothing you just said dignifies them; they just appear [unclear values].

The therapist is beginning to open up the issue of values. This client has no motivation to experience his feelings. His motivation could be increased by linking the experiencing of these emotions to things that are important to him.

T: Well, it dignifies them because they're an aspect of a human choice to be about something. For example, if you were to get close to somebody, you'd have to face painful histories linked to other people: disappointment, betrayals. So as you start getting close to somebody, the escape route starts looking pretty good because it feels uncomfortable. Well, it's like the swamp here, and if I'm going to go in that direction, this discomfort is what I've got to find a way to be open to. It is kind of like this: Suppose you're driving a bus. There are passengers in the bus who have been picked up along the way. Some of them look very unattractive, and they threaten you with various things. So, like, maybe there's a stinky old bum with a switchblade knife and someone else with chains and others too. And they say, "You have to take this route over here," so you say, "I don't want to take that route; I want to take this route." "No, you better take that route because if you don't, we're coming up and coming after you." The basic deal that they usually have is "If you don't go in that direction, we're going to make you deal with us. You're going to see us, smell us, taste us, feel us, whatever." And so we kind of make a deal. "If you sit down and hide yourself, I'll go where you say," or we stop and try to throw them off. But they're hard to throw off, and to do it, the very first thing you have to do is stop driving the bus, which stops you from going in the direction you want. It's kind of like that. Do you know who some of those passengers are for you?

C: I only have sort of big ideas of what they are. They involve power, frustration, anxiety, anger, lack of confidence.

T: [Pause] You were just touching on something, were you not? You started to tear up.

C: Well, I was trying to think of a way to say I hate how I get paralyzed by fear and by confusion. I hate that in myself. I'm just thinking now about how hard it is to know yourself in spite of the amount of time you've spent living with yourself [acceptance].

T: So fear and confusion are two biggies. When does fear show up?

C: Fear shows up when I'm tested or challenged by any situation. Like that meeting we were talking about last time. "Is this a confrontation?" This is making me think about what I want, and I don't want to think about what I want [avoidance, acceptance; avoidance by content, but acceptance because he is talking about it].

This is a sign of increased acceptance in part because the client is talking about topics that would usually be avoided. It is a good sign that he catches the pull to avoid, and outs himself. There is another reason it is a big step forward, which we will see unfold.

T: Because if you did …

C: Then I realize I don't know what I want [unclear values]. And that seems very bad to me.

T: It could be that you don't know what you want, but are you sure that it's that? If you knew what you really, really wanted, what do you think you'd do?

C: I'd probably cry.

T: Inside your values is your own pain.

C: Mm-hmm.

T: And so what do you really want?

C: I don't want to tell you [avoidance].

T: It's kind of an intimate question actually.

C: Let's come back to that one.

This is really excellent progress. Obviously he is being avoidant. But he is framing it so clearly that he is actually approaching the topic of values. And note the dynamic. He is speaking of fear ("Fear shows up when I'm tested or challenged by any situation"), and suddenly up pop values ("This is making me think about what I want, and I don't want to think about what I want").

In an earlier session this happened, and the therapist did not follow the lead. Instead, the therapist took it into self as context. Now the therapist feels the time is right, but the client is backing away. What the therapist is going to do instead is to go after choice.

The reason this is theoretically important is that research is showing that values work that is fused, compliant, or avoidant is ineffective. Real values work is defused, accepting, and active, but in lay language, the concept of "values" is very close to that of "evaluation"—which is almost the exact opposite of what we mean in ACT. Choice is a selection among alternatives without verbal defense and justification, not verbal evaluation, and values are choices. Going in this direction is the long way around, but it does lay important groundwork.

Choice

T: So, now those kinds of things are what I'm talking about. It is really neat that you see it. If you go back to the bus metaphor, it's kind of like, if you would stop being controlled by the passengers, then you'd have to deal with this sign up on the front of the bus. Where are you going? That's your call, not the passengers'. Because it would be like the bus is supposed to go to New York but the passengers are saying you've got to go to Miami. It does not work like that.

C: Where do I want to be going? Where do I want to be?

T: That is the issue in front of us. Yeah. In the normal structure of things, we make these deals with our own minds, basically, that certain kinds of thoughts, feelings, memories, bodily sensations—"Well, I can't have those." But that means you can't drive. You can't be about anything. I mean, after all, "This would make me afraid, this would make me nervous, this would make me insecure, this would make me feel lack of confidence, this would make me feel confused," or whatever. There's a list of passengers that are going to come up. So now we have an issue: how to deflate the passengers. That's what we've been working on so far. Turns out that the main power that they have is that they will come up and be seen. That's enough for us, usually, to give away control. It's like, "Tell me where to go. I'll go there as long as you don't come up." And there's a big cost. Life's going by. The clock is ticking. Whose life is this? And that's the issue of "Where do I want to be going? Where do I want to be?"

C: I thought that was what we are coming back to later, not now.

T: Okay. We will, in a couple of sessions. We can let it be for now. You'll work on it in between sessions anyway.

C: Hey.

T: But I need to lay the groundwork. Right now it feels like this is not so much your life; it feels like it is your emotions' and your thoughts' life. Just for in here, I want to make a distinction that we can use. It's just for in here because it's not a distinction that's in the dictionary or anywhere else, and it's kind of an idiosyncratic thing, but I want to make a point. What I want to distinguish between is making a choice and making a decision. I want to define it this way. The *decision* is a selection among alternatives that you do for a reason. And you can explain and justify and, you know, give reasons for your behavior that are linked to your selection, sort of like "Why did you fill out your taxes that way?" "Well, because this regulation says that, these receipts say that, and so that's like that." But I want to define a *choice* as a selection among alternatives that is made usually *with* reasons and yet is not made *for* reasons. Okay? All right? You with me?

This concept can be difficult to understand, because it is very unusual—it is not how we live our lives. Almost every decision we make is done for reasons, and that process works rather well in most situations. But in some cases, such as clinical issues, making decisions for reasons leads to inaction because there are too many reasons not to follow a value. Reasons could include "I will get hurt," "It won't work anyway," and so on, and if these can't be disproved, then some clients won't move ahead. Making a choice and following it with reasons—but not because of reasons—allows change to occur without the need to justify it cognitively.

The following dialogue takes up most of the session. What the clinician is doing is trying to establish the possibility of defused selections among alternatives. Without that, values become heady, avoidant, and socially compliant. To work well, values have to be intrinsic, owned, and undefended. The client is going to see if it is possible to do *anything* without verbal defense and justification. This exercise is borrowed from the human potential movement, and it is not an easy one for highly rational people. For this client, it is undoubtedly going to be very, very difficult.

C: Mm-hmm.

T: So let's just see if it is possible to choose. We will start with something trivial, and then we will link it to values. Okay, so let's see. So, you drink sodas?

C: Mm-hmm.

T: So over here I've got a diet cola and over here a ginger ale. Do you drink that stuff?

C: For sure.

T: Okay. I want you to choose one of them.

C: Okay, I choose the diet cola.

T: Okay. Why do you choose the diet cola?

C: Because I like it.

T: Okay. Except you could have noticed that you liked this more and still have chosen that, right?

C: Yeah.

T: Could have. It's a free country. Nobody would have sued you, right?

C: As far as I know.

T: And the other thing is, I didn't ask your *likes* to choose. I asked *you* to. So, over here I've got a diet cola and over here I've got a ginger ale. Which do you choose?

C: Oh brother.

T: Let's see if I can get away with this without having you pop me one. Which do you choose?

C: I still choose the diet cola.

T: Okay. Why do you choose the diet cola?

C: Because I never drink anything else.

T: Okay. Except you could have noticed that your history is that you hadn't had anything else yet still had this, right? Possible? Could you have done that?

C: Mm-hmm.

T: All right.

C: Could have chosen that.

T: You could have chosen that. So noticing that you had that history didn't make you choose this, did it?

C: Mm-hmm.

T: Besides, I didn't ask for your history to choose. I asked you to.

C: But I am my history and my thoughts and my ... [fusion].

T: That's a thought.

C: My thirst and my budget. That one costs more.

T: That's a thought, too. Could you have all those thoughts and still choose the other one? Can you make a choice? It's real clear you can make a decision. I get that. And you're actually pretty good at it; you're very logical and very smart, I mean, you're good at it. I'm asking you to do something else. I know this is a trivial choice. But if you can't choose

144   ACT Verbatim for Depression and Anxiety

when it is trivial, when can you? So over here I've got a diet cola. Over here I've got a ginger ale.

C: I feel that I am making a choice based on what you told me. Okay, right now, just to be perverse—that is, making a decision to be perverse—that I choose to be that one; I mean, is that what you'd say if I chose that one?

T: Let's see; which do you choose?

C: I choose the diet cola.

T: Okay, why do you choose the diet cola?

C: I think it was to be perverse.

T: Except you could have had the thought "I want to do this to be perverse" and done that.

C: Well, I can have thoughts and make choices.

T: Yes, I agree. I've said, "with reasons, not for reasons." Yeah, you'll have reasons. It's "blah, blah, blah" from morning to night. You will have "reasons." I'm with you on that. Usually for some milliseconds you might have some peace in the sense of silence, but most people don't have peace of mind in the sense of silence. I mean we believe there are such people on a mountaintop somewhere, but I wish they'd come and talk to me because I've never met any. Peace of mind must mean something other than silence. This is probably one of the most important things you'll do in here. I mean, in this silly game we're playing, if you can make a choice, you've got some power here. If you can't, then let's just let the programming roll, let's just let your mind run, just turn over the keys.

C: Well, if you were to ask me, I have "happy" and I have "sad," which do you choose to be, I would say no, I can't do that [defusion].

T: Yeah, I agree. I agree.

C: Because no matter how much I want, or all the times I've tried, it doesn't work that way.

T: Right, it doesn't.

C: Okay, but let's review what making a choice is.

T: Okay, a decision is a selection among alternatives done *for* a reason. You can explain, justify, rationalize, make sense out of why you do things. A choice is the selection among alternatives done with reasons and not for reasons.

C: If I choose ginger ale to say, "I want to be different; I want to make a different choice," it's a reason.

T: Is it?

C: I don't know how to pick one without having a reason.

T: You'll have a reason. Sure. Watch your mind. But is it *for* a reason? We're trying to do something that actually your mind does not know how to do. You do know how to do this. Minds don't like this. The fact that minds get what I'm asking, they're going to tantrum. Because they know where it leads.

C: Mine doesn't.

T: The very fact it doesn't understand means it's not 100 percent in control. Your mind thinks you're going to die if it isn't in control. I mean, your mind actually thinks that it *is* you, never mind that it's good for you. So this is dangerous. Can't you sense it? What I'm asking is seemingly dangerous, crazy. But the mind isn't good for everything. So, usually you can decide between these two things. I'm not saying there's anything wrong with deciding between cola and ginger ale. But if you can't make a choice with a silly thing, when can you? So let's see if we can do it. Over here I've got a diet cola; over here I've got a ginger ale. I'm asking you to notice your mind giving you all that stuff, and pick one. *With* all that stuff. Not *for* any of it.

C: Every time I want to pick one, there's a reason for it.

T: That's right. Let it give you the reasons; just listen.

C: Okay.

T: [Pause] Okay. And then without linking it to any of that, reach out and take one of these things.

C: I can't [fusion].

T: Who's in control here? Whose life is this? Are you an automoton? I mean, are you telling me that your hand can't reach out and grab one of these things?

C: Sure.

T: Try it and find out. Okay, which one did you choose?

C: A diet cola.

T: Okay, why did you choose it?

C: Because I'm left-handed, and it's easier to grab that way.

T: Thank your mind for that interesting thought. And then slap it around because we're going to have to do the whole thing all over again. You probably don't know why that was. We'll set this aside and come back to this. Let's just see. Let's do the first round—You said, "Because I like it." Okay? Now, I'm going to make a prediction. All right. Why do you like it?

C: Because it has no calories.

This is incredible if you step back and watch it. Every other creature on the planet makes choices, not decisions. Yet this thin cortical overlay, this evolutionarily more recent acquisition, this veneer of reason and logic, claims that it is impossible to do even the slightest thing without its having the final say. The therapist decides to show how thin the veneer is.

T: Okay, I'm holding something behind my back, which I will show you in a second. Why do you like the fact that it has no calories?

C: Because I like to have refreshment, and it's nice that it's not adding weight while I'm having refreshment.

T: Okay, and why is that so important to you?

C: Because I am overweight.

T: Okay. Why is that so important to you, not to be overweight?

C: Because I would like to look good.

T: Why is that so important to you?

C: That I don't know.

Arrogance of Minds

T: [Quickly pulls hand from behind back with three fingers up] Okay, we went three steps before you said, "I don't know." It's always three to four. Three to four levels out, and people don't know what in the hell they're doing and why. You could have started anywhere, any path, and we go a few levels down, and this is just stories. You don't really know why you're picking one or the other. You tell yourself stories. But you pursue them, you say, "Okay, mind, let's see how much you know," and it's about that thick [holds up thumb and finger barely apart]. There's nothing to it. That's going to run your life? You're going to turn yourself over to that?

C: Well, it's easier to listen to those reasons than it is to look under them, because I know a little bit about what's under there [fusion]. It's fear and uncertainty [acceptance].

Ironically, the purpose of this course of treatment, in part, is to let go of the struggle with fear and uncertainty. Yet here we are, and through a very indirect route. Relational networks are tangled webs, but they have just a few organizing principles.

T: I told you the mind won't like it. Do you really think you know why you do things? Sometimes you do in some sense. My kids can tell stories about their behavior. "Why did you do that?" And they'll tell a story.

C: Mine too.

T: Sure. Do you think they really have any idea why they do things? I want to know why because I want to be sure they can rationalize and justify their behavior so that if they're out there doing something completely ridiculous, they'll feel kind of nervous. But the tragedy is that they're going to actually believe that they know why they do things. If so, give everybody a Nobel Prize because the bag lady on the street is then as talented a psychologist as the greatest psychologist who's ever lived. I mean you can raise a bird in a cage and you still can't predict half of its behavior. And people were there for everything that's happened to them in their whole lives. What happened four days before your eleventh birthday?

C: I have no idea.

T: How about seven days after your tenth birthday?

C: Nothing.

T: This is the arrogance of minds. Minds know everything. It's like, "How do I touch my nose?" that I was doing in our fourth session. Okay. So let's see if we can put this mind of yours in its place. I don't want to hurt it or to get rid of it. It's a nice thing to have. You definitely want a mind. But is there no limit? Here's the cheating way to do it. I'm going to ask you to do something, and you have a half second to respond [puts two hands out, each closed as if it contained something]. Quick—choose one. Okay [client chooses one]. Why did you choose the left one?

C: Because I like it.

T: Oh, you're going to go down hard: kicking and screaming.

C: I am. What is the purpose of choosing if there's no reason for choosing? Why would I be interested in choosing?

T: Because otherwise it's all verbal programming. Nothing else can be part of it. You've done that. That's what brought you in here in the first place. Okay, we'll play this rationally. I'll get in there and sort of play intellectually with your mind for a minute, but then we're going to come back out. If we're sitting on top of Mount Olympus, we can see that our lives have something to do with everything that's happening in the universe and that the universe affects our lives. There probably is some grand order somewhere. I'd presume that.

C: I wouldn't.

T: Then I don't know why you're fighting me on it because what you're saying is "Why would you do X?" as if it should all be rational. Maybe there is a reason in some grand scheme; maybe my choices are the result of things that have happened to me. But that does not mean much. Don't you have a cat?

C: A ferret.

T: Oh yeah. Your pet does pretty well. If you're kind to him, feed him, he's not cold or hungry, gets some pats, hey, it's cool, right? But you can have everything your pet needs to be happy and you can be miserable. What kind of deal is that? I mean you're coming to the shrink. You're paying me big money. Your pet's not doing that. He's just waiting for you to come home and be kind to him.

C: Okay.

T: Okay, but your pet is not going, "Well, the pros of this are, and the cons of this are." It's just choosing. You can do that too, but you have to do it with reasons. Without this, you cut yourself off from your dog-and-cat wisdom. And you cannot do values, but I'd be getting ahead of myself to walk through that.

C: Well, I know that there have been times when I've done things and haven't been able to see why. I don't know if that's the type of thing you're talking about or not, that you just make a choice without a reason.

T: That's one. I'll give you another one. Let's see if we can get this one handled. Over here, I've got a diet cola. You probably haven't heard this before. But, over here I've got a ginger ale. Now the game is to see if you can, *with* your mind, *but not because of* your mind, reach out and touch one of these. You don't have to kill your mind; you can listen to it, even. And as you listen, just reach out and touch one.

C: It's too difficult [fusion].

T: What's going to happen? Is your mind going to reach out and kill you? You can listen to its reasons and respectfully decline to link your action to what your mind is giving you. So that you don't explain, justify, or interpret your action as linked to this because of this, justified by this, explained by this. I mean, who makes that link? Does your mind make a link, or do *you* make a link? Resistance is a link. Compliance is a link. But there is freedom within the link.

C: Okay, so I can hear my mind and ignore it.

T: Ignore is a little bit too strong. Listen to your mind *and* choose. What is the power that your mind has other than to talk to you?

C: Let it talk?

T: Yeah, just like the passengers on the bus. You don't have to link it to what you are doing. Do you? This can be done. Over here I've got a cola, over here we've got a ginger ale; which do you choose?

C: I choose neither because I'm not thirsty.

T: Mmm. You're a tough case.

C: Well, I can appreciate the fact that physically my mind has nothing to do with the fact that my arm is moving [defusion].

T: Right.

C: But that's as far as I can separate my mind from me.

T: Okay. Now flip a coin: heads or tails?

C: Heads.

T: Why heads?

C: Because I formed a mental image in my mind and that's the picture that I saw when it landed on your hand.

T: It wasn't even a coin. Okay. Could you have had the picture of heads and still said tails? Or tails and still said heads? I understand that you had the picture, if you had the picture; I believe that you said you did.

C: I could have.

T: Okay. Heads or tails?

C: Tails.

T: Okay. Why did you say tails?

C: I don't know. That just popped out.

T: Whew. Okay. Can you do that without the world stopping? No fundamental law of the universe broken? It's a trivial thing, right? Can we say this: you don't have to choose heads or tails *for a reason*, right?

C: Right.

T: Okay. This is possible. Is it not?

C: It is.

T: Okay. Now the only thing that you have to do is to add the reason back in and see if you can still chose. Let's do it this way: Your mind says, "Choose heads, choose heads, choose heads." Okay? Get it going. And then do whatever you're going to do either way, not linked to that. Heads or tails?

C: Heads.

T: Okay. Why did you choose heads?

C: I just kind of grabbed one.

T: Okay, but you had lots of "reasons," right? "Choose heads, choose heads, choose heads."

C: Yeah. So I did.

T: Did you do it because your mind told you to choose heads?

C: No [defusion].

T: It's harder, though, right? That was harder than the first one.

C: For sure.

T: Because your mind is telling you something, and it's like, "I have to do what it says." Now finally: Over here is a cola and over here is a ginger ale. Choose one.

C: Cola.

T: Why did you choose cola?

C: Just did it.

T: Awesome. Here's the connection I want to make, and then that's enough for tonight. If you can't do this, how can you choose your values?

Choosing Values

C: Back up.

T: How can you choose your values?

C: But aren't your values based on learning and decision making?

T: Sure, in one sense—I'm not saying that choices are disorderly and chaotic. But values are a metric. We measure our selections by them. How can we select a metric that way? If I say, "Why do you value that?" do you see what will happen?

C: I can think of lots of reasons for all the examples that pop into my head.

T: Okay, let's do it. Give me something of value.

C: Then we're going to go down three to four, and then I won't have a reason.

T: Let's see.

C: So, I'm thinking, the first thing that came to mind was that I value honesty.

T: Okay, and then why do you value that?

C: Because more often than not, if you're not honest, it's trouble, problems, bad feelings, and whatnot.

T: Okay, and why is not having trouble, problems, and bad feelings something that you value?

C: Because those are all, well, wait—avoiding them? Why do I want to avoid them? [defusion] Because they are not harmonious in the social fabric.

T: Okay, and why is a harmonious social fabric something you value?

C: Because chaos and whatnot are disruptive … Sheesh. I'm going around in circles.

T: Okay and why is avoiding disruption valuable?

C: Because … aw gee. I don't know the answer to that one.

T: Do you see it? Let's look at this logically, so just put your intellectual hat on—just flat-out intellectual hat. Values are things that you use to evaluate things, right? They are a ruler that you apply to events. If you were going to evaluate your values, you would have to have some other values to evaluate them with. So if I'm going to measure a ruler, I have to have another ruler, right? Well, if I was going to measure that ruler, I'd have to have another ruler.

C: I get it.

T: If you don't make choices, you can't have values either, not values that really work. Values are not preset, hardwired things—you have to choose yours. Values are pretty important, and if you don't have them, it's hard. Without choice, we have nowhere to start. What would you like your life to have stood for? What is it if it is not about being approved of? It's kind of like, if you were going to write your own tombstone, and you're going to put what you stood for on it, what would you like it to say?

       I'd ask you to look at this as a choice—as an undefended, naked, and in-the-wind choice. Not defended, rationalized, explained: This is what I'm about. Why? Because this is what I'm about.

       Think about it over the week.

C: I will.

T: What do you want on that tombstone?

FINAL COMMENTARY

This session will make those readers nervous who like doing therapy without taking charge. And given this client's sensitivity to being told what to do, what this clinician did is a risky move in some ways. But in the past, the therapist has gotten away with a dance of structure and lack of structure, taking control and giving away control.

It is worth noting that the client is much, much more willing to tolerate ambiguity. The entire last half of the session in some ways was like a gigantic exposure exercise in which a long, almost experiential exploration of an issue without a clear point was walked through. The client would never have tolerated this three or four sessions earlier, and it is a sign of progress that he did.

At this point the therapist needs to step up to the challenge of values and continue exploration of the client's pain. If those two can be linked to action, the full ACT agenda will be fleshed out.

The next obvious step is to go strongly into values. But as you will see, that is not where the clinician goes next.

Figure 7.1 Time spent addressing ACT processes in session six

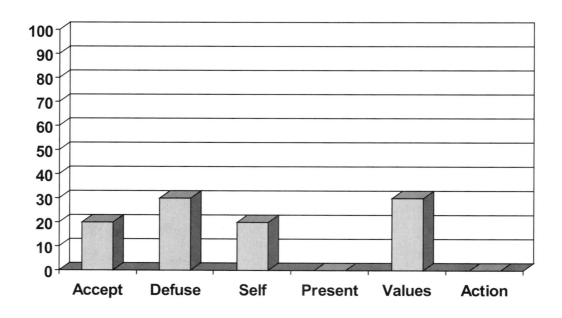

Figure 7.2 Status of client's ACT processes by the end of session six

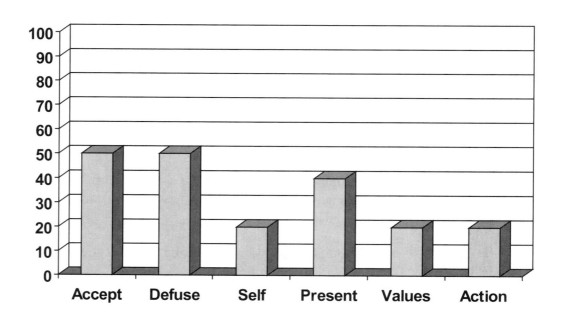

CHAPTER 8

Self-Compassion

In the last session, the therapist pushed hard on choice to set up the values work. But in this session, the therapist does not immediately take the client there. Instead, the therapist goes through all of the other props that may still be keeping the client standing (continuing with the sand-washes-away-until-you-topple metaphor). The therapist will link many of these props to the tin-can-monster exercise in session five. Although the most recent session is mentioned, it is as if it is in the background.

We were surprised when we first saw the transcript. This is an odd choice, but on reflection, it makes odd sense too. What took place two sessions ago was potentially transformative. The client saw something about pain and emotion and their connection to values. The client pushed off on considering what he really wanted—almost begging to postpone that issue. In hindsight it seems that the therapist may have gone to choice not to set up values immediately, but to get back to the emotional core behind the values work, and to bring to that effort a greater sense of choice available to the client, probably fearing that this highly intellectual client will turn values into another stick to beat himself up with unless that emotional touchstone is psychologically present. As a cork is pushed out of a bottle by first pushing on one side and then the other, the therapist is going back to the emotional issue in this session, and going back to values work, per se, in the next.

One reason to base a book on actual therapy transcripts is to illustrate the emergence of twists and turns like this. ACT is a flexible model, not a rigid set of steps. It is interesting to watch the flow in the hands of a therapist who obviously understands the model well enough to create sequential decisions on the fly. That does not mean that the therapist's decision was the right one—just that it was a coherent one.

SESSION SEVEN

T: I was trying to remember back when we were doing that exercise two sessions ago, we're following back to that strand that came out of that core feeling from the meeting. You remember? Tell me again, what exactly did you say? We were doing this exercise and we came up on something. You began tearing up. Later on you said, "That didn't have anything to do with that."

C: I said I was just having a hard day. I was really wound up. I have been sleeping poorly. At some level I felt really pushed to the wall in here. It wasn't so much that I felt you were responsible for how I felt; I was just like, "This is too much," you know?

T: Yeah.

C: And we were thinking about old images and things I think about all the time. I felt like I didn't follow your exercise. It's like, you want me to see something your way, and I don't have any idea what you want.

T: You said something like "I don't know what you want me to do" or "I can't do what you're asking me to do."

C: Both. There were some things that you asked me to do, and I think I understood what you were asking and I couldn't or wouldn't do it, and there were other times when I'd think, "I really don't understand what you're asking me to try" [fusion].

Fusion is pretty easily detected when someone needs to "understand" something before going forward. It is very likely that this is not just an issue in this one situation in his life but is present in many others. He likely does not move forward in many other areas unless he feels pretty sure that it will be safe or a good idea. The therapist will work to help him take some steps without the client being sure it is a good idea. In fact, the therapist might want the client to do this work *while* thinking that it is not a good idea.

Creating an Openness to His Experience

T: That was important because it was related to the content of the memory in some way. What was the memory? I remember making the connection, but I can't remember why. What was it?

C: One was the kid up on the roof, but the one before that was Dad.

T: Dad looking in, and he's lecturing you about something.

C: For sure.

T: It was something about what you're supposed to do, or how you are supposed to behave. And you're like, "Why is he telling me this? What am I supposed to do with it?" It's interesting. It seems like how you felt about the session … and how you feel in here regularly, for that matter. "Why are you telling me this and what do you expect me to do with it?" It's kind of an interesting parallel.

C: Exactly the type of stuff I don't like.

The last statement is said with a touch of irony. This interchange is a clue that treatment is helping him do things that he is not sure about, while noticing that he is not sure whether this is the right thing or not. We would know this process is really changing things when he does something spontaneously and without certainty that it is a good idea.

It is generally a worthwhile move, during the session, to connect behaviors to issues being worked on. It grounds the work in larger issues. You notice that the therapist is deliberately seeming to be somewhat confused, which is creating a space for the client to step forward, recapturing some of what was there two sessions ago. And as he does, the relevance between the content and the claim that the reaction had nothing to do with content is very clear.

T: And that's good. Because, well, because it means buttons are being pushed that are old and probably meaningful in some way or another.

C: You said something like "I'm not your father telling you what to do," and it's like, yeah, I know that. I felt that you tried to say something like, "It's okay."

T: We were talking about the feeling that comes up in association. Anyway, I need a little help getting clear.

C: Do you write notes afterward? Because I notice you don't write much in here.

T: I try not to write them in here; I want to listen and to focus on you.

C: It's very easy to lose memories. In classroom settings where I've taken notes later, it's like, wait a minute, a big gap there.

This last statement is a poke and perhaps an attempt to move the topic. There is likely some anger in the room over the focus of the session so far. The client would rather avoid these feelings and move on. The therapist stays on the topic.

T: We are trying to back up a little bit from thoughts so that they don't pull you in quite as fast, number one. And number two, see if we can carve out a place where you can do something else with your thought rather than just believe it or disbelieve it. But more like, let it put you in contact with your own history and what's going on emotionally in the moment as opposed to a big struggle. We are doing things to shift the relationship to the words that are going on in your head, with a little more room to feel anxious, angry, sad, hurt, uncomfortable, mad, whatever. That's the content. It's just that there is another way to interact with the content other than just what your head tells you literally.

C: I've been thinking about this concept of "you." You said several times, "Who's in charge here?" It's real hard to separate any part of what's going on inside. I'm aware that my physical responses to what I'm thinking are separate from me. But my mind says that means I should be able to control them, but then I think, "Trying to control them is not helpful." Still, somehow I manage to divert myself most of the time from crappy thoughts. But I don't do it by grabbing it and solving it and shaking it and saying, "I'm done with you." It's more like just going someplace else.

T: More like distraction, don't you think?

C: For sure, it's a distraction-type thing.

T: And that can be helpful if it is not meant to subtract anything. But then there is this third option, different from struggle or distraction, which is to think the thoughts as thoughts.

C: But they're not thoughts, they're feelings.

T: Same deal: feel the feelings as feelings.

C: And just accept them. Leaves floating on the water.

T: Yeah. Not accepting them in the sense of twiddling your thumbs ... but letting them be as they are. But where I'm taking this is another place.

C: Don't give me your cola and ginger ale again.

T: Okay, though choice is important.

C: That felt like this humongous concept that was sort of thrown in toward the end of the session. You could spend six weeks in a seminar on it. I can't grab that in five minutes [fusion, avoidance].

This is a poke too. But there is also a bit of humor in the interaction, so there is a self-reflective quality even to the pushing back: "Oh no! Not cola again!"

T: Sure. But we shall see if we can use it, even so.

C: Gotcha.

T: When thoughts and feelings are really sticky, I suspect issues of right and wrong are there. We have touched on this topic a few times. Right and wrong can only appear when you take thoughts like "He's wrong and I'm right, and somebody has to acknowledge that and agree with that" literally. This would not be an issue if that statement were experienced as words in your head—are you with me?

C: For sure.

T: I just wonder this: have you mixed up right and wrong with hurt or anxiety or anger? If you do, it sticks to you. Suppose it were like this: You've got two craps tables and you have to pay somebody to play at them. This one over here you can play for being right, but you have to pay in some chips of vitality; or here you've got another one, and you can play for vitality, but you've got to turn in right and wrong—you've got to pay with self-righteousness. Which do you choose? Back up and look at that and see if it isn't true. See if this is how it works for you. If you're playing for being right, there's some significant loss of vitality that's associated with those moments.

C: I know what you're saying. I don't know how to say it, but when I'm doing that, I'm doing something that's dangerous. When I'm doing that, I know that I'm making a choice of some very heavy things, and I know that there will be repercussions, there will be costs. The outcome will change something. Do I want that right-and-wrong thing to be what I'm about? [values]

Letting Go of Right and Wrong

T: Let me ask you this: if a miracle were to happen and you would be able to move from here, living the kind of life you really want even while experiencing all the stuff you have been struggling with and were trying to change—but without any change in circumstance, your history, the environment—who would be made wrong by that?

C: [Pause] Gee ...

T: Magically, the struggle clears up, and yet your history is the same, the circumstances are the same, everybody else is the same, the world is the same, everything is the same—it's just that you're moving on.

C: I'm wrong. It means I'd be thinking I've been looking at everything the wrong way [defusion; this could be fusion of course. See the next note for an explanation].

T: Right on. So basically you're in a situation where you better not let things change very much because look what it means about you.

C: So that's why it takes so long for people to change—they have to very slowly change these pictures so that they save face, sort of.

T: Is there some of that in there? Sometimes it's blaming others, sometimes it's just all the struggle you've been through. If this stuff could just clear up, I mean, what does that mean?

C: Then I would be wrong. Then that previous mind-set was wrong [defusion; this could literally be scored as fusion, but listening to the tapes, it feels as though he sees his investment in being right. If you see the pull toward the right-and-wrong game in flight, that is defusion].

T: Right. It kind of constricts things and squeezes them down; it's like chewing on a molar coming in—it hurts so good. Self-righteousness feels good. But it hurts too, and there's not much power in it.

C: Why is it that way? It's so consuming, it's so narrow, it shuts everything else off.

T: But one of the things we ran into is how much of what you struggle with is historical. So this move basically says "Things can't change unless things change that can't change." How is that for some psychobabble? Yet it's actually right. So here are these two tables. You can play for right and wrong, but you've got to pay with vitality and aliveness. Suppose it really were a cola versus ginger ale deal? You really could sidle up to either one of these two tables just as a matter of choice. So which would you choose?

C: Well, I would choose being vital and alive and present ... but there are times when you just get sucked into this whole right-and-wrong thing [defusion].

One of the things you are beginning to see is that the client is grabbing onto ACT issues and is just running with them. This is more than superficial agreement—things are falling together for him. He sees that right and wrong is a verbal prop that holds verbal patterns in place. It is in the nature of relational networks that we learn to value their coherence. That is fine when taking a chemistry test. It is a sure route to inflexibility when dealing with your story about your life. The therapist nicely rolls this forward into the linkage between this issue and defusion, acceptance, and behavior change.

Linkage to Acceptance and Action

T: Right. So what is it that sucks you in?

C: Good question. I've been trying to identify it for some time now.

T: Part of it may be when we start interacting with those thoughts literally. And right and wrong is all in there. You had a conflict with one of your waiters a while back. It got real sticky. What percentage of your thoughts do you think have a strand that goes through right and wrong about that waiter?

C: [Pause] All of them. Every one [acceptance].

T: Nice.

C: "Why didn't he do this? Why is it like this? He should do X. I should. He should …" [acceptance, defusion].

T: I'm not saying there's anything wrong with right and wrong; it's just— what is the function of it in a given moment and does it really serve you?

C: Oh man, most of the time it has absolutely no useful function [defusion].

T: What would happen if, when you'd sensed you were in one of those times, you'd let all of the thoughts go by? I don't mean that you argued with them or changed them; I mean, you'd simply sort of kept your hands off them and just let them be like leaves on a stream. What if you had respectfully declined your mind's invitation to fight for self-righteousness? What would it look like to do that? What would show up?

C: The immediate thought or picture that comes to mind when I think of these things going around is of me holding on to a string and then letting them go and then letting them kind of fly out farther and farther. Feelings as well, "I'm hurt" or "I'm being pushed," you know, and they want to have a form so that they can be solved. They would just be sitting there all whiny and grabby, and I'd be going, "Well, here I am" [acceptance, self as context].

His description is very ACT consistent. The therapist will have to pay attention to see if the client behaves in ways that are consistent with the grasp of the work— speaking and doing are different—but this is a nice step forward.

T: That's really cool. That's exactly what would happen [pause]. Could I say it another way? To some degree it protects you against "hurt" to go into the world of right and wrong. Yet it loops back on you and it hurts you in another way. So it's kind of like right and wrong pull you up into your head and get you out of your body, feelings, and emotions—true? So do you need to do that?

C: I sometimes feel like I need to … but it has a cost [this is a mix of the processes, but in context it seems relatively accepting and defused].

Sometimes an ACT client will say, "I feel like" or "I think," which is very different than "I need to" or "I will." It involves labeling the process. We are not entirely sure yet what this client means. He could be saying that he "feels like he needs to" in a defused sense of noticing the pull to avoid and to be right; but it could also mean he is still invested in avoidance. Our intuition is that fusion is starting to break down, though he has a ways to go.

T: Okay.

C: It's very uncomfortable to let go [acceptance; this is acceptance because he acknowledged it]. That's about all I know. It's scary [fusion]. I get afraid if I let go that it could take me over [conceptualized self]. The rational, thinking part of me has done pretty well so far, and there's no way we're going to let the second string come in until we're down and out [conceptualized self; this is scored because it seems like he is identifying with "the thinking part of me." At the same time, the use of the term "second string" is highly encouraging because it means he is beginning to see his various moves in flight, which is a defused place to work from].

The mix of an attachment to his ability to control his thoughts and feelings and a defused, self-reflective quality gives the therapist two options to pursue. The therapist pursues the second view.

T: This is cool. Exactly right. So have you suffered enough?

C: One part of me, my rational mind, wants to be able to pick up emotion and use it when it wants to, for the fun part of it, the joys, the highs, whatever [values], but to keep it safe at some level. It's very buried.

This is an interesting and encouraging statement because it shows that the client is aware of not just the pain that avoidance has caused but also the loss of joy.

T: This choice, who's first string and who's second string, how old is that?

C: I think that's probably going back to teenage years. But it's gotten much more defined, for sure.

T: Well, and you have done well.

C: Oh man [defusion; in part because this is said with irony].

T: What your mind tells you is that the reason you've done well is because you use the first string—control and suppress and avoid, right?

C: My mind says that. Actually it thinks that *and* it's very insecure [defusion; it is usually good when the client refers to his "mind" like that because there is more flexibility around the content].

T: If you were to allow the second string in, is there a fear of who you are, or what you'd be like? You might be a completely different person.

C: Oh, people that I know would not want me to let my actual feelings out! [This is also a mix because the content is avoidant but there is humor in the statement, which the therapist reacts to, which indicates some defusion about it.]

T: Right. Right. Be afraid. Be very afraid. So your mind says it will have a big cost.

C: For sure.

Exposure Exercise from Session Five

At the beginning of the session the client spoke about not being interested in going back to the exposure exercise, but the therapist goes back into it here. You will see that the client repeatedly tries to change the topic or to avoid working. Doing this kind of work is like doing exposure with an anxiety client: you have to nudge a little, but pushing too hard will often backfire. The next series of exchanges is a gentle dance of keeping the client in the exercise while fostering acceptance, defusion, and a sense of self as context.

T: "You'll lose me and all the good things I've brought," plus it's dangerous, plus who would you even be? Yeah. And, if you go back, go back as a teenager, or even earlier, if you can find it, when you made that choice of who's the first string. Can you find an emotional component to that choice?

C: Anguish. I don't know. I just have this very vague, very quick flash of a child realizing that Mom and Dad were not going to nurture that emotional part of me. I was going to be criticized or abandoned: it was like, "Well that's fine but we don't have time for that."

T: Right.

C: It's a very unstructured picture.

T: "Anguish" is a pretty powerful word. That image of being a kid, essentially being told, "You put that part away and we need you to be more rational about this." Bring in the first string. It is a painful image isn't it? Although your mind says you need the first string, isn't it also true that as you do that, you're doing to yourself what was done to you those many years ago? The same move, right?

C: Yeah. But it's a survival thing. It's very strong.

T: Is it survival, really?

C: That's how it was interpreted by the child. You either go with the flow or you lose it.

T: Oh yeah. We can understand the child being put in that position. We don't get very good training at all as to what to do with our emotional side. And we usually have bad models because we have people exploding or suppressing around us.

C: For sure.

T: So you don't know much about the second string we've been working on here?

C: Unh-unh.

T: Why would you?

C: There has been little to no reinforcement of "Hey that's good, let's do something with it. Have fun with it, nurture it, bring it out, and let it play" [acceptance].

T: Nice. Very nice. "Play" is an interesting word. There's something in what you've been saying inside the struggle that seems very nonplaylike.

C: Yeah, it's a real thing of not being yourself. It's being what other people are telling you to be [self as context, values; values fit here because if you let go of who others tell you to be, you are confronted immediately with what you yourself want].

T: How young are you here?

C: The kid?

T: Yes. How young do you feel, right now, saying that?

C: Like nine or ten or something like that.

T: Ah. I was guessing teenager, but it's younger. Nine or ten. Gee, kids that age really do need to play. That's kind of their job; not their *only* job perhaps, but it's a big part of their job. Would it be fair to say that your logical mind has sort of beat up on that nine-year-old?

C: I can see my logical mind sort of picking up on management trends, and I've taught my logical mind not to speak to the other part of me as cruelly as it has in the past. It's a politically correct logical mind.

T: Oh, good [slightly sarcastic]. As you even talk about this, do you feel it in your body anywhere? Do you kind of feel like this is available to you in other ways, other than just logically? Conflict, struggle, top dog, and so on.

C: I feel, sort of the back of my head and the back of my eyes, that sympathy for the kid [defusion]. I want to be recognized and I also feel excited to be talking about this stuff. So it's all kinds of stuff. Yeah, this is what I'm thinking about [values].

T: Last time we did the little things, we brought the kid in, the one that was up on the roof. Up on the roof is a playful thing.

C: It's an escape thing; it's a hiding thing. For sure [acceptance].

T: Yeah, well, that's true.

C: I have lots of dreams about hiding. Getting away from people. Running and hiding and then they're walking by and "Oh, they're not going to see me" and stuff like that.

It is always a good indicator that acceptance is there when people admit things that they normally would not. He is talking about wanting to hide from people. This is a thought that he has probably rarely expressed to others. It is also interesting and hopeful that he says he is excited to be talking about this. It indicates a level of importance of this thought and willingness to experience the thought that may be helpful if it gets rough.

T: Is this connected up to this anguish? Kind of a depression quality there?

C: It's definitely connected; I'm on the outside: ostracized [acceptance].

T: When we got the kid in the room, I was a little surprised by one thing.

C: That I didn't want to tell the kid anything? [acceptance]

T: Yeah.

C: I've had too much experience with kids. There's no way that you can talk to them about this kind of thing. They don't want to listen [avoidance].

There is a lot of avoidance about talking to this child. It is not about not knowing what to say; it is about not wanting to say it because of the discomfort in it. In fact, he said as much in that original session (see chapter 6).

T: Who's talking right now?

C: It's the adult talking.

T: Yeah.

C: The kid wanted something from me, and it's hard for me to look at it; I want out as quickly as possible [acceptance; this is acceptance because he admits it]. I want to hide because I feel threatened [acceptance].

T: Right.

C: "I'm uncomfortable and I've been pushed and betrayed by adults before and I don't like you."

T: Ah, very nice. Super. Suppose you could say something that would really, really be heard. Suppose God comes down and says, "Okay, you get a paragraph, and it will be heard and not just heard with ears." So if we took the nine- or ten-year-old here, so we actually have him here—what would you want to tell him?

C: One thing that passed through my head was "Your parents really do love you." I don't know where that came from because I never, certainly consciously, doubted that they did. What I was conscious of was that they were "providing" with a vengeance and they wanted me to know it. At least my Dad wanted me to know it. "I'm doing my job; I want you to know that" [acceptance; he is more fully participating in an exercise he was avoiding].

T: Is that a way of saying, "So you better be thankful and you better not have any problems because I'm doing my job here."

C: For sure, it's like, "If you have problems, it's your fault because you can't process what I've provided, which I know is right for you. You have all the tools that you need if you don't make it."

T: Whew! That's a bit heavy for nine years old.

C: Yeah, but maybe I was imagining it. It wasn't nearly as coherent then. I'm sure if I really was feeling that, it was kind of more like, oh, confusion. I'm sure I was getting mixed messages. "Everything is fine, and we're civilized," and then there are the fights at night, and you can tell when your parents are mad at each other. That kind of thing.

T: Were both of them intoxicated when they were fighting?

C: Yes.

The client's parents abused substances, but he rarely discusses this. Avoiding talking about it indicates that he is still fused and avoidant of painful memories and emotions. His parent's substance use is not a central issue of therapy, but if he ever talks about it in greater detail, it would be a good indicator that the ACT processes are moving. The therapist should also keep this topic in mind for future emotional-exposure exercises.

T: Yeah.

C: So obviously they're not happy. Obviously, what they say they're doing right isn't making them happy. So, what's going on here? And yet they're my parents. They know more than I do. I'm healthy. I'm happy. I'm housed. As an adult now, I can think of what I want to say to the kid. I think I'd want to say something more basic, more concrete, like, "You know, it's okay." That's the kind of thing I'd want to get across. Maybe, "You're going to be all right."

T: So what do you think he wanted at nine or ten? I know I asked you this before.

C: Well, what I said last time was that he wanted to be left alone.

T: Yes, but then I asked what he really wanted, and you remember it was hard to get a clear answer. You said he wanted to get away and stop pretending that everything is okay.

C: I think part of it's like, "Quit these mixed messages and this thinly veiled expectation stuff because I don't know what you want. I'd rather just have nobody."

T: Right. Go another level down. In terms of—okay, he wants to be left alone, I understand that. He wants to run away; to stop pretending. Good. But he's nine or ten. Can you come down to his level?

C: You're just a child, and carrying a heavy, heavy load [acceptance; note, however, the use of the second person, which indicates that he is not fully open yet].

T: So in your mind's eye, can you get down on his level? Can you do that for him?

There is a lot of pain associated with thinking about himself at that time in his life, pain that he does not want to experience now. The therapist keeps on it, saying through actions, "What you are experiencing is okay; we don't need to run from it."

C: Can I be at his level? Or can I can be me looking at him at his level?

T: At his level, yeah. You looking at his level.

C: I think so. Every time I see a kid, I feel some sort of appreciation for them. I like them in some way I guess is what I'm trying to say. Even the teenagers that come in the store; you can just tell they're trying so hard to be somebody, but inside they're squeamish. I make eye contact with them. "I see you in there; it's okay, whoever you are." "What do you need?" "You want to be an asshole? Fine, be an asshole, I can't help you when you're being an asshole; come back when you're ready." "You're confused; yeah, I know you're confused. Let's talk about it." I don't know. I just try to be one-on-one as opposed to one on top of one or something [avoidance].

T: A lot of what you said I think is just very, it seems very sensitive to what this is about.

C: Well, I think I can say, "I'm really mad; I'm still mad at my parents for how I perceive that they treated me." On an intellectual level there's no point in being mad at them. I have a totally different relationship with them now.

T: Sure, but it ties into feeling like there's a lot of injustices that have happened to you and he's mad and he still wants something to happen before he moves on.

There is a heavy right-and-wrong issue in this. It is so close that it has become part of the conceptualized self—probably something like "I was wronged and I can't change until someone says they are sorry." The therapist sees it and carries it forward.

Resistance to Forgiveness

T: So take that anger and see if you can find the strands of "right" and "wrong" in there. See if you can let go of those strands and see what happens. Take your time; don't rush this. Get in touch with feeling mad, with your thoughts about how you were treated and how they parented you.

C: It keeps coming to "I'm mad, and they shouldn't have done this and they shouldn't have done that," and if I let that all go, then I feel alone. I can't just let go of that [conceptualized self].

T: Okay.

C: I think I'm thinking they shouldn't have done what they did, but even if they thought what they were doing was the right thing, they didn't give me what I needed to be here and now, so I'm still mad [conceptualized self].

T: Right. Except that last part, that's your responsibility. They couldn't have done that for you anyway. This is a little twisty, because if you were to step forward with what part of you needs—in order to finish that and let that go—then it means that you've kind of healed all that. But then you take them completely off the hook for another thing. It's like that question: if a miracle were to happen, who would be made wrong by that? You can't go back and do your childhood again. You know, if they're off having fights while a nine-year-old is kind of cowering in the bedroom hearing them, that's never going to be undone as a fact, that that happened. So if you kind of hold on to it in terms of content, there isn't any way to do anything with it, because if you move on, it lets them off scot-free. And yet part of you fantasizes that they step forward and say how sorry they were and how wrong they were and all that kind of stuff. Even if they did, the problem would still be here. It's between you and you. It's between this nine-year-old and you. What's standing between you and delivering on what the nine-year-old needs and didn't get? Because it isn't just that he didn't get it—he's *still* not getting it. Do you agree?

C: Mm-hmm.

T: Don't you think he mostly gets ignored, lectured, patronized, told to make do. And who's doing that? It's not Dad at the doorway. It is this middle-aged guy right here ... not that one then. This guy right here in front of me.

C: That part of me is kicking and screaming about what I didn't get, you know; I'm expecting somebody else to do something, I guess, at some level. The brain is saying, "That's not going to happen," and so I hate my brain for talking to me like, you know, the way authority figures did [defusion].

T: Right.

C: My thoughts. But that little kid and those hurt feelings are still there, in the way. It's like he's still not getting something. I don't know [acceptance, defusion].

Comments like "I don't know" and others in which the client seems confused by his thinking are often good indicators of defusion. The client is noticing his thinking as an ongoing process and not as literal guidance that he must follow. The therapist is about to bore in on an issue. Forgiveness in an ACT model is for the client, not for others. Without it, attachment to the story is so strong that people nominate themselves to be the dead bodies proving a crime happened. The therapist is going to go back to that nine-year-old, sensing that his pain (still present in the client) will provide the motivation needed to take a responsible and accepting stance with the client's own emotions, "delinking" them from a rationalized inability to take action. This is the very core of forgiveness within ACT.

T: Let's just take this nine-year-old. What would it take for you to do what he needs? What would come up if you did?

C: Well, I can't, I can't.... Part of me is going, what is this psycho shit, you know, talk to the nine-year-old stuff? [avoidance!]

T: I know.

C: But this little kid is looking at me and going, "You're full of shit" and "You're not what you say you are" and "You're pretending" and "You don't know any more than I do."

T: Okay.

C: And hurting the kid, I don't want to hurt the kid.

T: Right.

C: I don't want to disappoint the kid.

T: So you have this "psychobabble bullshit—so what" reaction. But yet there's somehow something real to it. I mean not all psychobabble is truly nonsense. And I sense that you know we are on to something. If you could kind of look into his eyes and get connected with him, what is it that you don't want to be present with? Check it out: if you can get up in there, you'll find there's resistance, there's a barrier, there's something, some place that you don't want to go. Just guessing; see if that's true. And if so, see if you can find out what it is.

This point may be a little beyond the scope of the book, but it seems worth addressing here. ACT uses some techniques that are unorthodox within behavior therapies. There will be fewer times that the client will provide praise to the therapist for what she says because the work covered in an ACT session will usually contradict the client's verbal system. We are usually challenging the way clients interact with their thoughts and feelings. We can't just straight out say, "Your problem is that you take your thoughts too literally and that you would function better if you knew these were not true things," because that would only be heard as "To make these thoughts lesser, remind yourself that they are not true." That would not work to control them any better than what the client was trying before.

ACT therapists end up doing these kinds of exercises, such as the gestalt-like process of having clients talk to themselves as a child, in order to go into previously avoided pain. People poke fun at ACT for it, but it can do important work by allowing difficult experiences to be explored, accepted, and defused from. The use of *deictic frames* (relations in terms of the speaker, e.g., I/you, here/there) and the perspective-taking inherent in exercises of this kind are also helpful in establishing some compassion in the client for herself and for her history. This client would readily reject and minimize his own needs, carrying forward the pattern his parents established. But it is much, much harder to do that when looking at a nine-year-old who is hurting. If we can let that image represent his desire for love, acceptance, and play, we can give a form of the alternative to that pattern of avoidance and suppression that has lead him to own a successful business but also to feel miserable.

This next long section is painful to read. What the therapist will do is to unearth how the client's conceptualized view of himself as a hyperrational person is preventing him from being present with his own emotional life. The nine-year-old represents part of that. There is a kind of suppressive, self-denial within the next section.

Avoidance and the Conceptualized Self

C: I'm not following you.

T: Is he still here? Have you lost him?

C: Well, he's kind of here.

T: Well, let's get him in the room. Get him in here. Picture him right here in front of you.

C: Okay.

T: Okay. Take your time to really look at him. He's feeling something. And he does want something; isn't it obvious? He is pretending he doesn't because he doesn't believe he can get it, and he's not about to ask for it. Given that, he'd just as soon hide. But all that is part of this layer that he's got around him. Go another level down. You were this little boy once. You know what is going on inside him. Stand with him. What does he want from you? You said something about getting down on his level. See if you can kind of go into his eyes, sort of get down on his level, get up next to what his life is like. And as you do that, see if you notice where you'd start finding some resistance.

C: Well, if I sort of figuratively crouch down with him, I'm afraid that he is going to see something in me that doesn't ring true and that will scare him off [acceptance]. It's a fear of not being genuine and not being whole and deceiving myself.

T: Okay.

C: Not liking myself.

T: Okay. So can you take all of that and still sort of crouch down? I mean after all, that's your issue; that's not his issue. He still needs something. What about him?

C: So, you're asking me why I'm hesitant to get down to his level?

T: No, I'm not. No "why" is needed here. Kids need things from the giants around them. The nine-year-old can't solve these adult problems. As you get into your head about "why," the nine-year-old is still left hanging. I mean that's probably what happened to you in the first place, right? You had all these adults around with all these problems, and what are you going to do about that? It's a kind of neglect really. But it is happening right now. So I'm asking you to go down there and get with it. Take that insecurity with you and get down on his level and then see if you can kind of get up next to what his life is like and what he was feeling and what he needed. What's going on for him, what he wants from you, what he's feeling, what he's thinking. What's hard for him? What does he want?

C: I think I'm trying to be both people at once, and it's just not working.

T: Don't abandon him out here. That's what everyone else did. He's still out here.

C: My struggle is still trying to see exactly what you're trying to get me to do [fusion, avoidance]. If I'm getting down and seeing what it is he wants, all I can do is guess what he wants from my adult.

T: You don't guess with the teenagers who come in to the store. When you look, it's real evident. Just look at him. You can see them; look at him.

C: I can see that he's curious. He doesn't understand where I am coming from and is hesitant and wary. He trusts me much more than he trusts himself because I am an adult. So he's just waiting.

T: Okay.

C: He's letting the adults call the shots.

T: Okay, so call a shot.

C: So I would say something like, "Before I got here, you know, I'm visiting, I noticed you came in from outside. Let's go out there because it's nice to be outside. Let's go out there." And I would try to look at things, what interested him. I'd say, "There are some cool trees here. When I was your age, I would probably be climbing those trees." I'd probably try to make him feel better by saying, "You know, I'm not sure I can do it now because I'm fat and old but you could." Ask him about what he does during the day, ask him to show me something. Try to play, admire what he's doing outside. Try to let him know I want him to be himself. Try to let him know I want to hear what he has to say, as opposed to what most adults ask because they're uncomfortable with children. "Well, how old are you getting these days? My, you've grown two inches." I'd say, "You're a person, and I know you're in there. Let's play."

T: Yeah.

C: "You can talk to me, or not; I know I certainly can't make you" [acceptance].

T: This is good stuff. Stay with it. Take your time. Take him on his own terms [long pause]. Suppose in that context, he lets you know what's actually been going on, what his life's like, especially when it's hard or it's difficult. What are you going to do?

C: Well, it depends on what he says. I can't imagine me at that age telling anyone that my parents kept me awake all night or something. I mean, sometimes they had bad fights, but I'm trying to think of what he'd be concerned about at that age and I ... really ... I can't think of anything.

T: Try to stay with it ... You are slipping into a story. Let me ask it this way: is there anything that he's feeling, especially things that he does know how to talk about, that is confusing to him? I mean he's in a difficult situation, is he not?

C: For sure. For him it's a big deal.

T: Then stop minimizing it. He sounds alone, he sounds frightened, he sounds sad, his parents are not giving him much room to just be a kid. He's got to be worried about things you wouldn't want a kid to be worried about.

C: I would take it for him if it would help [acceptance].

T: Can't do that. He's got to feel what he feels.

This may have been an error. If the client in fact "took it for him" meaning that he would feel his feelings without rejection, that would be perfect because it is a metaphor for acceptance. By saying "Can't do that," the therapist is trying to get to the raw emotion, but it would have been more effective to flow with that relational network. A response like "Awesome. But to take it honestly, you have to feel it fully. What feelings of his will you take in that way?" might have been more fluid. Note that the client picks up on the mistake in the therapist's response.

C: I can. If his feelings could be transfused into me, wouldn't I be willing to take them? [acceptance]

T: Is there anything in there that you wouldn't be willing to have?

C: No, because they're his and not mine. And I'm not responsible for them [conceptualized self].

T: Except he's you. Let's start letting right and wrong go. Take all the literal language that you've got wrapped around this and start letting some of that go. Let the feelings come up even if they are confusing, ill formed, and not easily labeled.

C: The adult is looking at those feelings and going, "Ick, disgusting, I don't want those."

T: Exactly. You are not just doing it here, but you do it looking at the nine-year-old. If we took this nine-year-old and put him on our lap, he's just going to blend right into you because he's not out here; he's part of you. You walk around with him all the time. Think about what you're doing when you go to something like "Ick, ew, I don't like it." It would be like if you said to him directly, "Ew, ick, gross, get out of here, I don't want you." I mean this is the kind of harsh way you've been treating yourself and your own emotions.

C: For sure. Exactly.

T: It's a self-attack, is it not?

C: Sure.

T: Well, how long is this going to go on? How much abuse and neglect for how long?

C: It's like one or the other is going to die. Or you go nuts or something. Because it's not working, that doesn't mean I don't keep trying [fusion, conceptualized self].

This is a rather shocking response. This is the issue of a conceptualized self. The client is sensing that opening up to the pain within and moving forward will indeed mean the end of the attachment to the story of "who I am." He is actively playing with the idea that it might be better to be "right" and lose contact with his own experience rather than open up to it and lose being right about the conceptualized self.

T: Would you be willing to let go of the decision you've made that your logical mind is you, and that it's the primary way that you have to interact with everything, and if you don't hang on to it, you're doing something very dangerous and you might even die?

C: But I need something else. I can't just let go. If I let go of my logical mind and I say that's not me, then, "ew" [conceptualized self].

In other words, this attachment to the self-conceptualization is a way for the client to avoid the pain of being present with his history. The only thing that can compete with this, if compassion for himself is not enough, is values. The therapist senses that and begins to draw this to a close even without the hoped-for deep compassion for the suffering the client had endured. The therapist will leave the client with an exercise designed to reduce the attachment to the conceptualized self.

T: Who are you?

C: Yeah. And my intellect pops right back in and says, "Well, you are the sum of many, many things [fusion]. You're just an organic being, consuming air and struggling along on the planet in this absurd quest to find meaning in your life, and you're nothing but a blob."

T: So thank your mind for that one. Are you avoiding something? Notice we are leaving the nine-year-old and his needs behind. Because they're too disturbing, because they're too *something*.

C: I'm thinking that this is similar to being on the bank, and you're about to go into the water. Makes me feel weird.

T: The question is, who is in charge here? Whose life is this anyway?

C: What do I do? There isn't anything there that I can see to answer that [fusion].

T: Do you need to answer?

C: My mind wants an answer very much [fusion].

T: Invite it to come along; it's welcome to come along. If you try to answer it, that's the trick, that's one of many, but it's one good mind trick. If you do try to answer, you get pulled into the content world that it's laid out, and that's exactly what the mind thing is.

C: I can't hold on to that.

T: I can't either. Would you be willing to do this? We could feel how a self-concept was getting in the way of really stepping forward for that part of you. Would you actually write down that list. I'm a person who …

C: I'd go on forever.

T: Do fifteen or twenty major ones, okay?

C: Okay.

T: And after you've done that list and we've kind of looked at it, write down the opposite next to each of those attributes. Then look and see if you can't find that opposite in your life somewhere too. Somewhere. See if sometimes that's also true. Okay, so now you've got two lists. The first one is the one you've defended with the idea of yourself. It's what your mind tells you that you are. Second one may also be true, sometimes. Let's see.

FINAL COMMENTARY

The therapist is doing a good job of staying on message and staying within an ACT space, but you cannot say that the therapist hit a home run in this session. The client is shifting in and out of the key ACT processes. There were nice stretches where he was seemingly on board, but he could not quite get over that last hump.

It is hard to evaluate this session. There are clear signs of progress, but also the deal has not been closed. Ninety-five times out of one hundred, this approach at this point of therapy would have broken the system wide open because of the compassion a client would feel toward herself as a child. But this client is very dug in, and the key choice has not yet been made.

The key choice is the choice to be accepting and loving toward yourself, and to shift the focus from being right, and getting apologies from parents and so on, to living well *with* your history and programmed reactions exactly as they are. In the next session the therapist will return to that issue of values, and we shall see if more progress is possible.

Figure 8.1 Time spent addressing ACT processes in session seven

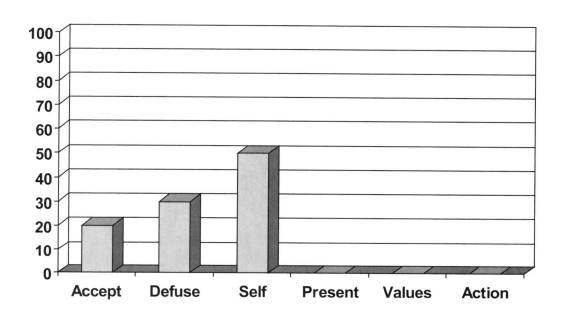

Figure 8.2 Status of client's ACT processes by the end of session seven

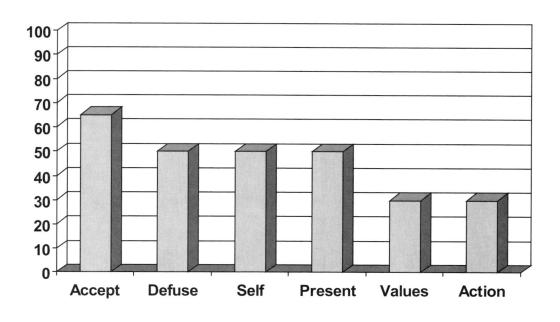

CHAPTER 9

Choosing Values

The last session was designed to eliminate a number of remaining barriers to moving ahead: right-and-wrong issues, attachment to the conceptualized self, and avoidance of early and almost traumatic pain. The therapist went back to a variant of an exercise (the little child exercise) used successfully in session five. While progress might have been made, the client was not really willing to step up to a key choice using the metaphor of the child who was hurting. There were moments when the client seemed to be more accepting and did not define himself as his private events, and there were other times when he seemed still very much dug in.

Session six was mostly about choice, which normally sets up values work. The therapist did a detour, seemingly sensing that more needed to be done before getting to values work, but given the struggle at the end of the last session, the therapist now brings values back front and center.

SESSION EIGHT

T: So how are things?

C: Not liking my business much lately and I have to watch my attitude while I'm there. I feel like I have a short fuse. I'm kind of thinking, "I need a change, I need something, I need a kick in the butt," or whatever.

T: Yeah.

C: But I don't think that will be good enough either. I think I am a perpetually dissatisfied person. I feel less depressed than I was, but I still feel a little pissed off.

We are not certain what the functions of these statements are, but they have the feeling of being about not knowing what direction to go in life. Life can feel pretty unfulfilling if your day-to-day work is not about something meaningful. We get the sense that this client is ready to move ahead, which fits the agenda the therapist appears to be warming up for.

T: Have you watched whether right and wrong shows up linked to being pissed off?

C: I haven't really gotten much beyond the fact that it makes me squirm to follow those thoughts very far [avoidance]. And everything gets all kind of confused, and whatnot, in my head [defusion].

T: "Follow the thoughts" meaning ...

C: Meaning this situation, or that person, is wrong, and I deserve better, and I follow it back, and it just makes me uncomfortable [avoidance].

T: Okay, when you're hooked and pissed off, how often do you find that right and wrong is in this situation?

C: I'd say not all that often. Usually what comes first is self-criticism: "You're doing it again; you're wrong" [avoidance, fusion].

This is an odd response because self-criticism is obviously a right-and-wrong issue, and he even says, "You're wrong," in association with it. We added avoidance because his self-criticism is likely about that. Our guess is that he criticizes himself because he is having a feeling that he believes he shouldn't be having. This is confirmed in the next couple of lines.

T: That counts.

C: Oh, okay.

T: Okay. Well, give me the self-criticism loop. That's the most common one. Give me the flavor again. It goes ...

C: "You're an idiot. Why can't you control your feelings better than this? This isn't getting you anywhere" and "This is the same old thing" [avoidance, acceptance; avoidance by content but shows acceptance by talking about it].

T: Right there, those are your usual things. Is there anything else you could do based on things that we've done in here?

C: I can't think of any [avoidance, fusion].

T: Okay. When you're in the middle of that criticism, do you think you are looking *from* that process of criticizing yourself or *at* it? When you're looking from that posture of self-criticism, self-blame, is that your dominant mode or are you commonly able to watch your mind doing its critical habits? What's your posture? Know what I'm asking?

C: Not really.

T: Are you in the thoughts?

C: Yeah.

This is disappointing. At this point in therapy it is unusual to be struggling so much about mindfulness and defusion. If you look over the sessions, however, the client often comes in highly fused and avoidant in the early minutes of therapy.

Mattering as a Choice

The discussion of choice has a couple of functions in ACT. First, it promotes defusion. It helps clients experience that their minds do not necessarily have all of the answers about what they do, and that they are able to do as their minds say, or not. The purpose of the discussion of choice is to loosen the social/verbal forces that keep behavior more tightly tied to what a person thinks. Second, it makes it possible to follow that client's values more fully. This ties back into defusion because to follow the client's values takes some level of defusion. The evaluative mind will get in the way of moving in a valued direction because of its logical, problem-solving abilities. It will have things to say regarding the right move for the situation, and sometimes that gets in the way; sometimes it can be useful, but not all the time. The therapist is going to work with the client to help him choose his values and then act on them even when his mind is yelling at him.

Before the next exercise starts, we thought it would be a good idea to give an overview of its proposed function. It is an exercise borrowed directly from the human potential movement, but it has not been written about in other ACT texts. This exercise has to do with choice and values. It is liberating to see that you do not need to prove that something is "actually" important in order to care about it; it only needs to be important to the person who is doing the caring. But verbal convention puts importance in objects, not in the people who hold things as important. That may be an effective mechanism for society in driving certain actions (such as putting a value on human life to prevent violent crime), but it means that sometimes values become something visited upon us unwillingly, and we may resist rather than be motivated by them.

T: I'd like to look at something. Are you up for a tangent?

C: Sure.

T: Suppose I take the position that nothing in the world matters; can you dissuade me of that?

C: Nothing in the world matters to you, or in general?

T: In general.

C: Things matter because if they didn't, there would be chaos.

T: So?

C: And most people find chaos uncomfortable [avoidance].

T: Maybe. But being uncomfortable doesn't matter.

C: Things matter because you have an obligation to participate in the structure of society.

T: Yeah, so we've been told, but prove it to me.

C: Well, it gets back to my chaos theory: If you don't participate and go along with things, then there is a lack of order. Everything that human beings depend on in our society requires cooperation, and that involves a certain amount of commitment and believing that things matter, following through, and otherwise being engaged. If it doesn't matter, then it means that you don't have any connection to anything else. You want to be connected because you'll go nuts if you're not.

T: Well, that's an interesting thought, but I don't care; going nuts doesn't matter either.

C: Oh man. If you think that nothing matters and that's the position that you want to take, then nobody will talk to you, so it doesn't matter anyway.

T: Okay. Would you admit that you're probably not going to be able to prove that it's something that everyone must care about? [The therapist is trying to help the client experience that values are chosen areas of life rather than facts. We do not have to value any specific things; we get to choose what we care about.]

C: Probably.

T: All right. Now take it to the next step: Suppose that you see something in the world that you think is unfair, that you care about, that you're mad about, that's like, "This is bad business" or "It's good," whatever. But let's take bad. "This is bad." Whatever it is—there is a densely populated area and many people die as a result of floods there. Now take that picture and remove all of the living creatures from the planet and out of the universe. All you've got left is the aftermath to the buildings. If there are no people, what happened to its importance? Do you suppose the buildings care?

C: What you said was very weird, but I think I understand what you're saying.

T: So, here's the thing: what I'm asking is, is the caring, the valuing, the mattering, in the event?

C: No.

T: So, where is it?

C: It's in your mind looking at the event [defusion].

This is nice. There is a clearer separation between him and his thoughts. It seems like the client is becoming more defused.

T: Okay. We usually talk about it as if the importance is in the thing. But once you do that and then it's out there in the world, it is as if the thing actually has this property.

C: But I think it's understood that it matters to me.

T: Even to you, the direction has gone this way: from it to you. Isn't it more like from you to it? I mean, who is doing the caring?

C: I care. I mean something [conceptualized self].

T: "I care about that."

C: Yes. The caring is in me.

T: And so caring is put on whatever you value. Which is what makes it human and all of that. But if you take the process of caring about something from here and put it out there, then what happens? You notice what happens when you're watching TV at three in the morning and the disease of the month is coming on asking for money. Next thing you know, you are looking for the channel changer but you are feeling slightly guilty. My guess is you don't write a check to all of them. I mean you feel some kind of "ew." It's almost oppressive. Have you ever found yourself turning the tube off?

C: For sure.

T: Where I'm going with this is, if caring's all out in the world and we're almost, like, victimized by it, it's like all these things are literally important. Caring is more like there's a verb here, there's a "doing," we're "importanting" about this thing. I mean, you wouldn't want to say that in normal discourse because it's too ridiculous, but if you were to be more accurate, we're the ones who are doing the caring, doing something about it, evaluating, and "importanting." Are you with me?

C: For sure.

T: Okay, so if you imagine a world in which there is no right and wrong in an objective sense, you can value whatever you choose. And if you don't value something, you don't. What if *valuing* is something that you do and not something that's done to you, and what if you're free to do whatever? And what if there's not a real rule book out there that says, "Here are the things you have to care about, and you're bad if you don't." Well, the question would be, what do you choose to care about? If it were a choice, what do you choose to value? If it was a free choice—you could care about anything and not care about anything—what would you want to care about?

This statement above really shows the defused stance that values can come from. The therapist is saying that the client is free to care about anything that he chooses. Often the world seems to dictate that people should care about particular things, but they may not be the things that matter to a client. It is very likely that this client values something that is valued by other members of his social group, yet research shows that valuing because others expect it is not a very useful tool for changing behavior.

C: Well, I'd want to care about my business, but I find myself caring too much about my business [values].

T: Suppose caring is a choice.

C: I understand that it is, but I don't seem to be able to control the quantity [avoidance].

T: It may not be just quantity. It could be—let's actually get into it—it could be that you've made a deal where you've put the fact that you care out and forgotten that you've done it, and then it's coming back at you. The fact that you care has to be handled because it can't be allowed to be like this, as if reality is being violated in some way. There's a kind of a trick that happens. "Importance" gets put out in the world; then it's like, I'm sitting in the chair, and the light is on, and *that's* "important." It is that level of reality. You know, it's like the importance of all things becomes a fact. There isn't any of my choice in it at all. And if it's important and it's not given its proper attention, then it's like some law of nature's being violated. That's one part. The other part is, I'd want to know what you are *actually* choosing, say, with the self-criticism thing; come all the way back to that. The thought comes up that says, "You're being bad; you didn't do it right. What's the matter with you; why are you so agitated?" whatever, right? The normal diatribe. Well that's automatic; you can't stop that. There's a habit of mind that is historical, and all verbal creatures do it. I've never met anybody who could ever completely quiet the self-criticism—"blah, blah, blah, blah"—have you?

C: No.

Values

T: I don't think it's possible to quiet the criticism, number one. But then number two, there's a choice in there. You are choosing to care about something. I hear it in how you say it. If you could catch this microsecond-long action, you'd have this tiny little window where you could do something. Once you're into it, then it's just a train on tracks— you have a very hard time stopping it. But there is this little window you have, when, if you can actually slow it down, maybe we can catch it. So let's slow it down. We're in this situation. You "care too much about your business" supposedly, but let's see. What is your mind giving you? Pick a situation. You're getting pissed off and you're getting agitated; let's go through it again, but we're going to try and slow it down.

C: Oh man, I'm criticizing this employee because he forgot to turn on this one machine in the general store when he came in that morning. He's doesn't think. He doesn't care because it is not his store; it's not his business [fusion, not present].

He gets emotional every time he talks about this one employee. He is not present with the conversation but is in his head thinking about the employee.

T: So first thing, you noticed some things that happened around you and you had some thoughts come up about them. And somewhere in there, there's some judgment about what he should be doing, and so on. And somewhere in there, as you get agitated, what are you in fact caring about?

C: Me being in control [avoidance, acceptance; avoidance by content but acceptance in the moment because he is talking about it openly].

T: Cool. That feels right. Very nice.

C: And it's not what's happening. It's "I'm losing it." And I hate that [acceptance].

This is a wonderful example of how a response can be used to illustrate one of a variety of ACT processes. The client's response shows high levels of fusion and not being present, but the therapist uses this response to illustrate what the client actually focuses on in terms of values. The therapist illustrates that the client is *valuing* getting his emotions and thoughts under control over other activities. He is holding that as an important quality of living.

It should also be noted that the client is clearly much more fluent now with ACT processes. He is talking about thinking as a process and having an easier time labeling what is occurring in his head. These are positive signs.

> T: And you know something about your history, about why that shows up as important. You came by it honestly, painfully. Wanting to be in control. It's a lot safer. Here's my question: do you have to choose to care about being in control? Over here I've got cola, over here I've got ginger ale, and what are you going to do? It wasn't just the objective thing that "He's a jerk" and "This isn't right" and so on. You have a choice of how to behave. Once it gets externalized, you're oppressed by it, you're victimized by it, it feels like there isn't a choice. It's like the work is heavy and going in there is heavy and the whole thing is heavy and the employees aren't acting right and you're a victim and you don't deserve this and this can't be allowed to happen and yet it is, and so on and on. Right? Okay, so if we first catch what this process is, we can see that it is an illusion. It's not actually out in the external world; it's in what we *do*. We take the step, and furthermore, that's a choice.

> C: It is so unconscious, and automatic. I don't even see it when it happens [acceptance].

> T: Right on.

> C: I mean it clicks; I know that it goes from just observable to internalized, but normally I have no clue. I can't slow it down; I have no idea that it's happening [acceptance].

> T: Let's take the in-control thing. If you are caring about being in control, what is that in service of? What are you trying to do?

> C: Protect [acceptance].

> T: Exactly. What are you trying to protect?

> C: Me [conceptualized self].

> T: Really?

> C: For sure.

T: Let's find out if that's true. If you didn't care about that, where would you go? If you didn't care about being in control, but you did care about defending yourself, what would happen? We're not talking about a physically dangerous situation here; we're not talking, like, physical destruction, although in your mind, when you learned this, that's probably what you thought was going on. Part of why it's powerful is that some of that stuff probably goes back to kid stuff. It looks almost like survival is at stake, not rationally but emotionally. So, what would happen if you let go of that? You said you're protecting you. Who's the "you" you're protecting?

C: It's the "me" that's insecure about who I am and what I know [acceptance].

T: Awesome. I could say it this way: If you were less in control, various things would come up. You'd feel things that you don't like feeling.

C: Yeah.

T: And the way you've got it set up in your mind is that that's almost life threatening. You're protecting "you" by protecting yourself against the things that you have inside of you. Think about this. If you let go of the control issue, what's going to come up? Things that are in you, right? I'm not talking about external monsters coming over and tearing you limb from limb. We're talking about the monsters already on the bus. Right?

C: For sure.

T: Okay, so is it fair to say that the defense is against emotions, thoughts, memories, and sensations that are already in you?

C: Okay. I see that.

Defining Values

T: So who's the "you" you're protecting? You're protecting you from you. What, are you your own enemy? Your history is your enemy? There's all this stuff that is part of my history, and it is my enemy? So my own feelings, my own memories, my own desires, wants, wishes, plans, purposes, thoughts are my enemy? Well, where are you going to run that you'll be safe, if that's true? Short of a lobotomy, I don't know any way to subtract history. Time goes in one direction, not two. You with me? So let's come back to what you really want. There's this little microsecond thing that happens—the thought comes up, which is habitual, and then you're fully engaged. But in between, something happens. You choose something. I just want you to see that this is a free choice. That means you don't have to do it. You don't have to run it out habitually. If it was a free choice, what would it be? What did you really come in here for? What is it that you want, really? Let me say it in another way: If you think about people who are dead, that are notable to you, mostly what you know about them is not what they owned or sort of the details of circumstance. It's what they stood for, true?

C: For sure.

This is about acceptance and values. The therapist is pushing the client to choose following values over controlling certain private events. Most of the time, attempts at controlling private events take people away from their values. If this distinction can be made, then it can alter the functional properties of both events: controlling private events becomes more aversive, and following values becomes more reinforcing.

T: Okay, so that's the thing that really stays behind, the path they were on, and what held that together, what their values were—we say things like "who they really were" and things like that. So I don't mean it in a superficial way. I mean it in a deep-down way. This is what they were about. Well, if you were to write this statement any way you wanted, What would you want to be left behind when you die? It's like you are going to put an epitaph on your tombstone and you can write it out any way you want, and what you get to write is what you stood for, what you were about, what your values were. If you could choose it, it isn't what you have been doing. It's a free thing. You can write anything you want, and actually live your life that way. What do you want on there? Don't jump at this. … Take your time. Here he lies, he …

C: … finally achieved wisdom.

T: Okay. Cool. And is trying to be in control at every moment on that path?

C: No. But actually, yes it is! Because you have to tread that path to get here.

T: [Pause] I agree with that. Nice. Okay, cool. Absolutely. Exactly the path that frees you is the one in which you can learn the cost of doing otherwise.

C: I've been learning.

T: Nice. Does that mean all the lousy things that have happened to you and all the rotten things people have done to you actually end up being integrated into what you value?

C: I guess in some weird way [acceptance, defusion, self as context].

T: Good. But that is part of why this right-and-wrong thing competes with
        aliveness. To move freely, you've got to let go of keeping them all on
        hooks. I don't mean to cognitively forgive them, like "Oh they were right,"
        but to let go of the attachment to them that has prevented you from
        living. Even your pain is part of your wisdom.

C: Until recently, I have not been ready to let go.

This is a very encouraging way to say that because it means he is up on the edge
of letting go, looking down over the precipice.

T: Let's look at some other things that hold this system together. Did you do
        that exercise?

The therapist is referring to the homework assigned at the end of the last session.

C: Oh, that, yeah, yeah, yeah. It was weird. I'm everything—I'm all things
        and everything. I don't like some of the things that are on the list. I'm
        tired of thinking about it [self as context, avoidance].

T: Okay. Put that on the list too. I'm a person who doesn't want to think
        about this list. Of course, the opposite is true too. You did the exercise.
        I'm a person who does want to think about this list.

C: Well, when I look at that list, and I can't, I mean, I have the thought
        "Am I worth something, am I of value?" If I'm everything, if I'm anything,
        if I'm like anybody else, then who am I? [defusion, unclear values; self is
        mixed—both self as context and conceptualized self]

There are many ACT processes at play here, and you almost have to score both
ends of everything. There is a struggle with defusion in that the client sees little separation between what he thinks and himself. If he is what he thinks, then it will be difficult
to engage in behavior that is different from his thoughts and feelings. He needs some
separation. Conversely, he is noticing that very process as a thought. Similarly, he could
be rated as high on conceptualized self, but his agitation means he is seeing the "every-
thing/nothing" quality of self as context. He might score high on avoidance because he
is fighting against uncertainty and yet he is swimming in it.

T: Cool.

C: Am I or am I not a good person, or am I not anything? I want a label. I
        want to know that I'm good [conceptualized self].

T: And as you said that, when that little thing went up, who was the human
        being that was aware of what you just said inside you? Is there a part of
        you that's conscious of what you just said, that knows what you said?

C: Yeah. I feel like all of me is conscious of that.

Making a Choice

This last segment has a building and intensive quality to it. The therapist is trying to get over the hump and to see a choice being made.

T: And does all of you need that label? As you said, "If I let go, if I'm all of this stuff, then I'm nothing—who am I?" as if you have to be a thing, a labeled, evaluated, characterized, described, particularized thing. Except when you look at this honestly, there are some parts of you that no matter what attribute you use, the counterpart is also there. That was that homework, to some degree. Here's what I'm trying to get to: You have this sense that you are losing it when you get into this kind of stuff. I think you do have to lose it, but I don't mean go crazy. I mean lose the attachment. The place where that is about something meaningful is when you ask, "What do you value; what are you about?" Let me talk about this in another way. Choices are like assumptions. They're not defended. They're not "for a reason." They're where you start. You kind of started with a choice—that you have to be in control. It's an assumption. Right?

C: Mm-hmm.

T: You're afraid that if you let go of that, you're going to lose yourself. And to some degree you probably actually would. But not really yourself, just the attachment to certain attributes, to the story. I presume you're in some pain about it or you wouldn't be here. You hide it pretty well, actually, better than most. I mean you come in and you don't give me much of a handle. You often almost ask me to assume that actually things are okay, pretty much. I think you're feeling like something needs to be moved. Something is hurting. There's something that's preventing you from being who you really want to be.

C: For sure.

T: Okay, when I give you the choice over here and you say, "This one, because it's familiar, because it's safe," so, what if it is part of where the pain comes from? So how much do you hurt?

C: Very much [acceptance].

T: Your pain is our ally because there is this kind of jumping into the unknown. I mean, why would you do anything different if you don't know where you're going? You would have to have some pain about where you are. So how high is the cost? How much are you willing to pay? What's it worth to you? Suppose you had to turn in 90 percent of your vitality to be in control. Is it still worth it?

C: At some gut level, I feel like I'm right on the edge. Actually I don't even know what I'm talking about, I just ... there's a big something [defusion].

T: I know. I feel it too. If you go with that, just trust your instinct on it, and not in the service of craziness but in the service of what you really value, what you really want to be about. Do you really want that on your tombstone anyway? "He felt like hell trying to be in control." What are you defending yourself against? And how much are you willing to pay? You can get away with it, you can go your whole life like this, but you do have certain costs. What you are calling "depression" is maybe just part of that. See if this isn't right: Depression is part of what you feel when you're trying not to let yourself feel all of what you feel. And that's such a crushing place to be in; you're like a hole in the ground. Depressed. Anxious. Is it possible that's part of the cost you've been paying? You're a tough one. I've got to give it to you. Your mind is like a steel trap. It is very strong; it's well practiced. You've got to admire it, how good it is at hanging on.

C: I'm frustrated and intrigued by this concept that there's this split second, there's this window, and there's this choice that is made to hold whatever it is as important. To be engaged by a problem [pause]. I have no idea what you're talking about, and it's pissing me off [defusion].

T: Good. I'm dancing, because I don't want to give your mind too much logic. I don't want to give your mind very much because you can't trust it. This is a very well-exercised mental apparatus. And part of it is real comfortable because it's done a lot for you. In some ways it's been such a pal and such a friend, so we've got to kind of sneak around it like we're kind of doing now. Part of it knows what I'm saying. That's what you were saying earlier, "I feel like I'm on the edge. I don't even know what the hell edge it is that I'm on." Right? Which is probably good because if you did know the edge that you're on, that would mean that you'd gotten all ground back into the mental apparatus, and once it figures out the system, it's not going to let you do anything about it. Because your mind thinks it's trying to protect you because you told it long ago, "This is me; protect me." You've taken this primitive survival mechanism and hooked up this thin cortical layer of verbal abilities to a concept of who you are, what your life is, and what you need. Now you've got millions of years of evaluation and survival protecting *the idea* of you, not *you*—that you have to be a certain way, you can't have certain feelings, there are places you can't go—just attributes. You did those opposites in the homework. Each opposite in a pair is true, but there are parts of those that you can't explore, you can't touch, you can't recognize. And your mind thinks it's trying to protect you because it thinks it is you.

We'll come back to this thing of trying to be in control of the situations, in control of your emotions, in control of your mind. There's a possibility in here, if you're willing to look at it. This little window in here has to do with our purposes. What has been the purpose of what you've been doing? Do you have to be about "in control"? It's a choice—do you have to choose that? Now if you really look at me and you say, "Okay, I'm with it" and "I see there's a choice here" and "I know there are consequences of the choices we make" and "I know I've been choosing this side, and the consequences are the ones I've been experiencing" and "I know about them in my life. This is it. These are the consequences. And given all that, I'm going to stand up here naked and in the wind, undefended, and declare I'm choosing this: I'm about being in control." You know, then all I can do is applaud and say, "Cool, you know, I hope life works well for you." There isn't any rule book here. You don't have to do anything different. It's just, there are two things happening: The coming down here, you're paying me money, you're saying with your feet, "I'm in some pain," and then I say, "Let's look at how well this is working." And you respond, "I want to do what I've been doing." I know that you want to, and you're saying, in the language, "I'm choosing it," right? And I know you have been choosing it.

C: Show me something better [fusion].

T: Thank your mind for that one; that's cool. This is why pain is important—all I can do is show you what it is. And I just do that by holding up the mirror. Suppose you're in an airplane and you've got a parachute on, and the airplane is on fire, and you're standing by the door, and I'm saying, "You can either stay here or jump." And you say, "Prove to me that it will be good if I jump." And I say, "I don't know, but I can prove to you that it won't be if you don't. It might be lousy to jump. The parachute might not open." So this is why pain is your ally here: there isn't any other reason that you'd do this.

C: Do what?

T: Turn a corner. Take a leap. Make a choice. What do you really want to do in your life? Look at what you've been doing in terms of its purpose and see if this purpose is serving your larger purpose.

C: I don't know if I can. I'd like to try. But I don't know if I can [avoidance].

T: You're a person standing at the airplane door saying, "I don't know if I can do this."

C: I'm not accustomed to making choices without knowing what the outcomes will be [fusion].

T: Yeah. It is tough business; it's rotten that it has to work that way. Dig, dig, dig: the hole gets bigger. Will you stop? And do what else? I don't know. Dig, dig, dig: the hole gets bigger. Will you stop? And your experience is telling you something.

C: I will if I can. Is that good enough? I'm aware that I want to be and I'm trying to be in control, but I don't know exactly how to let go of doing that.

T: [Makes an airplane noise]

C: I'm not going to have my life be about being in emotional control [values].

T: [Long pause] Okay. And then what? What path are you on?

C: I want to be true to myself—to be honest with myself. I want to do something else. I want to live. I'm not exactly sure yet what that is [all processes: psychological flexibility].

T: Your mind will think that you're going to die if you do this. It is going to think that you're going to die. Can you feel the resistance?

C: For sure.

T: [Long pause] I have a feeling I should wrap this up in a bow or something. I don't know if I can.

C: I feel like I want you to give me something to chew on.

T: Okay. In the major domains of your life, I'd like you to look at what it is you really want. Just between you and you. We have forms and stuff. I'll send them with you. The major domains are things like work, family, intimate relationships, health and exercise, spirituality, education, finances, recreation. In those major domains, ask yourself that tombstone question. Make room for the counterpunching, cynicism, and all that. Answer as if it really were a choice, you know, if you could be about anything, and this may be a little hard for you because there's some vulnerability in realizing there are things that you do care about.

C: There is. A little bit.

T: Little bit, or a lot? I think sometimes that's what's being protected—a vulnerability of caring. Because it hurts as soon as you know that you want anything, you care about something. So I'd ask you to bring all that with you and not fight it and yet still do it. Really try to allow yourself to connect up with what you care about. You can care about anything, but make sure you have a sense of choice in these domains.

C: Gotcha.

T: Have we done our work?

C: For sure.

FINAL COMMENTARY

The end of this session had an almost missionary feel to it, which may not be comfortable for all readers. But it helped carry the client over a rough hump. It would not be surprising to have a backlash from this client in the next session because the therapist is clearly being very active. Nevertheless, this dance seems effective at this point. A choice has been made. If it holds, that is a foundation for the remaining work.

Figure 9.1 Time spent addressing ACT processes in session eight

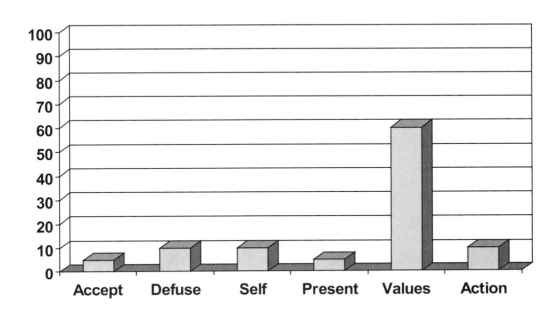

Figure 9.2 Status of client's ACT processes by the end of session eight

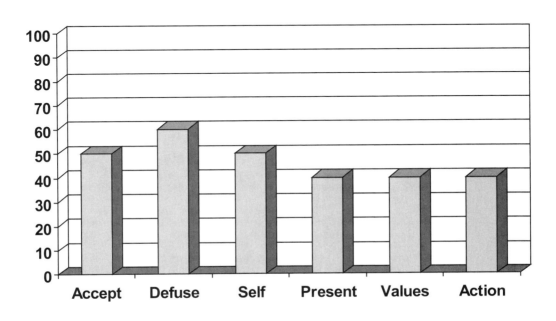

CHAPTER 10

Values, Defusion, and Back

It is clear from the last session that the client is moving nicely on many of the ACT processes: acceptance, defusion, and self as context. There is still work to be done on values and making larger behavioral commitments linked to those values, although the client made some progress in this area in the last session. The focus of this session is on picking larger values that can direct the client's behavior in the future, but these types of commitments need to be made from a defused stance, which is going to be the difficult part of this session. The client is less fused than during the beginning sessions, but his fusion will likely continue to interfere. We will be able to get a sense of the client's level of fusion by how he responds to the values homework that was assigned at the end of the last session. If the valued directions that he chooses feel honest to the therapist (that is, if they are what the client would choose if his mind was not in the way), then it indicates that fusion is less present, but if the valued directions feel socially driven (if they are what other people think he should do or what his parents would have wanted him to do) then more defusion work would need to be done. Let's see how the assignment went.

_____

SESSION NINE

T: Think about things at all?

C: Sure did.

T: What happened when you thought about it?

C: I worked on the homework you suggested [he was asked to define his values in a number of different domains, such as work, family, intimate relationships, health and exercise, spirituality, education, finances, recreation]. My reaction was "This is going to demonstrate a failing on my part." I know that things are pretty out of whack in my life. I am sort of realizing that is why I am in here—only part of the reason perhaps but a big part [values, defusion].

T: Cool.

C: I am pretty critical of myself. I find myself trying to get myself under control during an exercise like this. I am saying, "Just do the best you can; don't worry about it." I think I was anxious that I would find that there are things I want to do, things that I can't or haven't done, or won't do, or whatever [acceptance; showing more acceptance because he is noting it].

T: Yeah. That's cool. Well I think that's how it is, right? "Better not think too clearly here because it might be painful." What was your mind trying to protect you from? You'd think it was just working on your interests; it would say, "Well, what are your interests?" I want to know that. Enough on how your mind was getting in the way of this exercise. What did you chose as your values?

C: There were a number of areas on that form that you gave me. I felt as though there was some overlap between the different topics. Plus there were some that had little to do with me. I mean, I am not in a big relationship right now and because of the divorce I'm not sure I'm even ready for one. I have my children, and I love them. I still have to work with my ex on things regarding the children, but I guess the worksheet felt like it did not fit me as well as it could have [avoidance].

It is likely that the client is pushing back against talking about the homework because it is embarrassing or painful to talk about what is important to him. The therapist catches this and redirects him to the exercise without arguing about the validity of the worksheet.

T: Okay. Tell me about what you did get done. I see that you have the sheet right there in front of you. Let's talk about this, with the mind chatter back there.

C: Well. There were a number of different areas; do we need to go over each one?

T: The exercise was more in having you think about what is important to you. There is no right or wrong here—or anywhere. Let's go with the heaviest hitters. Which ones felt the most important or relevant to you?

C: Hmmm … [pause; looks at sheet]. I guess family—my children, work, and play: what you call recreation.

T: Okay. Tell me what you value in terms of family.

C: By family I meant children. My three kids are really important to me. I don't show it the way that I want to, but it is hard with my ex having them half the time and with me working so hard on the business. You know, part of the reason that I work so hard is to support them in what they want to do. I mean if one wants dance lessons, I will cover them—stuff like that [avoidance; this is avoidance because he is not stating his values].

T: What do you have written there?

C: For "children" I wrote that I want to be a father who is there emotionally. I want to be there to help my kids with the things that they are struggling with. I don't want them to have to go through the stuff that I went through. I mean my ex and I had our fights, but we were nothing to call the cops about [unclear values].

T: Is that what you would put on your tombstone?

C: It is a parent's job to take care of his children. I feel I do that. I guess I could do better, but they have everything they should have. I wish I supported them more emotionally. I had pretty bad models of that one. If things were different in my upbringing, then I would be a different parent [conceptualized self]. You should see some of these families that come into my store. There will be a dad who you can tell is an alcoholic and does not take care of his kids. They will come in and buy two twenty-four-ounce beers—and you know they are drinking them as soon as they get home—and the kid asks for a candy bar. It is always the same: the dad gets his beer, and the kid gets nothing. Sometimes I'm tempted to just give the kid the candy, but I don't want to deal with the parents.

It is possible that the client is unclear as to what values are, but a more likely possibility is that the client is still too fused and chooses his values based too much on what "should be." Values need to be chosen by the person living them—not by his history. The therapist notices this and leads the session back into defusion and self work. There is no point in arguing with the client. Instead, take what he says and roll with it.

T: This was a difficult exercise for you. How much do you feel that your modeling gets in the way of you making these choices? What I mean is, we are all products of our histories. We learn by addition not subtraction. What was put there will always be there. Think for a second of one of your memories of your parents. Got one?

C: Yeah.

T: We don't need to talk about it, but just tell me, is there an emotion tied to it?

C: For sure.

T: How about a rule? Is there a way it should be? Either Mom or Dad told you to do it this way, or you learned not to do it that way because they did it like that.

C: Yeah.

T: Yeah. It can be hard to choose your own direction with all that stuff getting in the way.

The client is still quite fused and too tied to his conceptualization of self to choose values that are his. At the moment we would get values that are mostly rule governed. We want his values, not his history's values. There is further discussion on values and their origination, and then the therapist takes the next opportunity to continue defusion and self-as-context work.

Trouble Committing

The following dialogue has to do with the client's verbal programming getting in the way of his making a decision. This process is made clearer to the client in what follows.

C: When I was thinking about what I want to do differently, I decided, "Well, I'm willing to fight the status quo." I do that in my life. I stir the pot and I say things to people that make them uncomfortable on purpose because I don't want the status quo. I think that things will be better if things are brought out into the open. I don't mean to hurt anybody's feelings. So when we've been talking about "Can you make a choice between being guarded and in control and choosing the other," I think, "Well, yes, I think I can." I know I can, because I do it in my life.

T: Here's what I take away from what you just said: "Don't assume that I can't move, because I can; it's just that I need to sort of get behind it, I need to choose it, and then I can do it, will do it, have done it." I'm with you on that. In fact, it's knowing you are able to move that confirms that it's worthwhile to do things like ask, "Well, what do you want?" you know? But the problem is, your mind is really not going to be a friend on that. It's not your enemy either; it just doesn't know what to do with that. Values aren't just programmed output. If you ask the computer, "What do you want to be about?" it doesn't have a clue. It doesn't have the capacity to do something that isn't preprogrammed and logical.

C: And all the things that I suspect are preprogrammed in my mind have to do with how things should be. I've sometimes had trouble going with what it is that you are teaching me [defusion]. You've said that we're trying to make a little space, and some of the exercises that we've done seem to be about that. Sometimes I feel like they are with me, and sometimes they are out of reach.

It is pretty common for a client to bounce back and forth between being in the verbal context that is supported in therapy and in the normal verbal context that is supported in the rest of the world.

T: Don't you think you are waiting for "What I'm supposed to do is do this, and as a result I'll have some clarity and I'll know what to do and I'll have some skills to be able to do that, and those are coming, so there's something wrong here, and I'm not getting what I need"? But there's another possibility, which is that the kind of clarity you need to get to is something that your mind interferes with, not because it's mean, but because it's only doing what it knows how to do. And so we've got to kind of fuzz things up and take things apart a little bit, rip holes in the fabric so you can sneak through. And that process won't feel clear; it will feel confusing. You are bouncing back and forth, you can notice your mind doing its thing, and right afterward you loop back, like, "What does this mean, what am I supposed to do with it?" The answer to both of which is, usually, nothing.

This is the defusion work that the client needs at this point. The therapist is putting nails in the verbal coffin.

C: Oh man. It is so confusing, you know? I feel like I have it at moments, and then it is gone [defusion]. There are times that I feel like I want some confidence—that there's something there that I can trust [notice he said "feel," not "need"].

T: Right. Okay. The normal response is one of fear because it feels like you're stepping into nothing, like you're going backward into a void or something. That's your mind talking; we need to get in touch with your experience. Suppose it turns out that there is an aspect of you that keeps going forever, therefore is nothing like anything you know about. It's going to feel like no thing. "Nothing" in English was actually written that way:

"no thing." It's pretty scary for minds to consider "no thing." It can feel like you are going to lose something—that you are going to fall into an abyss. Do you know what I mean?

C: For sure.

T: Nothing means zero. There's a flip side to it. If this table were absolutely everywhere, what would happen to it? If there wasn't any space in the universe where it wasn't …

C: What would happen to it? It wouldn't be a table—it would be everything.

T: Right. And what would you know about it through perception of its characteristics?

C: Not much.

T: Would you know anything?

C: I don't think you'd even know it was a table.

T: Would you even know it existed?

C: Probably not.

T: Right. So the flip side of nothing is exactly the same as everything.

C: Sounds like God.

T: Hey, that's scary isn't it? I'm not talking religion here.

C: No, no, no.

T: But there is kind of a spiritual dimension to what I'm talking about.

C: All right, so you're not going to answer my question. That's cool. I feel I am a little more ready for this abyss. But I have to admit that I really feel pulled to want to figure this out. Remember when I read that article on ACT? Well, I found myself looking up more articles on it on the Web. I know what that is about now. I wanted some certainty before I did this. I mean, why should I trust you? You said it yourself: you are just some wiseass shrink [this was said tongue in cheek].

T: Yeah. You said something quite reasonable, which is, "Gee, you know, if I'm going to leap into the void or something, I mean, I've got to have some confidence." That issue makes sense—mind sense—we don't usually do things without some certainty. A metaphor for what we are doing is like jumping out of a plane. If you wanted to practice that, you could do it from that table. Put on your parachute and jump, and it would be precisely the same thing you'd have to do when you'd be in the plane except the context is different. The actual action is the same. That's like some of these exercises; they're tiny jumps.

This is what happened last session—the client started out pretty fused but became less so as the session progressed. Note that he got unstuck a lot faster this time. He is also in a better place to start making a commitment based on a real value. We mean "real" as one that is not tied to his verbal machinery. It will be a value that is chosen. He still struggles with fusion, so the therapist tackles this with another defusion-focused exercise. There is no harm in washing a little more sand out from under the client's feet.

A Thought That Pushes You Around

T: What I'd like to do is get a thought that when it gets on you, it's like gum on the shoe. I want a thought that pushes you around, that you struggle with, that bothers you, that gets under your skin.

C: That thought is "What am I supposed to be doing?"

T: Okay. Good. "What am I supposed to be doing?"

C: I'm at this point in my life where something has to give. My relationships are not what they should be. And my business is killing me. You know, what am I supposed to be doing with my life? Am I doing anything good with my life? Am I contributing to humanity or am I killing myself?" All that stuff. This goes on and on in my head [unclear values].

T: Now when you think that, is it usually kind of a negative thing?

C: For sure.

T: Well, here's what I'd like you to do. These are eyes-open exercises. Let's do one little round like this: What I want you to do is to take that thought and to put it out there so that you can see it as an object. Then wait for the next one to show up. See if you can put it out there and try to let go of any sense of having to interact with it literally, to take it on its own terms, do what it says to make it go away or to believe or disbelieve it.

The therapist lets the client sit and watch his thoughts for a minute or two, then interrupts to see where the client is with the exercise.

T: Okay, so then what's the next thing that shows up?

C: What would my mother think? What does my mother think?

T: Okay, cool. So let's take that and put it out there on the floor. Notice that you had it, and there it is, and you are without any sense that you have to believe it or disbelieve it. It's just like watching a train on its tracks.

C: The next thought is "I must not be doing the right thing or I wouldn't be here—in therapy."

T: Oh, okay. Cool. That's great. Thank your mind for that one. Put it out there. "I must be doing the wrong thing or I wouldn't be here."

This continues for six exchanges. The client is having self-critical thoughts about not getting better fast enough, self-help books that might help, that he could not do this exercise on his own, pictures of objects, and then he has a thought about his struggle with depression and gets pulled out of the exercise. This is called "buying into a thought." He just gets fused with one of his thoughts and responds to it as though it was a real thing. We pick up on the dialogue there.

T: Historically, that's a big one right? So let's let that one be out there. Try to let go of any sense of struggle that you might have, maybe in your hands. You'll feel it, the pull of it. See if "This is depressing" can be a thought. Do you even know where it came from—"Oh, that's my dad talking" or "That's my mom talking"?

C: My depression is just one of those things. I feel I've been working on it forever and have not gotten too far with it. Depression can get me into these loops [defusion].

T: Okay, good. So this time, instead of looping on it by following its content, we're just going to let it sit out there. We're not going to be doing the loop. Because the loop takes itself seriously, and we're not going to take this seriously. We're doing nothing with it except noticing it.

C: You're distracting me from it. Just be quiet for a second [acceptance(!); he is actively seeking out the feeling of being depressed].

T: Okay [there is silence for a minute].

C: This one is old [defusion]. Maybe Mom or Dad. Maybe just me. I am not sure, but this is an old struggle.

T: Is there anything fundamentally threatening about these reactions?

C: Not when they're out there. However, my stomach has been hurting through this whole thing.

T: What does it feel like?

C: It feels like acid indigestion.

This part is pretty neat because there is not much written on ACT about how to respond to bodily sensations. They are responded to in the same way that you respond to thoughts and emotions.

T: Okay, see if you can get that feeling and put it out there. Not to get rid of it—we're putting it out there so we can see it. Let it know we're not trying to get rid of it.

C: I kind of, sort of can put it out there.

T: Okay. Is there anything in that feeling that's bad, dangerous, hostile, threatening, or that you can't have?

C: That's harder. It's not pleasant and it leads to other things [fusion].

T: Okay, that's a thought. That's two things. That's an evaluation, "It's not pleasant." Pleasantness is not *in* that. If I paid you a billion dollars to have that feeling, my guess is it would be pretty pleasant. So you have an evaluation that it isn't pleasant, so put that out there. So right next to the feeling is a little sign saying, "You're not pleasant."

C: Okay.

T: Let's see if you can get a shape or quality of that sensation. I want you to see if you can create that thing as if you were sculpting it, as if you were making it whatever it is, as if you could create it from clay. And for some reason you're doing this on purpose. Just choose to do this. Create that sensation.

C: Okay.

T: Have you put it there on purpose?

C: Mm-hmm [acceptance].

He would not have been willing to do this exercise at the beginning of therapy. There is some movement in acceptance.

T: Who's aware of what we were just doing? Who's aware of that?

C: I am.

T: Cool, and our minds formulate it.

C: And eyes, ears, and all that other stuff, not just your mind.

Defusion Exercise

T: Think of something again. I need something that you've been struggling with and trying to change. You could use a feeling that's associated with some sort of thought, event, situation, and so on.

C: A feeling: frustration.

T: Okay, cool. Can you get in touch with it? Put it out there in front of you. Let me know when it's out there.

C: Okay.

T: If it had a size, how big would it be?

C: Oh, much bigger than these thoughts. It's like a big ball that's almost as tall as I am. It looks like one of those four-square balls.

T: If it had a color, what color would it have?

C: It's dirty and it's kind of reddish blackish.

T: If it had a weight, how heavy would it be?

C: It's not that heavy; it's like forty to fifty pounds. It's just real big and awkward, nothing to hang on to.

T: If it had a speed, how fast would it go?

C: Real slow.

T: If it had a surface texture, what would it feel like?

C: Gritty rubber.

T: If it had an internal consistency, what would it feel like?

C: Well, I've got this ball image in my mind, so it's air. My mind is telling me, "It's just air. You're stupid; you could get rid of it."

T: If it had power, how much power would it have?

C: This image doesn't have much power; it's like gas—there's no speed, no power.

T: If it had a shape, what shape would it have?

C: It's two shapes: it's a big, round, bouncy, inescapable ball, and it is also gaseous.

206   ACT Verbatim for Depression and Anxiety

T:	If you could somehow use it to hold something, let's say, water, how much water would it hold?

C:	Thousands of gallons.

T:	Do you have a feeling toward this ball?

C:	Yeah I do: scorn.

T:	So I want you to get in touch with that scorn. Find it in your various reactions, and when you get in touch with it, I want you to move this ball to one side and put the scorn out there and let me know when it's out there.

C:	Okay.

The therapist goes through the same series of steps with this feeling. The client describes its size, shape, color, speed, power, weight, how much water it could hold, and so on. After it has been described as a different object, of the client's creating, the client is asked if he has a different reaction to the object in addition to scorn. Here is the client's answer.

C:	Can't think of a word for what it is. "Disappointment" I guess.

T:	Okay, good; so get in touch with that one. Have you got it? Put it out in front of you and move the other two to the side. Have you got it out there?

C:	This disappointment that I feel is like a big, big wall. It's a big balloon-thin wall, and it's yellow too, and it's bulging toward me, and it's holding back some big ball of water or something. It's not threatening; it's just sort of omnipresent. Powerful. Fast. Hot.

T:	I want you to see if you can just let that thing that you've called "disappointment" just be there. See if you can let it out there and just see it as an object, as a thing, and not something for this moment that you need to have inside you. It's not who you are, and it's not something that you own, resist, or comply with. I'm asking you to see if you can just let go of it, not to get rid of it, but to let go of any attachment. And then, with it out there, in that state, take a sidelong glance at the other two and see if anything has changed. Don't prejudge it, just look and see.

C:	They're much smaller [defusion].

T:	And so, when you're ready, we're going to take them back in. But before you do that, notice what happened in this exercise. What I want you to just gently file away is that some of the power in these things may come from the context you put them in and not from their mere existence. You can bring them back in the way you might bring in an old acquaintance whose relationship is complex, it includes some negative things, and yet, the person is welcome to be there. It is not because you like them but because you choose to welcome them [pause]. Welcome back; that was fun. Did anything come up that you are willing to share?

C: That *was* fun. That last one made me sad.

This is a clear example that the client is moving forward in ACT. The client would absolutely not have participated like this in the early sessions. He is way more willing to experience the emotions that are involved in these exercises—including the odd feelings that come with being asked to do these things. The client is certainly more defused than at the beginning of the session. The therapist will be able to go back to the issue of values that was originally targeted.

Unplanned Opportunity

T: Give me a little more on that—sadness.

C: It is more disappointment at just how big this is, how long this has been around.

T: Yeah. Lots of power there. Do you have any thoughts on the associations that come up with that feeling?

C: The word that comes to mind is "failure." I'm kind of thinking about my dad, and the next images that come to mind are of him talking to me and me sort of watching me listening to him, and feeling real disconnected, wanting to understand what it is that he's trying to tell me, what he's trying to pass on or something, and not being able to, and feeling a sort of sense of loss about that.

T: The inability to connect?

C: Yeah. And feeling sort of hopeless about it now. I mean I am a dad too right now, and I don't want to be like that with my kids. I want a real connection [values]. I don't want them to be my age thinking about how I messed them up [conceptualized self]. I do feel that my parents tried their best, but man, it is hard to stop thinking about how they treated me. It is harder when you really care about something.

T: This ties together. There are a number of steps that got us here. This all started out with, "What am I supposed to do?" Then later on we worked and we got "frustration" behind "scorn." Behind this comes "disappointment," which is linked to "failure," which is linked up to "disconnected." Which is linked up to "I was wronged and I am in danger of wronging someone." You can imagine some of this sounds very old, does it not? I mean, there's dust all over these things. How old would you say? What's the youngest you can find any of these things?

C: Oh, little—five or six.

Pain vs. Trauma

T: Yeah, exactly. So when you're asking yourself, "Who am I supposed to be?" there's a thread that goes all the way back to that five- or six-year-old. He was asking himself, "What am I supposed to be for these adults?"—your parents. But let me ask you this: if you knew not to run from your own stuff, your own pain, your own sadness, if you could go back, how much of what happened to that child was a trauma that was caused in part by a kid not knowing that, actually, it was okay to feel like that? Do you know what I mean?

C: Yeah.

T: Is there any of your pain that you can't have, that you're not big enough for?

C: Well, you're either alive or you're dead. So at this point, no, there is no pain that I can't have [acceptance].

T: See if this isn't true. If you have a certain amount of psychological pain that shows up, and then you add to it just one element, "I can't have this," that combination is traumatic. It's traumatic in the sense that there's some kind of sense of damage that's been done here. There's another way to look at the idea of trauma—physical trauma; it's an actual injury. There is hurt, fear, disappointment, sadness, whatever, and that in itself is not traumatic. But if you can combine it with "I can't have this," then it is.

C: The trauma is incurred by your rejecting the feeling that you're afraid is going to overwhelm you. So you squash it and shut it down [acceptance].

T: I think it's something like that, do you think?

C: Yeah, but I think it's very unconscious.

T: Yeah. It's kind of like "pain" without "willingness to have it" equals "trauma." There's one part of it that we do voluntarily and can choose, and there's one part that's just automatic. If you are a kid with alcoholic parents, you can't get through childhood without big-time pain, with that circumstance. Can you?

C: No.

Values from a Defused Stance

T: Let's go back to values. Knowing all these things and all the dangers that are associated with sticking your head out there and getting it cut off—what do you want? What do you want to be about? What do you want to do? What's important to you?

C: A lot of things are important to me. Where to start?

T: If you were to pick an area, not your mind, but you, what area would you pick?

C: Let's go with the kids.

T: Great. What type of father do you want to be? Not what type of father *should* you be. In here you are allowed to say whatever you want. These are your values, not mine, and not your parents'. Say it had to be written on your tombstone: "Here he lies, he stood for this as a father [pause]. Take your time. Don't jump to an answer [long pause]. What kind of father?

C: I want to be honest, open, and supportive. I want my kids to be close to me. I want to be there for them. I want them to love me.

T: [Pause] It can be tricky when doing values where other people are involved because you can only control what *you* do. They may not respond the way you hope, but even knowing that there are no guarantees here, what do *you* want to be about as a father?

C: I will be honest and there for my children. I feel I've been putting on a mask with them. I've been showing them what I think they are supposed to see. They don't see the real me. I was afraid that they would not feel confident in the real me—heck, I'm still afraid of that. I'm not a together person; I worry they won't love what they see. Look at me—I'm in therapy [said jokingly].

T: Great. This is great! Time is running short, and I want us to carry this forward into the week. If you were to do something in the service of this value, what do you think that would be? Do you have any idea?

C: You mean something with my kids—like take them out?

T: I am more concerned with how you do it rather than what you do. I think it would be consistent with your values to do something with your children, but the values you came up with also linked to a sense of honesty and openness. Be with your children and with your baggage. Be the dad that you want to be. You with me?

C: For sure. This is cool. I will do it. I have the kids this week. I'll take them somewhere this weekend. You know, there are some things that they have wanted to do but they either bore me or I am no good at them. Like they've tried to get me to cross-county ski. It feels like a waste of time. I can see how that thought has held me back from doing this thing with them. Sound like a plan?

T: They are your values. You don't need my permission. But I will give you some guidance on the way it is done. You hear the note. Follow this note.

C: As confusing as usual [again, said jokingly].

T: See you next week.

FINAL COMMENTARY

The client started out this session fused and providing values that were linked to categorizations of what he thought he was supposed to do. The therapist picked up on this and redirected the session into defusion. This was effective at helping the client get back to the place where he could make value-based choices that were his and not his mind's.

The defusion work brought him to a defused place that he had not been at yet in therapy. It was from this place that he started talking about his parents and how they had influenced him. He talked about how they had affected him. That opening set up the final discussion of values. This time the client was able to talk about values that were his and not verbally fused ones. Finally, the client made a behavioral commitment to doing something that he had been avoiding. Things are really coming together for this client.

Figure 10.1 Time spent addressing ACT processes in session nine

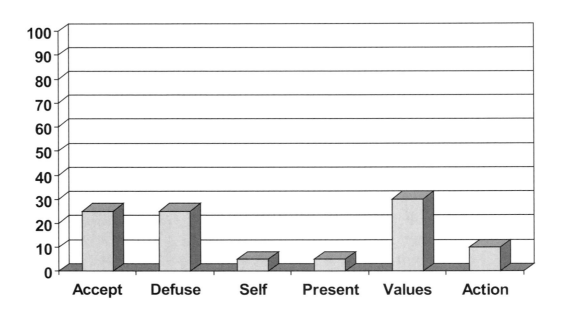

Figure 10.2 Status of client's ACT processes by the end of session nine

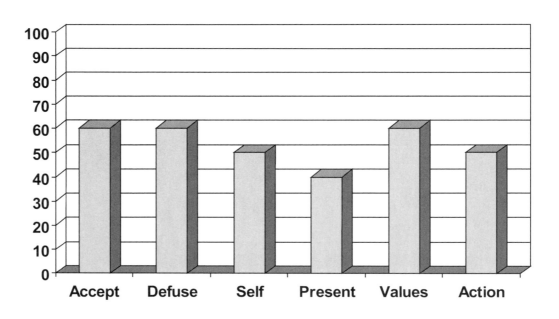

CHAPTER 11

Values, Commitment, and Wrap-Up

The last few sessions with this client have been a therapeutic dance. The therapist needed to go with the flow and make adjustments as it became apparent that certain ACT processes were sufficiently strong and to grab the processes that needed attention as they became available. You can think of this process using a hexagonal model. Each of the six areas is, in essence, a functional diagnostic dimension, going from weak to strong (Wilson, 2007). As each becomes stronger, the area in the middle gets larger and there is greater psychological flexibility. Because each supports the other, if one area is explored and found wanting, sometimes other areas can be worked on, making progress in the original area more possible.

At the end of session eight (chapter 9), the client had a kind of a breakthrough, declaring, "I'm not going to have my life be about being in emotional control. ... I want to be true to myself—to be honest with myself. ... I want to live." As homework he was asked to write out his values in different domains. The values that he came back with at the following session had a somewhat compliant feel to them, and the therapist seems to have dealt with that in session nine (chapter 10) by doing some additional defusion work and then returning to values. The client focused on one important area: parenting. Values in this area were clarified, and then they moved into a behavioral commitment exercise. The client committed to an activity with his children that focused on defusion and acceptance. The particular action wasn't specified, but the kind of behaviors that would fit the commitment were made fairly clear by the therapist.

SESSION TEN

It should be noted in addition to a clear sense of progress with the client, that therapy is now at session ten, which was the originally contracted number of sessions. At the end of this session, the progress of therapy and need for further sessions will be reviewed.

Homework Review

T: How did that homework go?

C: I'm not sure. I told you that I had my three kids for the weekend and that I would take them to do something that they liked—that I would do something that was unlike me. Well, on Friday night I said to them, "What do you want to do tomorrow?" They said that they did not know. You know how kids are—they wait for the parent's guidance. I usually make these decisions. So, this time I said, "Anything—you give me suggestions." They gave some of the usual suggestions like downhill skiing, shopping, movies, and then my youngest said, "We could go play in the snow, like sledding and snowman stuff." I thought it was so cute. I could tell this was something that she wanted to do but would not have asked to do. I am so into my sports and such that just going and goofing off is not like me.

T: Very interesting. So what did you do?

C: The other kids were into it, so we got up on Saturday and went up sledding. It was a sunny day. We went to the store and picked up a couple sleds and went up to the hills. There is a lot of snow up there.

T: Tell me about it.

C: I felt like I was out of my league. I did not bring all the right stuff for the kids. They got wet and cold. After a couple hours, they were getting hungry, and all I had were the drinks and snacks that I had picked up when we got the sleds. The other families up there had picnic lunches and stuff. You could tell they were more prepared.

T: So you weren't prepared, is that it?

C: Yeah, and I think I was not prepared because I am too selfish and did not think about them [conceptualized self]. I had *my* stuff ready. You know. *I* had warm enough clothes and I was fine being a little hungry, but the kids can't go without food as well as I can. I don't know what I was thinking. I'm sure my ex would have been better prepared.

T: What did you do with these thoughts when they showed up? I can see you out there, in the sun, with your kids, playing, worrying about if you are doing it right and not really enjoying the day.

C: For sure. I mean it seemed that the kids were having a good time. They got lunch at like one o'clock anyway. It was no big deal.

You can see the normal system at play here. The client feels as though he did not do well with the exercise. The one side of his mind is telling him how he did it wrong, and the other side is telling him how it went well. This is a struggle at the process level. This is not one of content.

T: You did the exercise in terms of action, *and* I want to know what you did with your mind while you were up in the hills. Were you with your kids or in your mind?

C: It came and went. Sometimes I was just there, and it was great. But that was the exception. Lots of the time I was in my mind. When I thought, "I'm messing this up," it pretty much hooked me, for sure. I am trying to do things differently, but I kept thinking, "Here I go and do it all wrong" [not present, fusion].

T: Right. It is hard to be in your head and with them at the same time, isn't it?

C: Right. I knew that at the time. That is one of the things that I was struggling with so much. It was like, here I am doing it; then I'm thinking I couldn't even do it and I was just the same [conceptualized self].

T: Yeah—and even that is just a thought. Your mind thought it was helping. It was trying to help you play with your children better. But it can only judge and evaluate—that is what it does—and this is not what is helpful when you are playing and being present. "Nice try mind—this is just not your game." Remember "Tell me how to touch my nose"?

C: So what do I do with it?

T: Maybe it is not a matter of getting control of minding. Maybe it is more about making room for your mind to do its thing while you do what you came to do.

C: Oh man. So this is just what is going to happen to me. I am going to have to live with my mind forever! [defusion; because, in context, there is a humorous sense of distance]

T: You can't have just one or the other. You get both. You okay with that?

C: Do I have a choice?

T: Of course you do. You can stay home and not have the struggle of "I am screwing up." But my guess is that will not be any better because your mind will beat you up about that too. Then you get, "You're not taking care of your kids" or "You're a bad dad."

C: Life's a bitch.

T: Take a minute though and look at this. Why were these thoughts "I'm selfish" or "Here I go and do it all wrong" so punchy? Why did they hit you so hard?

C: Because I was there to be with my kids and I wasn't doing it right.

T: Slow down a bit. Look inside what you just said [pause]. They were punchy because …

C: I want to be there for them.

T: See it? The self-judgments hurt because you care. That's a place you can be hurt—so your mind gets going one hundred miles an hour. You struggled with how you were taking your kids sledding, because it is important to you [pause]. So you have a choice. You can do things that are important to you, knowing full well that you can get hurt (and hear a lot of mind chatter sometimes), or not do them and have little risk of getting hurt. What do you choose: danger or safety?

C: My kids [values].

T: It's danger then. Are you sure?

C: My kids are what matter. The rest is crap.

T: And when you get all entangled with how you are not doing it right, knowing full well your mind will chatter about this, what are you actually *doing* inside that entanglement—kids or crap?

C: More crap.

The therapist just pitted avoidance and fusion on the one hand against values on the other. This is a good therapeutic move because it transforms the functions of the client's usual avoidance and fusion. Now not following his values involves avoidance, and following his values involves acceptance. Further, now fusion about how he is not living his values is itself not living his values; and defusion is in the service of having the room to step forward in the way he deeply wants to.

We are also going to step back and explain what that sequence was about. The client did the behavioral commitment as discussed. He designed a really nice exposure exercise, but the usual control and fusion stance slipped insidiously back into the process. He was doing something that he valued: he was taking his children out to do something fun, but he was not fully open to the feelings and thoughts that brought up. Because these reactions superficially presented themselves as being about how to do it "right," fusion and avoidance came in through the mental back door, disguised as values.

The result is that he did the exercise halfway. It is akin to a spider phobic holding a spider in his hand but thinking happy thoughts with his eyes closed. It is not really exposure. You have to be present for exposure to be helpful. He needs to be more open during his exposure exercises. It would be a good idea for him to do another exercise like this, but to be open to whatever shows up while doing the exercise. If he experienced his judgmental thoughts from a defused place, was willing to have them while being present with what was occurring, then he would be doing an ACT exposure exercise and he'd be actually living out his values more fully. We do not follow our values because it feels good; we follow them because we hold them as important.

A very positive sign, however, is that the client really seems to see the trap when it is pointed out. He is open to its implication and emotionally carries it forward without any sense of needless defense. Just like in session eight, in which the client says with a certain sense of anguished commitment, "I'm not going to have my life be about being in emotional control," so too there is a sense of depth to his statement now, "My kids are what matter. The rest is crap." All of the skills are in place for this client—now he just needs to bring them all together.

The therapist seems aware of the moment and the pivotal point the treatment has reached: if the client can apply acceptance, defusion, and mindfulness skills to his values and commitments, he will have created the engine of transformation that resides inside ACT. From there forward, life itself becomes the teacher. The client will be on a new path. Therapy is not about walking with clients from disability to permanent health—it is about liberating clients so that they can walk in the direction of greater and greater psychological flexibility. Life itself is that walk.

The therapist takes this moment in an interesting direction and one that seems to tie together strands from previous sessions.

In-Session, Values-Based Exposure, ACT-Style

T: Would you be willing to do another goofy exercise with me? It has to do with the work you did over the weekend.

C: What is it? [avoidance (slight); because the client is willing to do it depending on what the exercise is]

T: We are going to push the buttons that were pushed this weekend. I want to give you a chance to play with them a little. But I don't think that is what you are really asking. I think what you mean is "Will I be able to handle it?" "Will it hurt?" Are you willing to do the exercise not knowing what it will be like? We don't know the answer to those questions.

C: Hmmm.... Do I want to feel bad? No. But go ahead with your exercise.

It is evident he is not really agreeing to do the exercise. The therapist picks up on this and wisely declines to move ahead until the client's agreement is obtained.

T: I mean it when I asked if you were willing. This isn't like parents saying, "Do you want to go clean up your room?" That is in the form of a question, but it is not really a question. They mean "Go clean your room." I really mean this as a question. I am giving you the choice to step into this uncertainty, to walk through this swamp a little more. Should we do it or do something else?

C: [Pause] No. I am willing.

It is clear that the client is still hesitant, but the therapist senses that an agreement is there. This is important, because feelings and thoughts that show up during this exercise are more likely to be experienced openly if he chooses to have them.

T: Okay. What thoughts were you struggling with while you were out sledding this weekend?

C: Mostly "I am messing this up" and "I can't even be there for my own children." Stuff like that [acceptance]. It is not true, because I am a pretty good dad … [conceptualized self].

T: I am going to cut you off there. Your mind was pulling you into a literal discussion about the kind of dad you are, which won't be useful to us now [pause]. How old are these two thoughts: "I am screwing this up" and "I can't be there for my children"? I mean are these new or are these antiques?

C: I have always worried about making mistakes and how well I am doing generally. I feel like I spend a good amount of my time trying to avoid them. As for the one about what kind of father I am, well, that has been there since I first ever thought about children. So overall, I guess these are old—antiques. They certainly are not new for me.

T: Yeah. What do you feel is in the way of you having them as they are, without defense, without doing your normal thing where you fight with them and try to prove them wrong? What would have to change for you to have them as they are?

C: I am not sure I follow you.

T: What is it with these thoughts that is so hard for you to have? I mean, you can easily have the thought "I like to hike and run" or "I wear black shoes." You don't struggle with those thoughts, but these ones, "I am screwing this up" and "I can't be there for my children," really pull you in. What do you think that is about?

C: Easy. I don't want to be like my parents. I think they screwed up and I don't want to do that too. I mean, I seriously don't think I would be here if they were different [conceptualized self]. I am not really blaming them, I control my own life, but it keeps coming back to them in here.

T: Okay. Are you willing to do some work around that? Are you willing to push your buttons a little and see what we get? There are no guarantees here. We will just throw the dice on the table and see what happens.

C: Okay.

T: I know this may be a little weird, so it will take a little openness on your part, but I want you to conjure up a picture of your dad. Have you seen him lately?

C: Sure. I see him often enough.

T: Okay. Please close your eyes and get a picture of him. Can you describe him to me?

The therapist spends a couple of minutes having the client describe his father. The point of this is to make the functions of the father more present.

T: Now I would like you to keep your eyes closed and picture him coming into this room and sitting in this other chair that is across from you. He is sitting next to me. Nod when you have that image [client nods]. Okay. Now I want you to get in touch with those thoughts that you were having when you were parenting your own children. You were thinking, "I am screwing this up" and "I can't be there for my children," and you linked this back to your upbringing. You have a fear that you will be like your parents. Okay. Let's go right into that experience. You have your dad sitting across from you. Try and stay in contact with those thoughts you were having last weekend: "I am screwing this up" and "I can't be there for my children" and the feelings they brought up. Now in your mind's eye, look at your dad. If he was actually here and you were to speak from the pain of those thoughts and feelings, what would you say to him?

C: I don't know. You obviously don't know my dad. This guy is not easy to talk to [fusion, avoidance].

T: Take your time going into it. This is not about your dad really—it's about you and the dad you carry with you. That's who is in that chair. What is there for you to say?

C: Hmmm.... "Thanks for coming to see my therapist with me. Ummm. You and I both know that we did not get along as well as we could have." I am not sure what else. This is odd [dancing between avoidance and acceptance].

T: Make room for that thought if you can, and go into this moment. See his face; touch those difficult thoughts and feelings. And bring in just a touch of why we are even doing this—your kids. If you are willing, step it up a notch. Go in.

C: [To the dad, with a great sense of emotional presence] "I was out sledding with the kids this weekend. We had a good time and everything, but I kept having these thoughts that I would mess things up with them in the same way that I feel you messed me up. I am not sure how we got to the place that we got to, but I don't want to be that way with them and I am afraid that I have the innate tendency to be that way. I don't know. Your drinking and fighting probably was not a good influence on me. I know I don't drink, but I am divorced. I'm successful, and I provide well for my children, and things are okay with them, but I feel I am going through the motions—I'm so terrified I will screw it up, and another generation will be in pain."

T: What do you want from him?

C: I'd like an apology.

T: Let's see how that works. Go ahead. Put it on the table.

C: [To the dad] "I don't know. Did you ever get the feeling you messed me up?"

T: What do you think he would say?

C: He would say, "Nope. We all make choices in life. I took care of you and I think I did a pretty good job. You have three kids, a nice business, a nice house, and so on. What do you want?" [acceptance; because it is painful to hear, and he is participating in this exercise]

T: You have been waiting for an apology for a long while. At times life has been put on hold while you waited. You've kept Dad on the hook ... but that hook went through you first and then into him. There's no way off of it if you are holding him on it. What do you really want from him? What do you really want?

C: [Pause] I want him to love me, see me.

T: Okay. Tell him that is so; tell him so he sees it.

C: [Long pause, then through tears] "It was hard, Dad. It was hard. Hard watching you almost destroy each other. Hard feeling as though I was invisible; wondering if you and Mom could see me at all ...

T: [Pause] Go on.

C: "I've done a lot of things with that pain—a lot of things that have hurt me and hurt those I love. I know you didn't make me—I did that. I did that. Still it has had such a cost—to me, to my marriage, to my life, to my children."

T: [Pause] Anything else there to be said?

C: "This is my stuff not yours. How things are, or were, with you is not what I have to do with my kids. I've let it get in the way. I am done with that."

T: [Pause] Is there still more? Anything? I'm not fishing—I just want you to dig deep and see what is there to be said.

C: [Pause, still with tears] "I love you."

T: [Pause] Anything else?

C: [Long pause] "Thanks."

T: [Long pause] Okay. Picture the room and when you are ready to come back, you can open up your eyes.

C: Wow. Some of that came out of left field.

T: In what way?

C: I am not sure how to put words to it. I have thought that letting him off the hook does not feel fair. But keeping him on it is so hurtful to me and to others that "fair" is just not relevant. I see it in a different way. I knew this in a way. But now it's like it's not just a thought. It's like I see what I've been doing.

T: Anything else … from left field?

C: "Thanks."

T: Yeah. That surprised me a bit too. Neat though.

C: I don't really know what to say about that. He was doing the best he could even though a lot of hurtful stuff went down. But without him there is no me. In one sense I owe him everything. And yeah, I had a lot of pain as a child. But he is not me. What I do now is up to me.

T: Yes.

C: If my life really is okay, then I guess they did something right, despite all the pain I felt. Funny, that does not gall me the way I thought it would even an hour ago. I guess that's why "thanks" showed up. Weird.

T: Do you see any connection between what you just did and where we started? What about your own children?

C: I feel revved up. I can do this. There are some things that I have needed to say to my dad—I think I will actually do that. I do want him to know about how I hurt, but I also need him to know that I've been trying to guilt-trip him. I've been holding him at arms length. And that needs to stop. That will stop. The thing that is screwed up about that is that it means I go off into my head doing all of this right-and-wrong stuff, and that's exactly where his parenting really affects my parenting. I don't want it to be like that anymore.

T: Okay. So what do we need to "change" in your dad before you can parent differently—more consistently with your values?

C: Nothing. I need to approach it differently though. Him. My childhood. Mom.

T: And your kids? What are you going to do differently with your kids?

C: I am going to be open and honest with them. I am going to be there for them. I am not letting my mental and historical crap get in the way of our relationship anymore. Well, I know. That's unrealistic. So when it does, then I'll deal with it and come back to being there for them. I can't expect perfection … but I just see how I've been waiting for something to happen to make it all easy or natural. Nothing's going to happen. I'm just going to do it.

Homework

T: Are you willing to give that exercise that you did last week another try?

C: Well, I had them last week, so my ex has them this week, and besides, I am out of town for a week. I am game for the following week.

T: Right. My mistake. I knew that. Yes. Are you willing to work on this the next time that you have your kids?

C: For sure. And in a way it's not an "exercise" anymore. I know you know that. This is just me being a parent. They may not want to do that again [sledding], but whatever it is we decide to do, I will be there. Me and my mind.

T: I am way less concerned about what is done than the way in which it is done. Last time you came up with a really nice thing to do with your children that was tied to your values. In the midst of the day you found that you fell into entanglement with self-criticism, self-judgment, and so on. It is fine that that happened. Actually it was good that it happened, as I think you can see now. It gives you a chance to work on some of these things that we are working on. Maybe it is kind of like your history with your parents—even inside the pain, we can learn. So the important thing is just to be present and stay with the values inside that moment and let life be the teacher.

The client is showing a lot of flexibility. He is becoming aware of processes in which he is hooked, he is leaning into pain, and he senses the costs of not walking a valued path as much as he is aware of the pain of symptoms. This last interaction has a sense of "turning the corner" as all of the elements of an ACT approach begin to come together, moment by moment.

Only time will tell how well he will be able to do this outside of session, but he did such a good job inside of the session that it seems likely that these skills will carry over. That does not mean that things will be smooth—life isn't smooth. But the client is unhooked.

Shall We Continue?

This is the tenth session, and the client and therapist originally agreed to meet for ten sessions and then look back to see where they stood. Truthfully, the client could use a couple of additional sessions to really nail some of these processes down, but the therapist had said they would look at how things were going at the tenth session.

T: As I said at the beginning of the session, we are at session ten. The original reason for agreeing to a set number of sessions ties into this whole therapy rap: You should not take my word that this is helpful; follow your experience and see for yourself. I could be totally wrong. I don't want a blank check. I don't want to keep you coming here to maintain my lifestyle. I want you to choose therapy because it helps or to stop if it does not. What does your experience tell you about what we have been doing?

C: I'm swimming in the swamp. I am not to the other end, but I am in there swimming.

T: How does it feel?

C: It's good. Who would have thought? But it's good stuff [flexibility].

T: It is funny how your mind works, isn't it? Once you stop letting it drive the bus, you can finally start going where you want. It is not the way that the rest of the world teaches you that it works, but so far your experience is telling you that letting go of control where it does not belong gives you control where it matters.

At this point in therapy it is a little safer to be more literal. The client has learned these processes through experience, and the therapist is just reinforcing them.

C: For sure. Better late than never. Yeah, I was thinking about this being the last session. I know that you were thinking of this as more of a check-in point, but I have always been trying to look at it like the end. Not sure I ever told you that. I wanted to see if I could get this to help with my depression, anger, anxiety, whatever, in ten sessions.

T: So how did we do with those things? Are they gone?

C: You're funny. But seriously, they are better.

T: What do you mean, better?

C: They are still there, for sure, but they are not really the issue anymore. I still don't like them. But there is less hate there. And I'm more interested in my children and my work and relationships and living than in getting rid of all my passengers.

T: Is there more room for them?

C: Way more. Way.

T: So, what should we do with this being session ten? If you were thinking of it as an ending point, what is next?

C: I remember you warning me that this approach would be different than what I was expecting. It sure was different, but I feel that it helped me in a way that I needed. So thanks. Really. You've done a lot for me. More than I can say. So thanks [pause]. Do you think I need to keep coming in?

T: [Smiles]

C: Yeah, it's my life. Well, I have to miss next week anyway. And coming in every week can be difficult, and no offense, it is sort of expensive. So can we take a break and plan a check-in two weeks from now and just see how things have been going? I have a feeling that what I really need to do is to stop blabbing and get going. Is that okay?

T: Sure. I have done that before with clients. Let's skip a week and check in and then we can decide. Sometimes if things are going well, we then skip several weeks and see. But no matter what, I'm like the dentist: you can always drop back in for a checkup.

C: I like that.

FINAL COMMENTARY

You can see the client really progressing in this transcript. He came into this session somewhat fused and a little tied to the old control agenda. The therapist helps reorient the client to the function of this work: living a vital life. The therapist and the client did the most emotionally evocative cognitive exposure thus far: dealing with his parents has been one of his biggest avoidance areas. This is a big step forward for this client. The therapist linked this to the values exercise from last session and had the client recommit to doing another one.

They also agreed to make this the final therapy session. It was obvious that this was what the client wanted to say but that he was struggling with telling the therapist that he wanted to stop coming in. The therapist tried to hold off and make the client come to that decision on his own.

The therapist and client did indeed meet two more times: one session two weeks later and once a month after that. Recordings were not made—according to the therapist, these sessions had the quality of a checkup and were focused more on new behaviors than on struggles with depression, anger, or anxiety. At the end of these two sessions, the client felt that there was no need to have additional sessions—that the goals of therapy had been met. The progress over all ten sessions is graphed in figure 11.3.

Figure 11.1 Time spent addressing ACT processes in session ten

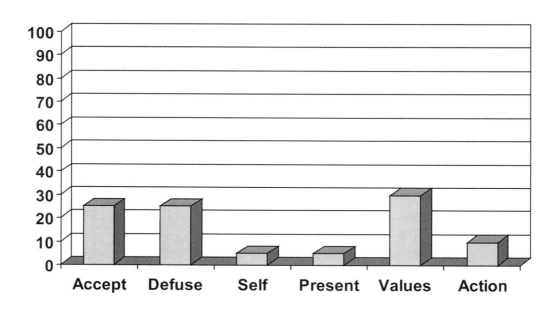

Figure 11.2 Status of client's ACT processes by the end of session ten

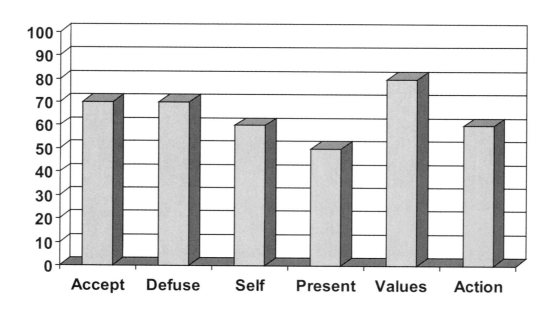

Postscript

As we conclude these ten sessions of ACT, we want to reiterate that this transcript should not be taken to *be* ACT. As this book is being written, there are published clinical trials of ACT with interventions as short as three and as long as several dozen hours. The protocols vary widely from problem area to problem area. Thus, there are many ways to do ACT. In addition, clinicians bring vastly different styles to the work, and in normal clinical work, when manuals are not central, ACT differs greatly from case to case and clinician to clinician. What is key about ACT is not the specifics but the targets, processes, and approaches inside an empirical model tied to a set of principles.

This is just one transcript with one therapist and one client. It is an example of the application of an ACT model, but it is only an example. Furthermore, we have modified some portion of the transcript (perhaps 15 percent) for confidentiality and training purposes, even making up sections when needed, so doing word-for-word analyses would not be wise. Also, the "data" we present at the end of each chapter is entirely subjective and is meant more to guide the reader about the transcripts (including the modifications) than to attempt formally to capture the client's full functioning. Thus it should *not* be cited elsewhere as "data" on the effectiveness of ACT—there are controlled studies for that purpose. Instead, our purpose throughout has been to train: to help readers to see ACT processes in flight so that they can use them inside their own work, using their own style, with their own clients.

You can use an ACT model of psychopathology (as presented in chapter 1 of this book) as one way to look at the course of these transcripts, summarizing all ten sessions, using our subjective estimates of what they reveal about the client's abilities in the six targeted areas. The graphs you have seen throughout this book are represented below, now in a new form, arranged according to the hexagon model (Wilson, 2007). Each dimension can go from 0 to 100, and each line on the six scales represents ten points.

Psychological flexibility is shown by the size and shape of the dark area in the center. As you can see, it is our impression that the client has gradually become more balanced and flexible.

That is the primary goal of ACT. This is not a matter of imposing a model on a client, especially if the results are seen in values and action. ACT seeks to help clients live a more vital and flexible human life defined against *their* values. That is our goal, and that is the justification for all other processes within the ACT model.

Thank you, reader, for sharing this time with us, and please let us know how else we might assist you in your work in helping to support human growth and to alleviate human suffering.

Summary of the strength of ACT processes in the client across the ten sessions

Session 1

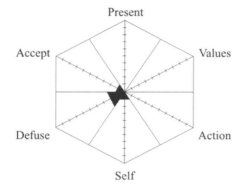

Session 2

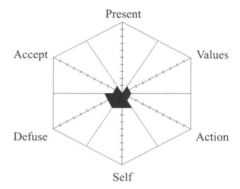

Session 3

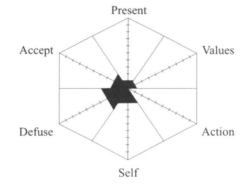

Session 4

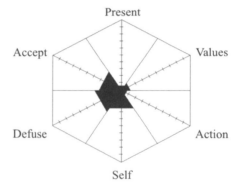

Session 5

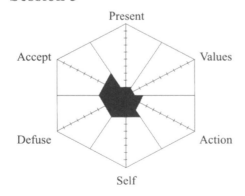

Session 6

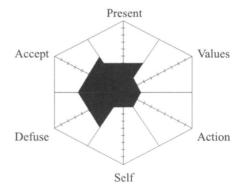

Session 7

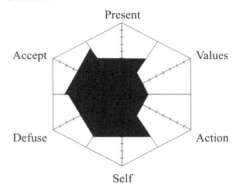

Session 8

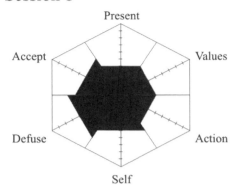

Session 9

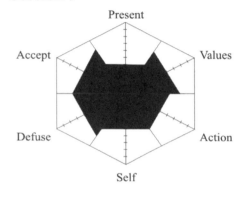

Session 10

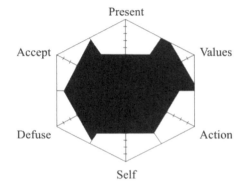

References

Chiles, J., & Strosahl, K. D. (2004). *Clinical manual for assessment and treatment of suicidal patients.* Arlington, VA: American Psychiatric Publishing.

Dahl, J., Wilson, K. G., & Luciano, C. (2005). *Acceptance and Commitment Therapy for chronic pain.* Oakland, CA: New Harbinger.

Eifert, G. H., & Forsyth, J. P. (2005). *Acceptance and Commitment Therapy for anxiety disorders.* Oakland, CA: New Harbinger.

Hayes, S. C. (1984). Making sense of spirituality. *Behaviorism, 12,* 99–110.

Hayes, S. C. (Ed.). (2007). *ACT in action* [DVD]. Oakland, CA: New Harbinger.

Hayes, S. C., Barnes-Holmes, D., & Roche, B. (Eds.). (2001). *Relational Frame Theory: A post-Skinnerian account of human language and cognition.* New York: Kluwer Academic/Plenum.

Hayes S. C., & Strosahl, K. D. (2004). *A practical guide to Acceptance and Commitment Therapy.* New York: Springer.

Hayes, S. C., Strosahl, K. D., & Wilson, K. G. (1999). *Acceptance and Commitment Therapy: An experiential approach to behavior change.* New York: Guilford Press.

Khorakiwala, D. (1991). An analysis of the process of client change in a contextual approach to therapy. *Dissertation Abstracts International, 52(5–B),* 2776.

Kohlenberg, R. J., & Tsai, M. (1996). *Functional Analytic Psychotherapy.* New York: Springer.

Luoma, J. B., Hayes, S. C., & Walser, R. D. (2007). *Learning ACT: An Acceptance and Commitment Therapy skills training manual for therapists.* Oakland, CA: New Harbinger.

Moran, D. J., & Bach, P. A. (2007). *ACT in practice: Case conceptualization in Acceptance and Commitment Therapy.* Oakland, CA: New Harbinger.

Walser, R. D., & Westrup, D. (2007). *Acceptance and Commitment Therapy for the treatment of post-traumatic stress disorder and trauma-related problems.* Oakland, CA: New Harbinger.

Wilson, K. G. (2007). The hexaflex diagnostic: A fully dimensional approach to assessment, treatment, and case conceptualization. Presidential address presented at the annual convention of the Association for Contextual Behavioral Science, Houston, TX.

Zettle, R. D. (2007). *ACT for Depression.* Oakland, CA: New Harbinger.

Michael P. Twohig, Ph.D., is assistant professor of psychology at Utah State University in Logan, UT. He is the author of more than forty scientific articles and book chapters, most of which focus on the treatment of anxiety disorders.

Steven C. Hayes, Ph.D., is Foundation Professor of Psychology at the University of Nevada, Reno. He is among the most influential figures in clinical psychology and has authored innumerable books and scientific articles, including the successful ACT workbook *Get Out of Your Mind and into Your Life*.